Women in the Medieval English Countryside

Women
in the
Medieval English
Countryside

Gender and Household
in Brigstock Before the Plague

Judith M. Bennett

New York   Oxford
OXFORD UNIVERSITY PRESS
1987

Oxford University Press

Oxford   New York   Toronto
Delhi   Bombay   Calcutta   Madras   Karachi
Petaling Jaya   Singapore   Hong Kong   Tokyo
Nairobi   Dar es Salaam   Cape Town
Melbourne   Auckland

and associated companies in
Beirut   Berlin   Ibadan   Nicosia

Published by Oxford University Press, Inc.,
200 Madison Avenue, New York, New York 10016

Library of Congress Cataloging-in-Publication Data
Bennett, Judith M.
Women in the medieval English countryside.
Bibliography: p.   Includes index.
1. Women—England—History—Case studies.   2. Women—History—Middle
Ages, 500–1500—Case studies.   3. England—Rural conditions—Case studies.
4. Sex role—England—History—Case studies.   I. Title.
HQ1599.E5B46   1987   305.4'2'0942   86–5122
ISBN 0–19–504094–5

1 3 5 7 9 8 6 4 2

Printed in the United States of America
on acid-free paper

This book came too late for my grandmothers, but it is, nevertheless, for them

Ruby Jenrette Bennett, 1897–1985

Anne Thompson MacKenzie, 1899–1984

Acknowledgments

Long projects accumulate many debts. I have spent many hours working alone on this book, but my work would not have been possible without the generous support of others. Graduate fellowships from the Social Science Research Council and the American Association of University Women provided early support for research and writing, and a grant from the American Council of Learned Societies allowed me to take a semester's leave from teaching at a crucial stage of revision. I have also received grants and fellowships from the institutions with which I have been affiliated—the Pontifical Institute of Mediaeval Studies, the University of Toronto, and the University of North Carolina at Chapel Hill. I am grateful to all of these agencies; without their support, my work would have been impossible.

The generous assistance of numerous archivists and librarians facilitated my research throughout this project. P. I. King and his staff at the Northamptonshire Record Office cheerfully provided me with a constant stream of materials on medieval Brigstock and promptly answered queries sent by mail. Elizabeth Elvey, the archivist at the Buckinghamshire Archaeological Society, and her husband, G. R. Elvey, were just as gracious in answering inquiries and providing access to the Iver records in their collection. The archivist at St. George's Chapel, Grace Holmes, not only shared her office space with me, but also personally transferred an assortment of Iver records to the House of Lords Record Office for my convenience. My gratitude also extends to the staffs of the British Library, the Public Record Office, the Institute of Historical Research, the House of Lords Record Office, and the Inter-Library Borrowing department at the University of North Carolina. I wish to thank the Duke of Buccleuch for allowing me access to the Brigstock materials that he has deposited in the Northamptonshire Record Office.

I must also acknowledge three publishers for permission to reprint portions of my previously published articles. The Appendix of this book draws partly on "Spouses, Siblings and Surnames: Reconstructing Families from Medieval Village Court Rolls," originally published in the *Journal of British Studies* (23, 1983, pp. 26–46). The discussion of brewing in Chapter V includes sections drawn from "The Village Ale-Wife: Women and Brewing in Fourteenth-Century England," in *Women and Work in Preindustrial Europe,* edited by Barbara A. Hanawalt (Indiana University Press, 1986). The social repercussions of the marriage of Agnes Penifader and Henry Kroyl of Brigstock were first described in "The Tie That Binds: Peasant Marriages and Families in Late Medieval England," *The Journal of Interdisciplinary History* (15, 1984, pp. 111–129). Parts of that description appear in somewhat different form in Chapter V with the permission of the editors of the journal and the MIT Press (copyright © 1984 Massachusetts Institute of Technology and the editors of *The Journal of Interdisciplinary History*).

Over the course of the past few years, so many scholars have read all or part of this study that I cannot thank them all individually. My teachers at the University of Toronto—J. Ambrose Raftis, Michael M. Sheehan, and John Munro—helped to develop my research at an early stage. Many of my colleagues at the University of North Carolina, and particularly Richard Soloway, made helpful comments on a completed draft. The generously offered critiques of Anne DeWindt, Edwin DeWindt, James Epstein, Cynthia Herrup, Sherryl Kleinman, Maryanne Kowaleski, Don Reid, Eleanor Searle, Richard Smith, and Keith Wrightson also guided my final revisions. I am grateful to all of these scholars and to the many others whose advice both enlightened my thoughts and saved me from many errors.

At an early stage of writing, Rosalie Radcliffe transferred the text of this book to a word processor, and she can testify to the fact that word processing does not automatically save either labor or time. She endured many revisions, and I thank her for her patience, promptness, and precision.

Moments of doubt plague most writers, particularly those of us who pursue our work under the peculiar structures of the American system of academic tenure. For their sustenance during such times, I owe thanks to many women and men in my generation of American scholars, particularly to Maryanne Kowaleski, Don Reid, Nancy Adamson, Sherryl Kleinman, and James Epstein. My debt to Cynthia Herrup, who has lived with this project from its inception, can be neither expressed nor repaid. Thanks also to Geoff Eley for good advice at a crucial moment.

November 1985   J.M.B.
Durham, North Carolina

Contents

Tables and Figures

I

Introduction

Historians who study European women typically focus on the nineteenth and twentieth centuries. Motivated by both feminism (the importance of explaining the current circumstances of women) and practicality (the archival abundance of recent centuries), these scholars usually recount how the dramatic changes of modern times have altered the lives of women. The burgeoning literature written on women during the last two centuries covers a wide variety of subjects, but particular attention has been paid to the working lives of women and the experiences of the poor and underprivileged; numerous published studies now detail, for example, the early effects of industrialization on working-class women, the growth of prostitution in nineteenth-century cities, and the movement of working women into the service sector at the turn of the last century.

The history of women in preindustrial Europe not only is more modest but also takes a different direction. Because of archival constraints, historians of medieval and early modern women generally examine the elite and the literate—the feudal ladies of courtly romances, the nuns and saints found in religious literature, the bourgeois wives who left diaries and letters. Although such studies greatly enhance our understanding of elite and religious culture in Europe before 1800, they seldom complement modern studies of the experi-

3

ences of ordinary working women. Medievalists, to be sure, have not completely ignored the experiences of working women, but such studies have usually taken urban women as their subjects.[1] Because the experiences of rural women remain largely unexplored, students of women in modern Europe have often relied upon unverified assumptions about the daily lives of countrywomen in earlier centuries. We know a great deal about how industrialization transformed the lives of working-class women, much less about how the commercial and agricultural changes of the early modern era affected women, and even less about the experiences of women in the medieval countryside.[2] By adding a medieval perspective to the history of working women in Europe, I hope to show how the choices that women faced in the seventeenth and nineteenth centuries were shaped not only by economic changes specific to those centuries but also by enduring customs that had long limited female opportunities.

Favorable judgments about the status of medieval women are almost a commonplace in historical literature because studies of the adverse effects on women of the commercialization and industrialization of modern Europe have thrown flattering light on the reputed status of women in the medieval centuries that preceded these momentous economic changes. As Olwen Hufton recently described the problem,

> feminist writing on the nineteenth century has tended to force upon historians of the early modern period one unenviable task, that of locating a *bon vieux temps* when women enjoyed a harmonious, if hard-working, domestic role and social responsibility before they were downgraded into social parasites or factory fodder under the corrupting hand of capitalism.

Because the "location of this *bon vieux temps* has proved remarkably elusive," the burden has increasingly passed from early modernists to medievalists.[3] If the golden age did not immediately precede the establishment of industrial capitalism in nineteenth-century Europe, then it presumably preceded the economic and commercial expansion of Europe in the sixteenth and seventeenth centuries. Implicit in many feminist studies of modern women, this notion of a premodern golden age also inspires anti-feminist theory. Ivan Illich, for example, argues in his book *Gender* that the equality of men and women in the medieval countryside has given way to inequality in the modern workplace. To Illich, the "rule of gender" in preindustrial Europe prescribed distinct, but complementary (and equally valued), roles for men and women, whereas the "rule of sex" imposed by industrialization has created a unisex standard (based on male norms) to which women are unreasonably expected to conform.[4]

In studies that have been usually both brief and problematic, medievalists have buttressed this appealing image of a golden age during which women enjoyed rough equality with men. But assessments of women's status in the medieval countryside have relied too little upon evidence reporting actual behavior and too heavily upon evidence prescribing ideal behavior. The realities of women's lives have often conformed poorly to what can be expected from a reading of the prescriptive advice found in literary, religious, and statutory materials. Medievalists have also often adduced picturesque, but atypical, examples to illustrate the supposedly wide opportunities granted women. Rodney Hilton, for example, used the very peculiar election of a few female officers in early fifteenth-century Halesowen, a manor in the English Midlands, to imply that politics in rural communities was not completely closed to women. The female officers of Halesowen, however, are aberrations to be explained, not norms to be used as examples. Finally, by focusing solely on gender, medievalists have mistaken the extensive activities of some women (especially widows) as representative of the condition of all women.[5]

Based on the everyday behavior of rural women of all marital statuses, the findings described in the following chapters suggest that a *bon vieux temps* will not be found in the medieval countryside. Despite the relative simplicity of their economic institutions, medieval countrywomen encountered political, legal, economic, and social disadvantages that distinguished them sharply from their fathers, brothers, husbands, and sons. This evidence is particularly telling because it comes from such a low stratum of medieval society. The complement to the search for a *bon vieux temps* has been the assumption that women of low rank enjoyed a rough equality with men of low rank. Idealizing the status of poor women has a long lineage that stretches as far back as the fifteenth-century feminist Christine de Pisan, who said of peasant women: "Albeit they be fed with coarse bread, milk, lard and pottage and drink water, and albeit they have care and labour enow, yet is their life surer, yea, they have greater suffi-

ciency, than some that be of high estate."[6] Yet the evidence that
follows indicates that rural women faced limitations fundamentally
similar to those restricting women of the more privileged sectors of
medieval society.

Norms of female and male behavior in the medieval countryside
drew heavily upon the private subordination of wives to their husbands, as popularized by such sayings as, "Let not the hen crow before the rooster."[7] Femaleness was defined by the submissiveness of
wives who were expected to defer to their husbands in both private
and public. Maleness was defined by the authority of husbands who,
as householders, controlled not only most domestic affairs but also
most community matters. The distinction between a private, female
sphere and a public, male sphere reached its fullest elaboration in the
nineteenth century, but a separation of the sexes—into private wives
and public husbands—was already firmly established in the households of the medieval countryside. As a result, women usually participated much less actively than men in the public affairs of rural
communities. Unable to act as members of peace-keeping groups or
as local officers, women seldom took part in the systems of mutual
dependency and reciprocity that bound men together into a political
community. Often considered to be legally dependent on their heads
of household, women used their local courts less frequently than men
to resolve disputes or quarrels. Inheriting land only in the absence of
brothers and receiving lower wages for their work than did men,
women were also less active as both landholders and workers. And
relying on public associations that were usually limited and focused
on family, women built social networks that were narrower than those
of their fathers, husbands, and brothers. Public reticence on the part
of women was explicitly encouraged in the prescriptive admonitions of
popular literature, religious sermons, and local ordinances. Medieval preachers criticized women not only for female foolishness and
disobedience to men, but also for their public vanity, love of gossip,
and tendency to walk about freely. Such exhortations were repeated
often in popular verse, as in the goodwife's advice, "Dwell at home,
daughter, and love thy work much."[8]

The public-private divide in medieval villages, however, differed
from the distinctions so common in the nineteenth century. Bound
together by close settlement, communal agriculture, and shared lordship, medieval peasants lived in a very public world—relying on their

neighbors, cooperating with other tenants, worshipping together in the parish church. Even the most private acts, sexual relations and marriage, were subject to considerable community interest and control. As a result, wives were never effectively isolated from public life because their ordinary daily duties brought them into regular contact with tenants, neighbors, manorial officials, traders, and many others. Although less publicly active than their husbands, wives were not in fact confined to a private sphere.

More important, the public-private distinction in the medieval countryside applied more to husbands and wives than to men and women. Despite the public reticence expected of wives, the public activities of a woman varied enormously according to whether "be she mayde or wydwe or elles wyf."[9] In preparation for establishing separate households at marriage, many adolescent daughters loosened ties of dependency on their parents, answering for their own offenses, acting alone in legal matters, and controlling independent lands. Widows, as heads of the truncated households left by their husbands, assumed many responsibilities normally left to males; they managed the resources of their households, accepted responsibility for the actions of their dependents, and dispersed familial properties to the next generation. Thus as an adolescent daughter or widow, a medieval countrywoman faced many more public opportunities and responsibilities than she encountered as a married woman.

Men's lives also reflected household position, but the changing opportunities they experienced were less dramatic and more continuous than those of women. Spending their adult years either becoming, being, or having been heads of households, individual men diverged slightly, but seldom significantly, from the expectation of male public independence. Adult men always approached in some measure the authority of married householders that defined their gender. In contrast, women's lives were discontinuous, since the dependency expected of wives fit poorly with their independent activities as adolescent daughters and widows.

These patterns suggest that the small, conjugal household profoundly shaped the social relation of the sexes in the medieval countryside. Recently identified by demographers as a pervasive feature of English life well before the advent of the modern era, conjugality promoted the ideal of public men (i.e., husbands) and private women (i.e., wives) that underlay the public subordination of women in the medieval countryside. Women needed no equal rights of inheritance because their husbands provided for them, they lacked access to peace-keeping groups and offices because their husbands represented the collective interests of their households, and they associated with smaller groups of friends and neighbors because their husbands dealt most often with matters outside the home. The political, legal, economic, and social disadvantages experienced by all countrywomen were rooted in the superordination of husbands and the subordination of wives. It is perhaps revealing that both "wife" and "husband" in Middle English denoted not only married persons but also simply adults, especially adults of humble status.[10]

Yet even while conjugality promoted an ideal of private women and public men, it also gave rise to many situations in which this ideal could not be effectively maintained. And some women, slipping briefly into roles provided by the inherent instability of the conjugal household, enjoyed extensive public rights and privileges that clashed with the public reticence normally associated with their gender. Because many daughters, like sons, prepared for marriage by developing resources separate from those of their parents, and because widows, bereft of their husbands, assumed the public responsibilities and privileges of householders, the ideal distinction between public males and private females was often confronted by the reality of women acting publicly.

As a result, the second-rank status of women in the medieval countryside was, in part, situational. Women as women faced certain handicaps that distinguished them, as a group, from men in the community, but these handicaps were based less on a notion of something defective in the female condition than on the practical presumption that women were normally household dependents, mainpasts of their fathers or husbands. It was, in other words, not the sex of Quena ad Crucem that prompted the court of Brigstock in 1315 to deny her the right to sell her land, but rather her dependent household status. Determining that "a wife's sale is nothing in the absence of her husband," the court moved to protect the economic unity of the conjugal household.[11] Sex was irrelevant, for the court similarly subjected the properties of minor sons to the supervisory authority of their householders.[12]

In short, conjugal households in the medieval countryside had a contradictory effect on the social relation of the sexes. On the one hand, conjugality defined gender by creating the expectation that males would be publicly active householders and females publicly passive dependents. On the other hand, it moderated the severity of these distinctions by sustaining many domestic circumstances that fit poorly with the expectation of male authority and female dependence. The fact that some women—in particular, adolescent daughters and widows—behaved in ways denied to wives suggests that household status often was more significant than gender. But it is always women and not men who are expected to subordinate themselves in the household.

Because medieval countrywomen have been little studied, many basic questions about their lives remain unanswered. Variations in women's opportunities in different regions and different local economies need to be traced. Were the lives of women in pastoral villages enviable in comparison to the lives of women in agrarian communities? Similarly unknown are the effects on women of a changing rural economy during the Middle Ages. Which setting better enhanced the status of countrywomen—the prosperous years of the thirteenth century, the economic stagnation of the early fourteenth century, or the underpopulated economy of the fifteenth century? The importance to women of socioeconomic distinctions within the peasantry also deserve study. Was the wife of a holder of 20 acres really better off than the wife of a smallholder? And the effects of such distinctions on women must be traced beyond the peasantry to encompass other classes. How did the lives of rural women compare to those of townswomen and gentlewomen? No single study can fully answer these substantive and complex questions, for each requires a methodological approach discrete from the others. But this book, as the first in-depth analysis of the social relation of the sexes in the medieval countryside, lays the groundwork for examining such comparative and temporal issues by considering the most basic question of all: How and why did the lives of rural women in the Middle Ages differ from those of rural men?

The answer to this question will be sought from the experiences of women and men on one English manor in the early fourteenth century. Such detailed studies have a long and distinguished place in medieval rural historiography because of the depth of analysis they afford. The medieval English countryside offered so many diverse circumstances and opportunities that only focused studies can uncover the nuances caused by such factors as ecology, custom, and settlement. As a result, medievalists have built case study upon case study to reconstruct the general patterns of the rural past. At the beginning of this century, scholars began to delve into the archives of specific estates to recreate the managerial and investment strategies of individual and corporate landlords. Although each study was specific to one landowning unit, together they have revealed much, not only about specific estates, but also about how landowners reacted to the economic vicissitudes of the medieval centuries.[13]

The same approach has more recently been applied to the humbler members of rural society—the peasantry and their villages. Case studies of villages are perhaps even more justified than studies of estates because they reflect real contemporary circumstances. Rural settlements before the plague were neither isolated nor homogeneous, but they were discrete, integrated communities. When medieval peasants spoke of the *communitas villae,* they meant something real, not abstract. Recognizing that the study of single rural communities is both efficacious and appropriate, students of medieval peasant society are slowly accumulating the case studies that will eventually come together to form a comprehensive picture of rural communities in the Middle Ages.[14]

In the following chapters, the approach that has proven so useful in reconstructing the histories of medieval landlords and peasant communities will be applied to the study of the social relation of the sexes in rural England. The use of a specific case study to examine this particular topic is justified by social anthropology as well as historiography. Drawing on a persistent notion that a society can be best judged by the status of its women, the study of women became a standard component of nineteenth-century studies and has remained a major topic of anthropological inquiry throughout the twentieth century. From Lewis Henry Morgan's publication of *Ancient Society* in 1877 to Karen Sacks's recent *Sisters and Wives,* anthropologists have relied on case studies to examine the complexities of relations between the sexes. Because the realities of women's lives are so often obscured by public pronouncements, prescriptive literature, and formal behavior, case studies allow the sort of delicate and detailed analyses required for a successful inquiry into the social relations of the sexes. Few subjects are as well-suited to the use of case studies as the lives of medieval countrywomen.[15]

Brigstock, the manor chosen for this close examination, lies in the heart of Rockingham Forest in Northamptonshire, about 75 miles north of London. By the time of the Domesday survey, Brigstock was already an old settlement. The Crown then held the manor, which included three and one-half hides, a mill, seven acres of meadow, and a wood fifteen furlongs long and one league wide. Portions of three other communities—Stanion, Geddington, and Islip—were incorporated into the final valuation of £20. Of the three, only Stanion remained closely associated with the manor. A daughter settlement of Brigstock carved out of deeper parts of the forest, Stanion lay two and one-half miles to the northwest of Brigstock proper, and many tenants in Stanion remained subject to the jurisdiction of the manorial court of Brigstock throughout the Middle Ages. The two villages were closely bound not only by settlement, but also by common customs and the annexation of the Stanion church as a chapel appurtenant to the Brigstock church of St. Andrew. Both socially and economically, the lives of the residents of these two communities were inextricably intertwined; families often held lands or offices in both villages. The clerk of the Brigstock court usually treated these two settlements as one community, and this approach, except where noted, has been adopted here.[16]

Surrounded on all sides by royal preserves, Brigstock's economy typified the diversity and flexibility of forest communities. Brigstock proper was an open-field village, a nucleated settlement centrally located between arable fields. Traces of medieval plowing around the village still testify to the agricultural labors of the peasantry centuries ago. And the records of the Brigstock court testify just as eloquently to the regulatory challenges of open-field agriculture. Villagers paid amercements for breaking hedges, moving strip markers, gleaning improperly, taking crops not their own from the fields, and even dragging plows across the planted strips of their neighbors.[17] But the forest location of Brigstock assured that its inhabitants could also expand their tillage by converting wasteland into arable land, and most assarts (or newly claimed arable land) became independent closes whose holders managed them separately from the communal regulations of the open fields. Although the extent of medieval assarting in Brigstock cannot be fully reconstructed, the provision of special rules for "newsets" in a late fourteenth-century custumal indicates that assarting remained an important economic resource for Brigstock throughout the Middle Ages. Aside from the unusual presence of such small closes, Brigstock's arable economy was also distinctive for its relatively small extent. At the end of the Middle Ages, Brigstock's fields covered only 1,400 acres, less than one-fourth of the land in the parish.[18]

Brigstock's small arable was offset by extensive pasture in the surrounding wastes, woodlands, and preserves. Animal husbandry was a vital complement to arable farming in all open-field villages, but it played an especially important part in the economies of forest communities like Brigstock. Although no manorial accounts or surveys have survived to detail the full importance of pasture (and even these would tell little about the animal husbandry of the peasantry), the records of the manorial court attest to the importance of pastoral resources in medieval Brigstock. Tenants were required to supply workers not only for plowing but also for herding. The right to pasture pigs in the woodland was carefully regulated through the payment of pannage. Owners of wandering animals whose trespasses damaged the property of others were liable to both civil suit and court amercement. And one crime regularly noted in the court of Brigstock was that of pondbreche—the illegal rescue of impounded animals.[19]

Aside from agriculture and animal husbandry, many other activities added to the diversity of Brigstock's economy in the early fourteenth century. The forest location of the manor offered both opportunity and temptation. Fuel was readily obtained both from the woodlands and from the digging of peat. At least one villager used the abundant woods to profit from the production of charcoal, and another sold timber. Food was also available for those who succumbed to the tempting presence of plentiful game and illegally took hare and deer from the parks. The abundance of untilled land surrounding Brigstock also proved tempting to some; traces of ridge-and-furrow in both Brigstock Great Park and Brigstock Little Park suggest that some villagers surreptitiously farmed parts of the royal preserves. Fishing in Harper's Brook, which created the valley in which Brigstock lay, probably supplemented the diets of many households; as specified in the listing of the manor's customs (or custumal) in 1391, all residents of Brigstock enjoyed the right to fish in parts of the stream. Even clothworking was not unknown; in 1303, Robert Moke sued Galfridus Lambin for failing to return promptly seven ells of wool mortgaged in a debt.[20]

The diversity of Brigstock's economy was unusual, but it did not save the residents of the manor from the demographic and economic

TABLE 1.1. Estimated Adult Male Residents in Brigstock, 1287–1348

Period	Number of Courts	Number of Adult Males	Adjusted Number of Adult Males
1287–1290	7	101	421
1291–1295	21	226	483
1296–1300	45	288	437
1301–1305	53	317	430
1306–1310	38	309	489
1311–1315	42	333	495
1316–1320	53	354	467
1321–1325	37	305	490
1326–1330	44	306	459
1331–1335	56	313	412
1336–1340	78	355	355
1341–1345	61	333	410
1346–1348	14	106	394

Note: See the Appendix for a full explanation of these estimates.

problems of the early fourteenth-century countryside. The English rural economy during these years was haunted by the classic Malthusian imbalance between population and resources; the rapid population growth of the twelfth and thirteenth centuries had finally surpassed the productive capacities of medieval agriculture. Grain prices rose, wage rates fell, and marginal lands came under the plow.[21] Poor weather between 1315 and 1322 aggravated the growing crisis, and possibly as much as 10 percent of the English population died in the famines and epidemics of these years.[22] Table 1.1 shows that Brigstock was not immune to these problems. During the six decades before the plague, the male population stabilized at a high level (c. 1287–1325), then fell quite dramatically (c. 1326–1340), and finally experienced a slight resurgence (c. 1341–1348). The local economy responded to these demographic changes. The proportion of field crimes associated with poverty and economic hardship—improper gleaning, stealing sheaves, pilfering hay—more than doubled in the first decades of the fourteenth century and then stabilized at the new, higher rate. The incidence of land sales, which partly reflects economic pressures that forced landholders to relinquish their properties, also doubled in the first decades of the century, stabilized, and then grew again. The frequency of debt disputes in the Brigstock court similarly rose in the early fourteenth century, leveled off for a few years, and then grew again in the years immediately preceding the plague. And the levels of amercements for the selling of ale—which likely reflect the abilities of offenders to meet their expenses—follow a pattern that also suggests economic problems in the early decades of the century (when the average ale amercement fell to one-third its earlier level), slight recovery in the 1330s (when the average amercement increased slightly), and a renewed crisis in the 1340s (when the average fell to a new low). When the population was stable but high in the late thirteenth and early fourteenth centuries, the economic prospects of the community seriously faltered; in response to the population decline of the 1320s and 1330s, the local economy briefly flourished; but it worsened again with the renewed population growth of the 1340s.[23]

In addition to shaping the local economy in a profound way, the influence of the forest shaped the peculiar inheritance customs of the manor of Brigstock. When a tenant died, his land was not solely inherited by either his eldest son (primogeniture) or his youngest (ultimogeniture or "Borough English"). Instead, the deceased's properties were divided between the elder son, who received all the lands his father had purchased during his life, and the younger son, who claimed the lands that his father had inherited. The custumal of Brigstock in 1391 explained:

> First, after the death of a tenant holding a semi-virgate of land and meadow with a messuage, his younger son will be his heir if any property shall have been left unsold. Because the said tenant, if he shall have need during his life, can sell all his hereditary lands. And his younger son, after his death, is the heir of the remaining unsold lands and will recover them. Similarly, the elder son will be the heir of any additional lands that the tenant shall have purchased and not sold to another. Because the tenant is able to sell all that he holds while he lives. And the elder son, after his death, is the heir of the remainder.[24]

A modified version of Borough English which left considerable discretionary power in the hands of fathers, this custom of inheritance is also evidenced in the court rolls of the manor before the plague.[25] The origins of the practice are unknown, but its causes probably "lie in the conditions of primitive settlement in a woodland region" since other communities in Rockingham Forest also followed this unusual rule of inheritance.[26] As in many rural villages, daughters only inherited in default of sons, and in such cases the property was divided among all surviving daughters.[27]

The seigneurial circumstances of Brigstock also reflected its forest location. Like many other communities in royal forests, Brigstock was part of the ancient demesne, and its tenants enjoyed the special privileges that accompanied this status—they were free from tolls and customs, they were not obliged to attend county courts, and they could use royal writs to obtain judgments in property disputes.[28] The Norman kings had been sufficiently interested in Brigstock to maintain a hunting lodge on the manor, which included a fishpond, hall, chamber, and mews. But no royal visits are recorded after the reign of Henry I, and as interest in the lodge declined, it slowly fell into disrepair in the fourteenth century.[29] The decay of the lodge reflected the waning of seigneurial interests. Although the crown continued to hold the manor either directly or as part of the queen's dower, by the thirteenth century it usually leased the manor to the tenants (often via third parties). In August 1318, for example, the tenants of Brigstock agreed to lease the manor at the cost of £46 yearly, to be paid to Margaret the widow of Duncan de Farendraght who owed the exchequer only 20 marks annually for Brigstock during the sixteen years of the lease.[30] The tenants of Brigstock were, as a result, relatively free of seigneurial control, but the king always remained an important presence in the life of the community. As testified by the constant mention of royal interest in the manorial courts, the tenants of Brigstock never forgot that they were leasees only, obliged to maintain the manor to the king's satisfaction. The royal parks that lay along the southern and western boundaries of the manor also assured that the tenants of Brigstock were perpetually subject to the royal officers of the forest; foresters, verderers, and wardens served as constant reminders of the king's special interests in Brigstock. And Brigstock, like all rural communities, felt the burden of the royal taxes, purveyances, and military conscriptions required by the wars of the three Edwards.[31] Because of such demands, the king's presence was probably becoming more, not less, evident in Brigstock during the late thirteenth and fourteenth centuries. But the king was more important as king, not as lord of Brigstock.

In its diverse economy, its unusual inheritance customs, and its relative freedom from direct seigneurial control, Brigstock was not a "classical" manor, raising the possibility that the experiences of women in Brigstock differed from those of other rural women in the early fourteenth century. To a certain extent, this possibility must be simply acknowledged, neither confirmed nor refuted. But the perplexing issue of typicality is somewhat militated by the fact that the classical manor—with an extensive demesne (those lands worked directly for the lord's use), considerable seigneurial supervision, and an agricultural economy based on the mixed farming of open fields—is more a historical illusion than reality. Manors varied widely in size, structure, and economy. And because no single community could represent fully the extraordinary diversity of economy, settlement, and custom found in the medieval English countryside, none was typical of all others. No case study can be a universal example.[32] As a result, this analysis of women in Brigstock is meant to be more stimulating than definitive. It is primarily hoped that the model provided here will encourage others to study the lives of women in different rural locales and to establish, in the process, how usual or unusual were the experiences of women in Brigstock before the plague.

The comparative dimension, however, has not been completely ignored in the following chapters. The very atypicality of Brigstock's economy, inheritance, and lordship provides instructive comparisons with the available published studies. To date, most research on rural society in the Middle Ages has focused on open-field manors under close seigneurial control that, more often than not, followed the custom of primogeniture; to the extent that these studies have supplied information on women, Brigstock provides a very different perspective. Moreover, the experiences of women as shown in the extant archives of two other contemporary manors will be directly compared, whenever feasible, to the findings for Brigstock. Iver and Houghton-cum-Wyton offered their inhabitants very different settings and circumstances from those found in Brigstock. Lying just below the Chiltern Hills in Buckinghamshire, Iver was a pastoral community whose residents primarily relied on animal husbandry and fishing for sustenance. Throughout the late thirteenth and early fourteenth centuries, the manor of Iver was held by a succession of local families. Houghton-cum-Wyton, favorably situated on the rich and well-irrigated soil of Huntingdonshire, was a classic open-field manor whose tenants focused on arable farming, with supplementary use of pastures and meadows. It was also subject to much closer manorial supervision than that found in either Brigstock or Iver; as part of the Ramsey Abbey estate, Houghton-cum-Wyton was under the constant, well-organized, and perpetual supervision of the Abbey's numerous officials. In both Iver and Houghton-cum-Wyton, eldest sons inherited the holdings of their fathers.[33]

The conclusions drawn from comparisons between Brigstock and other manors are necessarily more suggestive than definitive. But these comparisons do suggest that the general patterns of gender relations in Brigstock were broadly characteristic of most rural communities, with allowances made for nuances caused by different economies, seigneuries, and customs. Women in Iver and Houghton-cum-Wyton, for example, participated much less actively in their local food markets than did women in Brigstock; but daughters, wives, and widows in all three villages shared fundamentally similar constraints and opportunities. In the final analysis, however, neither published information nor data drawn from the archives of Iver and Houghton-cum-Wyton can establish definitely the typicality of social relations between the sexes in Brigstock. Until these comparative inferences are confirmed by research on women and men in other rural locales, the main value of this study will lie in the broad patterns it suggests, the methodological and theoretical models it employs, and the hypotheses for future research it generates.

II

Studying Women
in the Medieval Countryside

Rural England in the late thirteenth and early fourteenth centuries was a changing society. Because of the overcrowding of the countryside, land was scarce, rents were high, and labor was ill-paid. As a result, many peasant households were especially vulnerable not only to the famines and epidemics of 1315–1322, but also to the plague that began its ravages in 1348. This bleak situation was aggravated by royal policies. To finance their wars, Edward I and his successors sought new methods of directly tapping the resources of the rural population. The lay subsidies, purveyances, and military conscriptions of these kings further exacerbated the economic problems of rural dwellers. But not all the changes during these decades would have negative consequences. As landowners abandoned the direct management of the early and middle thirteenth century in favor of rental incomes, many peasants were able to replace labor services with cash payments, and others expanded their acreage by leasing demesne lands. The same decades also witnessed an enormous growth in local trade with the establishment of so many rural markets that most villages were probably within an easy day's walk from one such weekly emporium. None of the changes of these years, however, compared with the sweeping transformations that followed the mid-century plague. Rural society was under enormous stress in the late thirteenth

18

and early fourteenth centuries, but life in the countryside, although changed in many particulars, remained substantially intact until shattered by the Black Death in 1348–1349. The peasants of the early fourteenth century were still thoroughly medieval; their counterparts at the end of the century would be coping with the changes that would usher in the modern era. The society of Brigstock before the plague represents, in short, a rural society that was soon to disappear.[1]

The historical importance of the decades that preceded the plague is matched by archival abundance. In the middle of the thirteenth century, English lords began to keep detailed records of their holdings, and where such manorial archives survive in long and nearly continuous series, medieval villages can be reconstructed with a clarity almost unparalleled for historical communities. These records fall roughly into three categories. First, manorial administrators occasionally produced surveys detailing the manor's tenants, the rents they paid, and their customary rights and obligations. Surveys normally relied on information supplied by juries of male tenants, but they were not compiled on regular schedules and only reflect the economic organization of a manor at specific points in time. And because surveys were formal fiscal records, they listed tenants, not inhabitants, not even heads of households. All persons not legal tenants—wives, children, subleasees, servants—were unimportant to manorial officials and were, therefore, ignored. Second, manorial officers annually accounted for their receipts and payments at the September feast of St. Michael. Accounts, unlike surveys, were compiled on regular schedules and often survive in consecutive series that detail the economic rhythms of medieval manors. Accounts, however, like surveys, described only the economic structures of the manor, not the economic lives of the peasantry. The actual cultivators of the soil appeared in manorial accounts only if they directly figured in the official recitation of monetary obligations and their fulfillment—as renters of demesne lands, sellers of foodstuffs, wage-laborers, and payers of required annual fines.

The third type of manorial record, the rolls of seigneurial courts to which all tenants owed suit, reflects most fully the actual lives of the peasantry. Surveys and accounts provide supplementary insights, but court rolls are the essential sources for examining the social experiences of the medieval English peasantry. These courts were rural institutions, blending seigneurial desire for control with local need for community regulation and mixing the lord's law with local custom. The jurisdiction of manorial courts—requiring attendance by all tenants at meetings held every three weeks—ensured that court meetings were familiar and integrated features of life in the medieval countryside. The purview of the court was so broad that matters of even minor local concern were noted in its records. A typical court roll includes information about conveyances, leases and inheritances of land, about problems with maintaining the roads, fences and fields of the community, about animals or persons who had trespassed on the property of others, and about all sorts of agreements and quarrels between villagers. Elections to the numerous offices of local government were usually recorded, as were amercements paid by local brewers and bakers. On most manors an annual view of frankpledge supplemented the business of the triweekly seigneurial court. By the late thirteenth century, these views, although originally intended solely to identify those not in the peace-keeping system known as frankpledge, had expanded their overview to encompass all matters pertaining to the maintenance of local peace. Annual views of frankpledge amerced villagers for numerous minor offenses, such as thefts, assaults, slanders, illegitimate sexual activities, and unnecessary disturbances to the community. The entries of a single sitting of a manorial court, then, present a fairly full record of all the events and problems that had transpired in the community since the last court session. A few people would be formally excused from attendance, a villager or two would transfer or sell a parcel of land, a few others would record debt contracts or complain about unfulfilled agreements, a young man would inherit his father's property, a widow would claim her free bench, some ale-sellers would pay perfunctory sums, and a few people would be cited and amerced for disturbing the peace.[2]

These local forums differed from modern courts in their familiarity, use, and form. In the twentieth century, we attend our local courts only when forced to do so by crisis or summons; in the fourteenth century, many peasants probably knew their manorial courts as well as they knew their churches. Similarly, although we use our courts mainly to resolve interpersonal conflicts, most contacts in medieval courts involved cooperation and exchange rather than controversy and enmity. And the professional expertise that so dominates modern courts was minimized in manorial courts; the lord or his representative presided over the proceedings and provided a clerk to keep the record, but business was conducted by laypeople who usually acted without the aid of lawyers or other counselors. Manorial courts are windows, albeit circumscribed and clouded, through which historians can observe the action and drama of rural life in medieval England.[3]

The usefulness of manorial rolls for reconstructing social experience is enhanced when long and complete series are available, as is the case for Brigstock before the plague. Deposited in the Northamptonshire Record Office and the Public Record Office, the manorial archive of Brigstock includes the proceedings of 549 courts held in the community between 1287 and 1348. Court sessions have survived for all but eleven years of this period. Although account notations added to the versos of some rolls are too abbreviated to be of much use, one partial listing of tenants and their rents has survived for 1319. In reconstructing the social relation of the sexes in Brigstock, then, this study focuses on the 25 views of frankpledge and 524 seigneurial courts extant for the manor during the six decades before the plague.

Two problems complicate the usefulness of court rolls for studying the experiences of women. First, historians disagree about the proper methods of analyzing evidence taken from court rolls. The issues of technique and method raised by this historiographical debate are discussed in the Appendix, which describes how this study, while generally indebted to the methodological advances of recent years, uses analytical techniques specifically developed for the study of gender relations. The Appendix outlines the main features of the analyses of social organization, marriage, landholding, crime, civil litigation, and commerce whose results are reported in the main text. It also provides background information on two families, the Kroyls and the Penifaders, whose activities have provided special insights into the social relation of the sexes in Brigstock. Second, manorial court rolls, no matter how abundant and illuminating, predominantly report the activities of men. The manor court was the quintessential community organization, the nexus of public life; it was, in short, a male forum. In the absence of any secure demographic indicators, it is safest to assume that medieval rural communities boasted roughly equal numbers of adult males and females.[4] But even in Brigstock—where women were much better represented in the court than in either Iver or Houghton-cum-Wyton—only about one in every five persons who appeared in court was a woman (see Table 2.1). These aggregate trends were paralleled in the experiences of individuals; over the course of their adult lives, the men in the Penifader and Kroyl families of Brigstock averaged about 93 appearances each before the court, but their sisters, mothers, and wives managed only an average of 17 appearances each.[5] Both legal and social circumstances contributed to the vastly skewed representation of the sexes in local courts. On the one hand, women were second-rank constituents of these courts, lacking access to many of the political and legal options available to men. Faced with such disabilities, women brought less business before the courts than did men. On the other hand, women were also second-rank members of rural society, generating fewer matters that merited court attention. Less active than men in the economic and social networks of their villages, women found themselves less liable for legal prosecution or action.

Politics

In Brigstock, as in most medieval communities, political life was important and highly organized, but it was the business of men, not women. To begin with, no woman ever served as an officer in Brigstock. In addition to reeves and bailiffs to manage village and manor, the tenants of Brigstock also regularly selected messors to supervise field use, affeerors to determine court amercements and fines, tithingmen to oversee peace-keeping groups, and aletasters to regulate ale sales. The most common office, however, was that of juror, and many male householders in Brigstock served on juries impaneled for either general purposes or specific cases.

Official service was not an unmitigated benefit; in addition to time lost from other pursuits, officers in Brigstock were liable to amercements for dereliction of duty and to attacks from disgruntled villagers. As a result, some attempted to avoid official duties, as did William ad Stagnum who paid 20 shillings in 1314 to be excused from serving as reeve. But attempts to avoid offices were rare, and official service was generally a privilege reserved for only the wealthiest male householders in Brigstock. Serving as a sign of privileged stature, official activity also enhanced privilege because officers could use their authority to social, political, and economic advantage. As a general

TABLE 2.1. The Court Appearances of Women and Men in Brigstock, Iver, and Houghton-cum-Wyton

Category	Males		Females		Both Sexes	
	Number	Row Percent	Number	Row Percent	Number	Row Percent
Brigstock						
Individuals	1,149	58%	843	42%	1,992	100%
Appearances	24,298	78	6,983	22	31,281	100
Average appearances per individual	21.1		8.3		15.7	
Iver						
Individuals	704	70	306	30	1,010	100
Appearances	6,825	86	1,107	14	7,932	100
Average appearances per individual	9.7		3.6		7.9	
Houghton-cum-Wyton						
Individuals	488	65	236	35	684	100
Appearances	2,875	86	449	14	3,324	100
Average appearances per individual	6.4		1.9		4.9	

Note: This table excludes appearances by persons of unknown sex and by isolated individuals. Because many women have been unavoidably counted as two individuals under (a) their natal surnames and (b) their marital surnames, the count of female individuals overestimates the actual number of female individuals who appeared before these courts. This evidential bias does not affect the counts of female appearances. Percentages have been rounded to produce integral numbers.

rule, women never partook of the responsibilities and benefits of official service in the medieval countryside, and Brigstock was no exception.[6] Women also probably did not participate in the appointment of officers. Because clerks simply recorded the selection (*electi sunt*) of certain persons for certain offices, the methods used to choose officers in Brigstock are unknown. But it is unlikely that any females (even female tenants) participated in the formal selection of officers, because they were themselves ineligible for such positions.

Women were also not included in the basic peace-keeping system of medieval England, the frankpledge or tithing. Originally containing only ten persons, the tithing was a group of men responsible for bringing its members to court to answer for crimes and offenses. If a tithing, headed by a tithingman (*decennarius*), failed to produce an errant member, it was subject to amercement. This system of mutual responsibility was carefully maintained in Brigstock, as throughout most of the English countryside, by means of annual views of frankpledge, which inducted new members and amerced those illegally outside of tithings. With very few exceptions, all men in England, both free and unfree, were expected to join tithings at 12 years of age. But women, considered to be legal dependents (or mainpasts) of their householders, never joined these groups.[7]

Moreover, women were barred from a variety of legal actions that enabled men to solidify friendships and to enlarge their political influence. Men frequently assisted one another in court, acting as attorneys who stood in for absent litigants, as essoiners who brought other suitors' excuses for failing to attend court, and especially as pledges who guaranteed that a person would fulfill a stipulated legal obligation. Almost all persons judged liable by the Brigstock court to pay an amercement, perform an assigned task, or answer a specific plea had to produce a personal pledge who promised that the legal obligation would be met. If such persons defaulted, their pledges were liable for an amercement or other punishment. The private arrangements that preceded pledging are unknown, but most people probably pledged not for remuneration in cash or goods, but for ties of friendship and mutuality. The political ramifications of pledging are best illustrated by the fact that the people who most actively served as pledges in Brigstock were, as in most medieval villages, among the wealthiest and most influential members of the community.[8] Although men of all social ranks and ages were accepted as pledges by the

Brigstock court, women were rarely allowed to act in this capacity. Of the thousands of pledges recorded in the rolls of the court, only 46 were women, and most of these were widows pledging for their dependent children. Brigstock was unusual in this respect; on most medieval manors, no female pledges were ever accepted by the manorial court.[9]

The political inactivity of women in Brigstock was not firmly based on legal disability. Unmarried or widowed female tenants were as obliged as male tenants to attend all sessions of the manorial court, but they were never, despite their acceptance of the legal responsibilities of landholders, eligible for political responsibility. Because some female tenants were as wealthy as the male tenants who served as reeves, aletasters, jurors, and the like, it seems that sex was the major barrier. Usually as liable for their own crimes as men, women also sometimes lived outside the control of a male householder who could be trusted to bring them to court to answer for such offenses. But widows and spinsters were never inducted into tithings to ensure that they kept the peace, indicating again that sex was the excluding factor. Similarly, the acceptance of some female pledges by the Brigstock court demonstrates the legal sufficiency of a pledge proffered by a woman, but the court limited the political impact of female pledging by only infrequently allowing widows to pledge for their dependents. Although women sometimes held large properties, sometimes lived outside the authority of a male householder, and sometimes needed to act as sureties for their children, they had no access to formal political associations. F. W. Maitland's summary of the public functions of women under the common law in the thirteenth century applies as well to women under the customary law of communities like Brigstock: "In the camp, at the council board, on the bench, in the jury box there is no place for them."[10]

The clerks of the Brigstock court never recorded any protests by women about their lack of political involvement nor any formal efforts by men to exclude women from political matters. Instead, the relegation of politics to men was likely accepted as natural by both sexes. Just as medieval people expected wives to be submissive and husbands to be dominant, so they expected women to accept the government of men. Nevertheless, the political inactivity of women was an important aspect of relations between the sexes in the medieval countryside. Official service was an obligation that some men tried to avoid, but it also brought prestige, power, and the ability to exercise social control over the poorer and more marginal members of rural communities. As a result, women passed their lives subject to a system of communal regulation over which they had no direct control; men alone decided what pleas would be disallowed, what crimes would be ignored, and what customs would govern the devolution of land. All men did not participate in such decisions, but only men did so.

The ramifications for women of a male-controlled political process cannot be fully traced in court records, but one possible result was the low reporting of male violence against women in Brigstock. In the views of frankpledge sampled, reports of physical attacks against women were relatively infrequent, and many concerned assaults against women perpetrated by other women. Although women constituted 41 percent of all victims in the sample, they accounted for only 28 percent of reported victims of attack, and a relatively high number of reported female victims of assault were attacked by other women (17 of 44). Male violence against women might actually have been comparatively low, but it is also possible that male assaults sometimes went either unpunished or unreported because those in control of court processes minimized their importance. Consider that women numbered heavily among those found guilty of alerting the community with an improper hue and cry—an outcry alerting others to pursue a criminal—and that, in most cases, the objects of such putatively unnecessary hues were men; of the 15 alerts wrongly raised by women in the sample, 12 were directed against men. In other words, some women threatened by men might have been themselves rebuked when they tried to rouse the assistance of their neighbors (and the men went unpunished). Or consider the experiences of Matilda Coleman of Brigstock who was amerced in 1302 for unjustly raising a hue against Adam Swargere. The implication that Coleman's outcry was malicious or premature is belied by the simultaneous amercement paid by Swargere for mistreating Coleman's daughter (*maleficit*). (Under normal circumstances, Swargere would have paid two amercements—one for the offense itself and another for the hue justly raised because of the offense.) Swargere had clearly harmed the girl, yet the tithingmen considered that her mother had raised the hue against him without justification.[11] Such cases suggest that female accusations of male violence (and, indeed, female problems overall) were discounted or disregarded by their courts. Medieval women stood in relation to the men of their villages as those men stood in relation to manorial administrators; the medieval world was a hierarchical world with peasant women at the bottom.

The political complexity of medieval communities makes it unlikely that informal political influence compensated for women's lack of formal authority.[12] Public institutions in the countryside were highly articulated and stratified—every man belonged to a tithing, all villages regulated themselves with numerous officers and bylaws, and most seigneurial courts required the attendance of all tenants on a triweekly basis. Such sophisticated mechanisms of local government severely curtailed the ability of women to influence public matters in informal ways. Indeed, the integration of rural communities into larger units—estates, regions, and the realm—gave men political powers that extended far beyond their local authority. The same men who helped to govern a community and run its court also acted as brokers with the outside world—dealing with manorial officials, negotiating with royal tax collectors, testifying at county courts. Even in the unlikely event that some sort of political equilibrium had existed within rural communities between formal (male) power and informal (female) power, the balance would have been destroyed by the advantages that those men who held formal power exercised in the world beyond the village. Moreover, whatever informal influence women might have exercised was inherently limited. Usually existing only to compensate for a lack of formal power, informal power not only is less authoritative but also is more easily subject to erosion.[13] It is reasonable to suppose that informal relations were important in local society, that women sometimes manipulated public decisions from behind the scenes, and that women did not aspire to positions of public influence, but these suppositions do not belie the basic power held by the men who controlled the politics of their localities.

Legal Status

Because only tenants, most of whom were male, were required to attend the court of Brigstock, most women probably only went to court when they had specific business to transact. Once there, they encountered a variety of legal practices that marked women as second-rank constituents of the court. The legal distinctions that separated women and men are clearly illustrated in a sample of civil pleas brought before the court of Brigstock (see Table 2.2). Like men, women occasionally sought to resolve personal quarrels and disputes through court actions—pleas of trespass covering general problems for which plaintiffs sought redress, pleas of debt brought to force payment from recalcitrant debtors, and pleas of contract covering all agreements between villagers that had ended badly. Yet almost every aspect of civil pleading emphasized the legal disabilities of women.[14]

In medieval England, the customary law of seigneurial courts diverged often from the common law of the king's courts. But Brigstock custom apparently followed common law in limiting the contractual capabilities of women. Under common law, a married woman could neither loan money nor conclude a contract without implicating her husband, because she possessed no chattels (all marital goods being the property of her husband).[15] The same rules likely applied in Brigstock where women only rarely litigated suits of debt or contract; only one-tenth of the sampled female litigants pursued such pleas, as opposed to over one-fourth of male litigants. Women active in suits of debt or contract were either unmarried (3 widows, 2 women of unknown status), or married women acting jointly with their husbands (3 wives). A case recorded early in 1331 illustrates how the Brigstock court considered husbands liable for the contracts of their wives; John Hayroun sued both John Sutor and his wife Strangia for damages suffered when an agreement concluded with Strangia alone fell through.[16]

Legal procedures also emphasized the legal disadvantages of women. One major drawback of the courts was the length of time case litigation could take. Because postponements were commonly sought and easily obtained, litigants often faced months of legal action during which the case's progress had to be reported to the court at each triweekly meeting. Men, who were usually obliged as tenants and suitors to attend all court sessions, were probably little disturbed by the need to report a case's status to the court on a regular basis, but women, most of whom only attended court to transact specific business, might have been much more inconvenienced by lengthy litigation. Female litigants were also handicapped by the need for large numbers of assistors. Successful litigants relied heavily on aid from

TABLE 2.2. Women and Men in the Brigstock Sample of Civil Pleas

Category	Males		Females		Both Sexes	
	Number	Column Percent	Number	Column Percent	Number	Column Percent
Type of action						
Plaintiff	176	51%	33	38%	209	48%
Defendant	172	49	53	62	225	52
All actors	348	100	86	100	434	100
Type of plea (if known)						
Plea of trespass	225	73	70	90	295	76
Plea of contract	17	5	2	2	19	5
Plea of debt	67	22	6	8	73	19
All known pleas	309	100	78	100	387	100
Type of resolution (if known)						
Concord	167	79	28	53	195	74
Judgment/law	44	21	25	47	69	26
All known resolutions	211	100	53	100	264	100
Final outcome (if known)						
Actor won	105	50	25	47	130	49
Actor lost	106	50	28	53	134	51
All known outcomes	211	100	53	100	264	100

Note: Percentages have been rounded to produce integral numbers.

others—attorneys acted in their behalf, essoiners excused them from court attendance, oath-helpers assisted in the waging of law (or compurgation), pledges promised that they would abide by the terms of the final resolution. Because men were able to reciprocate such actions, they often drew upon large networks of friends and associates for such assistance. Women, however, were usually unable to act as attorneys, essoiners, or pledges, and they consequently had to rely on smaller pools of assistors, drawing on the goodwill of male relatives.[17] Women also lacked the legal sophistication to pursue their cases as successfully as men. Cases were often won or lost on the basis of minor errors—an essoin would be incorrectly proffered, a plaintiff would fail to implead both husband and wife, a defendant would misstate some part of the charge denial. Women, less familiar with court procedures, were more likely to commit such errors. In 1303, for example, Emma Morice lost her suit against Margery Cocus (whom she accused of slander, assault, and theft) because her charge lacked two required elements—a precise description of the slanderous comment (*non nomiavit specialiter dispersonacionem sed generaliter*) and a specific statement of the location of the alleged crimes (*non nomiavit nomine ville*). Women accounted for half of those litigants who lost cases on legal exceptions.[18]

Civil pleas so severely strained women's limited legal resources that they responded by rarely bringing such disputes before the courts; the Brigstock sample of civil pleas yielded only one female for every five litigants. Many potential female plaintiffs, known from presentments made at views of frankpledge, failed to seek compensation through litigation. As illustrated by Emma Morice's suit against Margery Cocus, civil pleas often sprang from problems reported annually by the tithingman; the perpetrator of a crime was liable not only for an amercement levied at the annual view, but also for any damages that the victim could obtain through litigation. But women, who accounted for 41 percent of crime victims reported in the sampled views (119 of 290 victims), numbered only 16 percent of the plaintiffs who sought redress through civil pleas. Clearly, women passed by many opportunities for litigation, either obtaining compensation through informal channels or dropping such matters altogether. Indeed, female litigants usually appeared under duress. Male plaintiffs roughly equaled male defendants; a man was just as likely to haul another into court on a complaint as he was to have to respond to another's plea. But female defendants outnumbered female plaintiffs by a 6:4 ratio. More often than not, a woman got involved in litigation not because she was using the court to seek redress for wrongs, but because she was forced to answer the complaints registered by another.

If a woman did pursue legal action, she usually did so only for particularly intractable disputes. Most civil pleas eventually ended with a concord rather than a judgment by jury or a formal waging of the law (which in the Brigstock court involved the defendant's attempt to deny the charges in a precise formulaic fashion). Courts actively encouraged concords by delaying cases, assigning arbitrators, and even sometimes demanding that compromises be reached. Few men had to take their complaints beyond these attempts at informal resolution; four of every five male litigants ended his plea with a concord. But women reached concords much less successfully, and almost half of their cases went to either judgment or law. Although the final award did not differ by gender (both men and women won about half the time), cases brought by women were so difficult that normal resolution by concord was frequently impossible.[19]

The settlement of disputes was a primary function of the Brigstock court, whose agenda included several such cases at almost every triweekly meeting. But women, faced with legal practices and court structures that worked to their disadvantage, used their local court to resolve quarrels much less frequently than men. The Brigstock evidence suggests that the legal disabilities of women sprang from two discrete sources. On the one hand, local custom limited the public presence of wives, anticipating that married women would be covered in such matters by their husbands; the private dependency of wives led to an expectation of public inactivity. On the other hand, the political inactivity of women limited their legal influence; women were infrequent and unwilling litigants because the structures of the manorial court were often both unfamiliar and disadvantageous.

Although the second-rank legal status of women extended beyond civil pleas to many other aspects of court business, it occasionally offered practical advantage, not disadvantage. The fact that husbands could join their legally dependent wives in civil pleas, for example, strengthened litigants who wished to delay the resolution of their cases, because a joint plea doubled the number of permissible essoins. For example, Simon Coleman's complaint against Gilbert son of

Galfridus and his wife Emma in March 1310 remained unresolved for several months because of delays by the defendants. Emma appeared to answer Simon's complaint in the next court, but declined to do so because her husband had essoined. In the following three courts, her husband appeared, but could not respond because she had essoined.[20] The more frequent use of joint actions by defendants (24 actions) than by plaintiffs (9 actions) emphasizes the special appeal of this delaying tactic to those loath to answer accusations. Similarly, the legal dependency of wives, whose husbands could be deemed liable for their offenses, occasionally allowed them to escape personal responsibility for their crimes. But in medieval communities, as in most societies regulated by laws, legal competence was an essential mark of social adulthood.[21] Those who were not legally competent approached the status of children—protected by the law, but not responsible to it. The second-rank legal stature of women in Brigstock both reflected their expected dependency on men and reinforced their subordinate status.

Economic Opportunity

The political and legal institutions of Brigstock were, of course, rooted in the economic and social circumstances of the medieval countryside. Politics and law are social constructs, not only mirroring but also affecting everyday life. As a result, the political and legal disadvantages of women in Brigstock were matched by economic and social disadvantages. Even though both women and men worked equally hard to support their household economies, the economic opportunities of women were, as a general rule, more restricted than those of men. Manorial accounts, the best records of rural wage rates, show that women's jobs were consistently undervalued and that women employed for the same tasks as men were often paid at lower rates. Women also clustered in low-skill trades and crafts, leaving most specialized occupations—carpentering, smithing, regional trading—to men. Women's economic opportunities, however, were limited most severely by their restricted access to and control of the most valued resource of the medieval peasantry—land. Women obtained land much less frequently than men. Rural inheritance customs—preferring sons to daughters and dividing land among all daughters in the event of no male heir—ensured that few women inherited large properties. In their *inter vivos* transfers of properties, parents similarly tended to favor sons over daughters. It is probable also that women bought land less often than men because their purchasing power was limited by lower wages. Moreover, women who did hold land, through inheritance, gift, or purchase, encountered many obstacles to their free control and use of such properties. Any real properties held by wives were administered by their husbands, and widows customarily could not transfer permanent title to their dower lands (or free bench).[22]

The Brigstock sample of land transactions illustrates the relatively restricted economic options open to women in the community (see Table 2.3). The Brigstock land market was an active component of the local economy; with parcels of land changing hands at almost every court meeting, several dozen households altered the size or configuration of their landholdings every year. But women only minimally took advantage of the opportunities presented by such a vigorous land market; of the nearly 800 actors studied in the sample of land conveyances, only about one in five was a woman. This figure accords well with the only available estimate of the proportion of Brigstock land controlled by women. The partial rental of 1319 listed 60 tenants of whom 11 (18 percent) were female. Probably one in every five tenants in Brigstock was a woman.[23]

Although female landholders might have traded their land as frequently as men (since they accounted for about one-fifth of landholders and one-fifth of those participating in the land market), they used their properties less freely. The typical land conveyance in Brigstock involved two unrelated males and a small parcel of land; grantors and receivers usually acted alone, intrafamilial transfers were unusual, and most conveyances involved less than 2 rods of land. Men treated real property as a manipulable resource by exchanging land to consolidate holdings, by selling small assarts and parcels, by offering land as collateral for loans, and by effectively using short-term leases. To be sure, many men controlled certain properties that they refrained from leasing or alienating (which, in Brigstock, were inherited by younger sons). But they also often possessed lands apart from the main holding that they freely managed in response to economic circumstances (and, in Brigstock, these lands were inherited by elder sons). Women treated their properties

TABLE 2.3. Women and Men in the Brigstock Sample of Land Transactions

Category	Men		Women		Both Sexes	
	Number	Column Percent	Number	Column Percent	Number	Column Percent
Type of action						
Grantor	299	48%	97	60%	396	51%
Receiver	318	52	65	40	383	49
All actors	617	100	162	100	779	100
Autonomy of actor						
Acted alone	546	88	97	60	643	83
Acted jointly	71	12	65	40	136	17
All actors	617	100	162	100	779	100
Nature of grant						
Not intrafamilial	512	83	102	63	614	79
Intrafamilial	105	17	60	37	165	21
All grants	617	100	162	100	779	100
Size of grant (if known)						
Less than 2 rods	446	90	99	80	545	88
Over 2 rods	50	10	25	20	75	12
All grants of known size	496	100	124	100	620	100

Note: Percentages have been rounded to produce integral numbers.

very differently. First, women acted more as grantors of land than as receivers; the land market offered males roughly equal opportunities for loss or gain, but women granted more often than they received. Second, women tended to transfer larger portions of land; when large properties or entire holdings were being conveyed, a woman was especially likely to be present. Third, women were often joined by partners who either granted or received land jointly with them; only one of eight males acted jointly, but three of every eight females conveyed land accompanied by another. Fourth, women often participated in actions that transferred lands between members of a single family; they were twice as likely as men to participate in an intrafamilial conveyance. Three-quarters of the men in the sample acted autonomously in a typical exchange—without a joint partner and with no intrafamilial transfer. Less than one-third of the women did so.

Legal restrictions partly account for the peculiarities of women's land conveyances, but legal obstacles buttressed economic realities. Many women acted jointly in conveyances because they were not, as wives, permitted to transfer land without the permission of their husbands. Many widows coped with restrictions on their free bench lands by only granting properties to their children or eventual heirs. Those women, particularly spinsters, who did enjoy unfettered control of land often held such small parcels that sales or leases were out of the question. When women recorded conveyances in the court, they were usually receiving small endowments from their parents, transferring familial lands with their husbands, or granting heritable properties to their sons. The land market, as a forum for the free and autonomous exchange of land between villagers, did not exist for many women in Brigstock.

Women's comparatively limited participation in the Brigstock land market was founded upon the economic status of wives, whose assets were merged into conjugal funds controlled by their husbands. Daughters less often inherited or received lands from their parents because they became dependent economic partners at marriage; sons more often received parental lands because they became independent householders. Wives never dealt autonomously in the land market because their properties were controlled by their husbands who administered all the assets of the household. Widows could use but not alienate lands because they were bound by the interests of their dead husbands to pass conjugal properties intact to the next generation.

But two forces counteracted the ideal of female economic dependency within the conjugal unit; female labor was vital to the rural
economy, and some women—either unwilling or unable to marry—
had to survive without the support of a male householder. As a result, medieval countrypeople never thoroughly excluded women from
any aspect of economic endeavor. Just as women sometimes held
land, so they also labored for wages, worked as servants, produced
goods for sale, and traded at local markets. Although the presumption that most women were dependent wives placed all women at a
disadvantage in the rural economy, the realities of survival in the
medieval countryside assured that women nevertheless participated in
most economic activities.

Because medieval countrypeople usually merged their resources
with those of other members of their households, the economic disadvantages of women were lessened by their absorption into a household economy. Enjoying access to the land and labor of fathers,
husbands, or sons, most women were not forced to rely solely on
their own limited resources. But women's disadvantaged participation
in the rural economy redounded upon other, more private aspects of
their lives. On the one hand, the economic status of women might
have encouraged them to marry or, if widowed, to remarry. Because
women controlled less land and received lower wages, marriage offered them the considerable advantage of access to the resources of
men. On the other hand, relations within marriage were probably
shaped by the varied economic assets of husbands and wives. An
heiress who brought extensive lands to the conjugal fund or an ale-
wife whose sales provided her household with extra cash likely com-
manded more respect within her household than did other wives
whose resources or skills were less valuable.[24] But the economic disadvantages of women, although mitigated by the rural household
economy, nevertheless reinforced the secondary status of women
within both the household and the community.

Social Activity

The everyday social experiences of women and men in Brigstock suggest a society that not only often segregated the sexes, but also offered many more associations and activities to men than to women.

Criminals usually chose both victims and accomplices from among their own sex, and persons victimized together were also usually of the same sex. Hence, the attack by three women recorded in September 1304—by Emma daughter of John Prepositus, Basille wife of John Prepositus, and Juliana Drake—against Isabella Figur was unusual for its concerted action, but usual in the single sex of the participants.[25] Women and men certainly worked together in crime and attacked each other, but, more often than not, co-criminals, co-victims, and pairings of criminal and victim were of the same sex. In addition, women were much more likely than men not only to enter civil pleas against other women, but also to grant land to other women. If a woman went to the Brigstock court to answer a civil complaint or to receive landed property, she was especially likely to face another woman as the opposite party in the transaction. Sexual segregation partly reflected the different economic duties of women and men. Working in the vicinity of their households, women associated closely with each other during the day, just as men, working in fields removed from their domestic crofts, spent their days largely in the company of men. But contemporary literature suggests that practical segregation was reinforced by social anxiety. The goodwife advised her daughter:

> Acquaint thee not with each man that goeth by the street,
> Though any man speak to thee, swiftly thou greet him;
> By him do not stand, but let his way depart,
> Lest he by his villainy should tempt thy heart.[26]

The social worlds of women and men in Brigstock, moreover, were dissimilar as well as separate. As a rule, the social activities of women were particularly narrow and oriented toward family members. Political and legal institutions contributed to the comparatively restricted social horizons of women by offering men opportunities for neighborliness that were unavailable to most women. When the suitors of Brigstock's court gathered together every three weeks, they not only concluded legal business but also doubtless caught up on news, negotiated deals, and exchanged information. Most of the people present on such occasions were males. By assisting one another in court—as pledges, as essoiners, as attorneys—men were able both to enhance existent relationships and also to enlarge their associations. Tithings offered men similar opportunities for expanding their social contacts. And by never acting as officers, women certainly escaped the liabilities of such duties, but they also failed to profit from the social prestige and economic opportunity of official service. The manorial court was so integral a part of rural society that the political and legal disabilities of women created social disabilities as well.

When women did attend court, they frequently dealt not with neighbors or friends, but with relatives. Although not legally obliged to obtain pledging assistance from male kin, women sought pledging assistance from immediate relatives about twice as frequently as men. Of those who proffered pledges, 46 percent of female criminals used kin (as opposed to only 23 percent of male criminals) and 24 percent of female litigants sought familial pledges (as opposed to only 13 percent of male litigants). Women's land conveyances, which were twice as likely as those of men to involve an intrafamilial transfer, betray a similar orientation toward family.[27]

Even more suggestive than patterns of pledging and land trading, however, are the reported criminal activities of women and men. Because the political and legal disabilities of women offered them fewer opportunities than men to reflect and reinforce social associations in noncriminal court action (i.e., through pledging, trading land, loaning money, and the like), accounts of public misbehavior reported by tithingmen at the annual views of frankpledge provide particularly clear insights into the daily activities of women. The frankpledge presentments surveyed in the Brigstock sample of crimes complained about a wide range of behavior—problems associated with the agrarian economy (unlicensed pasturing, improper gleaning, illegal encroachments or purprestures), actions directed against local authorities (insulting officers, harboring strangers, rescuing impounded property), conduct that caused the entire community to be roused by a hue and cry (raised either justly or unjustly), and crimes against persons and property (threats, physical assaults, hamsokens or housebreakings). These presentments suggest that women not only were less disruptive and violent than men, but also moved about Brigstock with less freedom and ease (see Table 2.4).[28]

Although women participated in all the varieties of misbehavior reported to the Brigstock court, only about one-third of all offenders were women. Indeed, if sex ratios in Brigstock were roughly equal, a man was twice as likely as a woman to be responsible for a reported crime. Men also predominated among victims, accounting for 59 per-

TABLE 2.4. Women and Men in the Brigstock Sample of Crimes

Category	Males		Females		Both Sexes	
	Number	Row Percent	Number	Row Percent	Number	Row Percent
Crimes against the community						
Illegal pasturing	12	86%	2	14%	14	100%
Misconduct in fields	33	33	67	67	100	100
Property damage	47	73	17	27	64	100
Insolence to officers	4	80	1	20	5	100
Rescue of seized property	20	87	3	13	23	100
Harboring strangers	30	86	5	14	35	100
Behavior that caused hue	67	72	26	28	93	100
Unjust raising of hue	9	37	15	63	24	100
Miscellaneous	11	52	10	48	21	100
Subtotal	233	61	146	39	379	100
Crimes against persons						
Attacks (and threatened attacks)	118	84	23	16	141	100
Hamsokens (housebreakings)	27	79	7	21	34	100
Subtotal	145	83	30	17	175	100
Total: All crimes	378	68	176	32	554	100

Note: Miscellaneous crimes include unspecified crimes, receipt of stolen goods, misconduct by officers, and general misbehavior (*malefactor in pluribus locis*). Percentages have been rounded to produce integral numbers.

cent of those reported harmed by the crimes of others. Yet compared to other activities noted by the court, women were better represented as both criminals and victims. Although women accounted for only about one-fifth of all appearances made before the court (a proportion roughly maintained in their activities as both litigants and land traders), they accounted for almost one-third of all criminals and two-fifths of all victims. Nevertheless, men appeared more often than women as both criminals and victims, suggesting that they moved about the houses, lanes, and fields of Brigstock with greater familiarity. The tithingmen who reported these offenses might have especially remembered crimes perpetrated either by men or against men, but it is just as likely that men, more active than women in village society, more often found themselves not only tempted to commit a crime but also victimized by a crime.

Men were especially prominent in frankpledge citations that betrayed the householding status of the perpetrator; they were frequently reported for damaging property by taking in unlicensed purprestures or obstructing the roadways, for pasturing animals illegally, and for harboring strangers in their households beyond the permissible stay. The few women cited for such offenses were either independent landholders or householders (unmarried daughters or widows); wives never paid amercements for such offenses because their husbands were responsible for all the properties and actions that pertained to the management of their households. Similar customs doubtless were responsible for the preponderance of men among reported victims of housebreaking (71 percent). When property or households were involved in reported crimes, men predominated.

Men were also responsible for a very high proportion of crimes against specific persons. Accounting for 68 percent of all reported crimes sampled, men perpetrated 83 percent of all physical assaults, verbal threats, and housebreakings. Henry Cocus, for example, was first cited by the tithingmen when he was a young man wandering about Brigstock at night breaking the peace. In the following decade, he attacked John Hog, hurt Galfridus ad Solarium, and assaulted his brother and sister-in-law. His later citations included separate attacks on John Hikeman and a woman named Wimark, and a combined assault and hamsoken perpetrated against Emma Wit. The violence that characterized Cocus' life in Brigstock was distinctly male. Men were also prominent in antisocial crimes that physically threatened the governing order of the community—the insulting of officers and the rescuing of animals impounded for trespass.[29] Some women did attack others, break into houses, rescue impounded beasts, and insult officers, but the tithingmen presented women for such offenses on comparatively few occasions. Even today, criminologists debate whether the low representation of women in reported crimes of violence reflects innate differences between the sexes, socially imposed gender norms, or biased reporting by legal officers. Patterns of reported criminality in pre-plague Brigstock raise the same questions, but two points are clear: women were physically capable of violent crime (since at least some women perpetrated such offenses), and men were reported for violence much more frequently than women.[30]

Finally, women were especially prominent in two types of offenses that disrupted the community—illegal activity in the fields and raising unjust hues. Usually involving pilfering of grain or improper gleaning, field crimes represent a classic category of female criminality—the theft of foodstuffs. Women always perpetrated the bulk of such offenses; of the 27 people accused in 1343 of gleaning improperly or otherwise misbehaving in the fields, 25 were women. Frankpledge presentments betray no motives, but it seems reasonable to suppose that many women guilty of field offenses were attempting to feed their families.[31] The predominance of women among those charged with disrupting the community by raising a needless hue and cry is more problematic. Women might have more often than men misjudged situations or accused persons maliciously, but they also might have sometimes had their complaints ignored by the court. As exemplified by the amercement paid by Matilda Coleman for unjustly raising the hue against Adam Swargere (who had harmed Coleman's daughter), it is possible that the preponderance of women among those guilty of improper hues reflects less the misjudgment or maliciousness of women than their disadvantaged position before the court.[32]

The everyday, social experiences of medieval countrywomen, then, complement their political, legal, and economic opportunities. Women in Brigstock were neither cloistered nor powerless, but their lives were less public and less autonomous than those of their fathers, brothers, and husbands. The inescapable image is of a community where men dominated public life, governing the village through its many offices, enjoying preference in inheritance and employment, solidifying friendships by pledging and essoining as well as by loaning money and trading land, and simply moving about the village with considerable familiarity and authority. With the exception of politics, women were not excluded from this community, but they were not a full part of it.

Assessing the Status of Women in Fourteenth-century Brigstock

Ever since Victorian scholars argued that a society's level of advancement could be best judged by the status of its women, the study of women's status has been a familiar feature of anthropological and historical writing. The longevity of the subject, however, has produced more confusion than clarity. Probably the most contentious issue has been that of selecting proper measurements of women's status. Because a specific activity might be valued in one society and denigrated in another, no universal categories of action can be safely assumed to confer honor and prestige. Researchers must also beware of taking "man as the measure of significance" by assessing the lives of women against a male standard to which women did not subscribe. Dictated by items reported in manorial courts, the study of women's status in the medieval countryside necessarily focuses on public activity—political power, legal status, economic opportunities, and social activities. This public perspective is both useful and problematic.

One problem stems from the inability of manorial court rolls to report on those many aspects of rural life that might have been especially important to women. Court rolls provide only minimal information on the demographic rhythms that shaped women's lives during these centuries; historians will never be able to pinpoint precisely at what ages countrywomen became sexually active or married, how many pregnancies they carried to term, and whether most of them could reasonably expect to outlive their husbands. Court records are similarly silent on the emotional setting of the peasant household; laconic notations of land grants from parents to children tell little about conjugal love and relations between parents and children, and rates of intrafamilial crime and litigation are so negligible that most households likely settled internal controversies in private. Court business was also transacted at a level so removed from the casual networks through which women probably exchanged advice, child care, and resources that historians will also remain ignorant about the informal female world hidden in its records. In short, the public focus of court rolls requires that the status of medieval countrywomen be assessed from a perspective that especially stresses the activities of men.

This focus on public activity moves counter to the studies of some historians who, drawing on the pioneering work of Mary Ritter Beard, have emphasized the unique contributions and satisfactions of women. Beard argued that a male standard denigrated women by trying to make them into men, and she attempted to evaluate the experiences of women in past times by using female attributes and functions. Her studies of women's private and informal contributions to their societies provided a much needed corrective to traditional studies of women, but she never dealt forthrightly with the reality of women's public subordination to men.[33] Although Beard demonstrated that women's activities were many and vital, she failed to show either that their activities were valued by contemporaries or that women enjoyed as much control over their lives as did men. An important study by Peggy R. Sanday has shown, for example, that female participation in productive work does not automatically lead to high female status. Concluding that control over produced resources is more crucial than production itself, Sanday determined that "female production is a necessary but not sufficient condition for the development of female status."[34] Because attempts to assess separately the experiences of women and men have sidestepped questions of control and power, they have led, in the words of Heidi Hartmann, to conclusions that are "relativist in the extreme."[35] The inescapable fact is that when men control public authority, it confers upon them advantages in both public and private.

Necessitated by the absence of sources that could illuminate the private lives of the medieval peasantry, the focus of this study on the public activities of Brigstock is not meant to imply that only public actions affected the status of women or the quality of their lives. Publicly inactive women were not necessarily insignificant, just as publicly active women were not automatically esteemed. We simply do not know. Aside from the public matters reported in manorial records, no other sources reliably report the experiences of the medieval peasantry. Uniformly illiterate, neither male nor female peasants have left diaries or memoirs that describe their private hopes and values. Living before the time of parochial registration, the medieval peasantry married, gave birth, and died without formal, written testimony. And generally despised by the literate minority, the peasantry's portrayal in contemporary literature is, at best, highly suspect. Literary descriptions can be useful as illustrations of trends established through other sources (like court rolls), but their probative use is very limited. Although the aspirations, attitudes, and values of medieval peasants will remain obscure, there can be little doubt that public activities were important in medieval villages and that the ability of women to act publicly was one significant component of their lives.

This is particularly true because of the indisputable importance of public opportunities in the very public rural world of the early fourteenth century. Medieval villagers lived surrounded by neighbors who cooperated in work and government, monitored courtship and marriage, and exchanged assistance and advice. Neighborliness was vital to rural living, and those whose public options enabled them to be better neighbors—through pledging, official largesse, loans, and the like—accrued both power and prestige. Manorial court rolls offer only a partial view of medieval rural society, but it is a view focused on essential activities.

Moreover, the public actions reported in court rolls often reflected private realities. Formal associations mentioned in court drew on informal friendships of lane and field; public customs regulating the devolution of land reflected private notions about the claims of sons and daughters to familial properties; male control of governance complemented male control of household affairs. Representing only one side of gender relations, public actions usually illuminate private matters. Indeed, the constellation formed by public and private relations between the sexes is so consistent that scholars like Jack Goody and Martin Whyte have predicted the whole pattern from only a few pieces. Comparing African and Eurasian inheritance systems, Goody argued that such public matters as the use and availability of land shape private customs of inheritance and marriage which, in turn, determine the status of women.[36] Whyte's cross-cultural analysis of women's status in 93 preindustrial societies led him to conclude that political, economic, and social structures crucially shape the opportunities of preindustrial women.[37] The studies of both scholars have shown that women most approach equality in their private relations with men when their public actions are more nearly symmetrical. As a result, the public activities recorded in manorial court rolls indirectly reveal much about private relations between the sexes.

Possibly even more problematic than the public focus necessitated by the archives is the issue of evaluating observed trends. Because of the absence of sources that describe the hopes and attitudes of medieval peasants, it is impossible to assess how highly women and men valued the particular activities of each sex. To the extent that medieval peasants absorbed the teachings and attitudes of the elite, however, they accepted a cultural tradition whose ideas about women were, at worst, misogynistic and, at best, ambivalent. Neither motherhood nor wifely status brought unequivocal prestige for women. Late medieval artists increasingly emphasized the loving interaction of Virgin and Child, but the elevation of ordinary motherhood to a praised occupation awaited both the Protestant reformers and the Victorians. Wives were similarly unappreciated—the Church preferred nuns to wives, the troubadours and goliardic poets valued adulterous love over conjugal love, and the writers of the fabliaux bitterly satirized the married state. Historians cannot reconstruct the private thoughts and experiences of medieval peasants, but nothing suggests that women and their activities were highly esteemed.[38]

An assessment of trends is also complicated by the fact that evaluations of dependency and autonomy vary according to sex and historical period. Recent studies have suggested that dependency has more positive value for women than for men, and it is possible that such varying judgments also occurred in the medieval countryside.[39] For a woman in Brigstock, the dependence brought by marriage was accompanied by the satisfactions of conjugal relations and motherhood as well as the protection of her husband. Similarly, neither dependence nor autonomy had the same meanings in the medieval world as they have for us today. Ties of dependence were basic to medieval life—barons pledged homage and fealty to their kings, serfs labored for their manorial lords, and wives fell under the authority of their husbands. In such relations, neither person was an autonomous individual; the vassal's service was matched by his lord's guarantee of support and protection, just as a wife's forfeiture of autonomous control over her property was complemented by the expectation that her husband would provide adequate care and support. Authority brought greater freedom of action but also more responsibility; dependency brought limitations on freedom but also protection.

Nevertheless, the authority of householders and the dependency of their wives, children, and servants were not equal sides of the same coin. Just as feudal lords were more powerful than their vassals and manorial lords exercised more authority than their serfs, so householders enjoyed powers not available to their dependents. The fact that the privileges of householders were accompanied by responsibilities and obligations does not negate the fundamental authority they wielded. The records of manorial courts like Brigstock clearly illustrate how the only social adults in rural communities were male householders; only they enjoyed the full range of political, legal, economic, and social opportunities in the medieval countryside. As heads of corporate enterprises, householders were not individualists, but they were much more independent than most medieval villagers, and they would also be much better able than their dependents to respond to the growth of an individualistic ethic in the modern era. The first true individualists were likely householders who subordinated the corporate interests of their households to their own personal needs.

A final challenge in assessing the status of women in the medieval countryside is posed by vocabulary. The English language can only poorly describe the nuances that were characteristic of householders and their dependents; consider how the descriptive term "dependent" carries modern connotations not found in medieval society. Terms such as "autonomy" and "independence" will be used to contrast the status of householders to the dependency of their wives, children, and servants, but readers should recognize that both householders and dependents were responsible to and reliant on each other. Similarly, modern English provides few neutral words for describing inequality, and readers should beware of applying the modern connotations associated with words like "restriction" and "disability" to medieval circumstances. Such words are used for descriptive purposes only and are not meant to imply either dissatisfaction or agitation on the part of medieval countrypeople.

Most students of gender have sufficient information to weigh the delicate balance of public and private worlds; sociologists and anthropologists can supplement public information with informal observations or interviews, and historians of more recent or more literate societies can weigh their knowledge of public sex roles against insights drawn from diaries, letters, and memoirs. But no private informants or memorabilia can counterbalance the public view offered by the records of medieval manors like Brigstock. No sources reveal the thoughts and aspirations of women in Brigstock—whether they felt limited by their choices, whether they ridiculed the public world from which they were so often excluded, whether they valued protection over independence. And the sources speak only indirectly or incompletely about the informal activities of rural women—how they participated in household decisions, how they weighed age, kinship, and neighborhood in forming friendships, how they privately deferred (or did not defer) to fathers, brothers, and husbands.

The basic characteristics of the public lives of women and men in Brigstock, however, are clear. Politics was a male affair in which women had no part, but women were included, although at a disadvantage, in the legal, economic, and social structures of the community. A young boy in early fourteenth-century Brigstock could expect someday to assume the public functions of a householder, eligible for local offices as well as tithing membership and pledging, competent in all legal matters, active as a landholder and perhaps also as a craftsman or trader, and socially at ease in the community. His sister could anticipate that she would move from the authority of her parents to the authority of her husband and spend most of her life as a dependent wife, covered in all public matters by her husband. She also likely knew that her public options would vary over the course of her life and offer, at their fullest extent, no participation in politics, second-rank legal status, disadvantaged access to land and work, and relatively limited social horizons. Behind the divergent public opportunities of women and men lay the expectation, rooted in the households of medieval villagers, that every woman was the mainpast of a man, needing little access to public matters. These rural households were, in some respects, surprisingly "modern."

III

Rural Households
Before the Plague

Historians of family life in the sixteenth and seventeenth centuries, eager to define the special characteristics of their own era, have often used the experiences of medieval countrypeople as a convenient starting point. They have sought "tradition" in the villages of the Middle Ages, portraying medieval rural households as large, complex groupings based less on conjugality than kinship.[1] Most households in the early fourteenth-century English countryside, however, were not large, were not extended by the marital families of the head's siblings or children, and were not embedded in their villages by intricate webs of cousinage. Instead, rural households in England before the plague were usually built from the discrete conjugal union of husband and wife, and with each marriage creating a new domestic unit, most households were small and nuclear. Although the conjugal family usually formed the basic core of the peasant household, actual blood relationship was a relatively unimportant criterion; shared residence and shared work were as important as shared kinship in household membership. The larger social context of the household was also comparatively freed from the constraints of kinship; friends and associates were chosen with almost as much regard to neighborhood and socioeconomic status as to kinship. Reconstructing the households of medieval peasants is a difficult and tenuous business, but all the steps

48

lead conclusively in one direction—toward small, simple, and autonomous households.

Medieval sources seldom speak explicitly about domestic structures and experiences in the countryside. Because the illiterate peasantry have left no personal memorabilia describing their private lives,
most features of rural households must be indirectly inferred from
the laconic entries of manorial administrators. But manorial clerks,
concerned with legal and fiscal matters, seldom paused to describe
the basic structural characteristics of rural households. They recorded
the labor rents due from households, the fines paid by fathers of recalcitrant children, and the licenses purchased for the marriages of
unfree women, but they were unconcerned with the composition of
households, with the organization of domestic economies, or with the
distribution of authority within domestic groups. Although their records reveal much about public activity in medieval villages, they
tell very little indeed about the households of these communities.

As a result, rural households are best studied not from the records
of only one manor, but instead from a variety of sources for a variety
of places. Because the records of a single community offer, in even
the best of circumstances, only one or two pieces of substantial evidence about household forms and functions, historians must rely on
many such pieces of evidence drawn from many communities. Although necessitated by the sources, this approach tends to obscure
the variability and heterogeneity of medieval households. As social,
not natural, institutions, households certainly responded to specific
social, economic, and cultural milieus in ways that are obfuscated by
an eclectic survey.[2] But such an overview does offer the advantage of
tracing general norms against which specific variations might eventually be compared.

Kinship and Community

Countrypeople in early fourteenth-century England valued both community and kinship. Living in close proximity to one another and
cooperating in agricultural and fiscal matters, medieval villagers necessarily respected sociability; an uncooperative neighbor could be
both burdensome and expensive. Kinship not only enhanced the
social ties of medieval people but also gave access to land because

property devolved on brothers or cousins in the absence of direct descendants. As a result, villagers cultivated ties of both friendship and kinship. Henry Kroyl junior of Brigstock, for example, developed a vast network of associations within his community, accumulating during his married years 322 different contacts in the manor court with 156 people. His closest friend was his brother John, with whom he associated in court on 17 occasions, but he also nurtured close ties with men to whom he was not related (including, for example, 10 separate interactions in court with both Alan Koyk and Henry Hirdman). Although the size of his network and the close relationships he formed with men like Koyk and Hirdman betray the importance of neighborhood to Henry Kroyl junior, his close association with his brother John underscores the importance of kinship.[3] A variety of circumstances, however, deemphasized both kinship and community in favor of the distinctiveness of conjugal households.

Communal solidarity was probably most severely undermined by distinct socioeconomic divisions within the peasantry. By the late thirteenth century, the legal distinction between free and unfree peasants had ceased to carry much importance in rural society; free tenants held unfree land, free and unfree intermarried regularly, and inflation had even, in some respects, economically advantaged the unfree over the free.[4] But medieval villagers were distinguished from one another by very marked socioeconomic disparities. As E. A. Kosminsky established in his analysis of the Hundred Rolls of 1279, most late thirteenth-century villages included smallholding cottars (possessing less than 5 acres), middling landholders (holding from 5 to 20 acres), and substantial holders of full virgates or more (20 to 40 acres). Kosminsky found that the proportions of small, middling, and large landholders varied according to size, type, and location of the manors (as did the economic viability of any particular acreage), but his overall figures suggest that the average rural community was divided into three groups of roughly equal size.[5] Case studies of social stratification in specific villages have regularly confirmed Kosminsky's figures; most villages were divided sharply between tenants who were so land-rich that they could afford to hire others, lesser tenants who possessed just enough property to squeeze by, and the nearly landless who pieced together a living from sparse holdings, wages, and charity.[6]

The inequitable distribution of land in medieval villages affected almost every aspect of rural life. Villagers blessed with virgates or even larger holdings have been often compared to the kulaks of pre-revolutionary Russia because they, like wealthy Russian peasants, essentially governed villages to their advantage. Virgaters dominated and controlled manor courts; they associated predominantly with one another to the exclusion of the less privileged; and they were much more successful than others at maintaining stable residence. The vagaries of economy and demography in the medieval country-side assured, however, that the hegemony of the privileged was more personal than dynastic. The families of wealthier peasants were often larger than those less advantaged, but very few were able to sustain socioeconomic dominance over many generations. Nevertheless, the inequities of village life prompted considerable social tensions as reflected, for example, in the high incidence of burglary and assault directed against members of the upper stratum by those of less fortunate circumstances.[7]

Social stratification on the pre-plague manors of Brigstock, Iver, and Houghton-cum-Wyton closely matched this general trend. In all three communities, a minority of traced surnames not only were associated with official responsibilities and powers, but also were disproportionately represented in most other influential aspects of local economy and society. Brigstock was typical. The privileged one-third of Brigstock's inhabitants (represented by those surnames linked to official duties) held almost all of the manor's substantial landholdings, dominated the business of the manorial court, managed more successfully than others to reside permanently in the area, and controlled much of the community's lucrative ale trade. The life of Brigstock, like that of all rural communities, was dominated by a small core group whose economic privileges supported their political, legal, social, and commercial advantages.[8]

The integrity of medieval communities was also undermined by the geographical mobility of countrypeople in the decades before the plague. Rather than remaining perpetually in the villages of their ancestors, medieval peasants, both free and unfree, constantly moved about and changed residence. Although lords attempted to restrict the emigration of their unfree tenants, they were usually unsuccessful. At best, manorial officials regulated such movement by taxing those who left legally, by seizing the goods of those who absconded by night, and by approving those who wished to settle as newcomers on the manor.[9]

Many peasants were doubtless attracted by the opportunities of urban life, but many others simply moved from one village to another—marrying into the new community, buying land, seeking employment. As a rule, most movement occurred within a limited regional area; when the origins and destinations of mobile peasants can be traced, they tended to move only 10 to 15 miles from their original homes.[10] Despite the limited mileage covered, the movement of rural people was frequent enough to shape profoundly the medieval countryside. In Brigstock, Iver, and Houghton-cum-Wyton only about one-third of each manor's surnames remained in use from the late thirteenth century through to the plague years, a similarity that is especially striking in light of the different economies and seigneurial circumstances of these villages. Although some surnames doubtless disappeared because of name changes or demographic failure, most probably disappeared because of emigration. The attrition included some of the most peripheral and some of the most substantial surnames in each village, but persons identified by surnames associated with economic and political privilege were, logically enough, less likely candidates for emigration. The instability of two-thirds of the surnames traced in Brigstock, Iver, and Houghton-cum-Wyton could have potentially caused enormous social dislocation, but the change was gradual enough to be absorbed without trauma. In early fourteenth-century Brigstock, for example, only 8 to 19 percent of the manor's surnames shifted in any five-year period.[11]

The permanent relocation of rural dwellers was complemented by daily movement between villages. All villages, no matter how isolated from the main roads, could count on the regular arrival of peddlers, pilgrims, laborers, and entertainers. Rural court rolls acknowledge this stream of itinerants in amercements regularly levied against those inhabitants who harbored such visitors in their homes beyond the permissible stay.[12] Even more important than peripatetic exchange was the regular meeting of people from different villages at local markets. In the thirteenth and early fourteenth centuries, an enormous growth in rural trade prompted such an explosion of markets throughout the English countryside that most villages were within easy reach of at least one weekly market.[13] Because these exchanges fostered much more than the trade of local produce and supplies, markets promoted the regional integration of the medieval peasantry in a variety of ways. A young woman might meet her future husband on market day; a young man might contract to work temporarily as a harvester in another village; two farmers from different villages might agree to cooperate in future sales; and peasants who had relocated could exchange news with parents, siblings, and friends. This constant movement about the countryside assured that even those who remained in the villages of their birth were well aware of the world that lay beyond the local fields—they dealt often with itinerant peddlers and laborers, they exchanged gossip at weekly markets, they knew neighbors who had moved to the village from elsewhere, and they probably had children or siblings who had married and settled in nearby communities.

The sense of community in early fourteenth-century villages certainly endured despite their inclusion of people with varied socioeconomic prospects and many different origins. Villagers still had to cooperate in meeting the demands of the crown, working with manorial officers, regulating the use of common fields, pastures, or waters, and living peaceably with one another. But by the early fourteenth century, the primacy of the village community in the lives of rural dwellers was limited both from within (by socioeconomic disparities) and from without (by regional integration). These same forces also limited the importance of kinship in the countryside before the plague. Because parents usually divided properties between their children inequitably, economic distinctions could undermine sibling ties. Henry Kroyl junior's closest associate in Brigstock was his brother John Kroyl whose social influence and economic power closely matched his own, but neither man ever associated in court with their brother Robert whose circumstances were considerably more modest.[14] Geographical mobility similarly limited kinship by assuring that most people had siblings and cousins who lived not in the same village, but only in the same region. When Cristina Penifader of Brigstock married Richard Power and moved about seven miles away to his village of Cranford, the social importance of her relationships with her brothers and sisters quickly waned.[15]

In addition, the descent system of the English peasantry worked against the influence of kinship. Descent was reckoned bilaterally with a person counting both maternal and paternal relatives as equal members of his or her kin. Only siblings shared the same natal kin, and since marriage provided them with separate groups of in-laws, even siblings had distinct sets of relatives. Kinship, in short, did not

define a discrete group (such as those formed when descent is reckoned unilaterally), but instead was specific to the individual.[16] Medieval peasants seem to have responded to the variability of kinship by
focusing on biologically close or socially important ties. When property or legal status was at stake, peasants could sometimes reckon
complex lines of descent through several generations.[17] But they
usually specified kinship only to close relatives; the most common
relationships specified in manorial courts were those of the immediate
household (*pater, mater, vir, uxor, soror, frater, filius/a, serviens,
ancilla*). Indeed, more distant ties of kinship not only were rarely
stated, but also were usually generalized (*consanguineus/a*) or spelled
out in a linked series of closer relationships—as when an uncle would
call his nephew not "nephew" (*nepos meus*), but "son of my
brother" (*filius fratri mei*).[18]

Kinship was certainly still important to villagers of the early fourteenth century; Henry Kroyl junior developed his closest friendship
with his brother John and also interacted publicly with most of his
kin in ways that tended to be more numerous and complex than his
public contacts with non-kin. Yet kinship was not so strong that it
predetermined the social experiences of medieval countrypeople;
Henry Kroyl junior's public activities completely ignored two of his
brothers, included very intense and enduring friendships with many
men to whom he was not related, and usually involved interactions with neighbors, not kin. It seems that ties of kinship provided
medieval villagers not with duties and rights, but with options and
choices.[19]

The Conjugal Economy

At the same time that such forces as geographic mobility and socioeconomic inequity undercut the influence of community and kinship
in English villages before the plague, other circumstances enhanced
the autonomy of the conjugal household. The Church's teaching on
marriage, formulated by Alexander III in the late twelfth century,
emphasized the independence of husbands and wives. By stating that
the approval of kindred, communities, and lords was a desirable, not
necessary feature of marriage, the Church focused on the free consent of the contracting couple as an essential element of conjugality.

Although the Church never ceased to encourage prospective spouses to consult their priests, lords, parents, and friends, it firmly acknowledged that a man and a woman could contract a valid marriage without the consent or involvement of others.[20] Rural people in the Middle Ages never fully complied with ecclesiastical prescriptions on marriage and sexuality, but by the fourteenth century English peasants were well aware of the de facto independence of marrying couples created by the doctrines of the Church.[21]

Royal and seigneurial policies might have similarly enhanced the importance of households. When Edward I and his successors began to tap the resources of the peasantry, they occasionally burdened individuals (conscriptions) or communities (purveyances), but the most widespread and enduring of royal demands were the taxes levied not against individuals, communities, or kindred, but against households. From the 1290s, royal taxes known as lay subsidies became regular features of life in the countryside, requiring most households to pay taxes on their movable goods. Even when the lay subsidy became a permanently fixed communal responsibility after 1334, most villages followed the established custom of collecting assessments from separate households.[22] Many seigneurial practices had a similar result as lords, seeking more effective and efficient methods of administering their estates, turned to householders as the most responsible, most powerful, and most distrainable segment of the manorial population.[23] Although ecclesiastical, royal, and seigneurial policies might have focused on the rural household, its autonomy was primarily supported by the diversity of the early fourteenth-century rural economy.

An active labor market especially buttressed the viability of conjugal households in the English countryside before the plague. Most households relied primarily on the work of their members, but they also regulated their labor supplies by taking in additional workers or hiring out superfluous members. Lords had long relied on the assistance of both day-laborers and salaried employees, and many land-rich households did the same, hiring wage-earners or live-in servants rather than relying on kindred or extended families to work their lands.[24] Because of the humble stature of such workers, they appear so sporadically in manorial court rolls that their importance in the pre-plague economy cannot be quantified. The labor market of Brigstock, for example, usually operated at a level that escaped the attention of the manor court, but occasional mentions of broken service contracts, unpaid wages, or misbehaving servants suggest that the employment of both day-laborers and live-in servants was not uncommon.[25] Their numbers were probably substantial. Zvi Razi found that 43 percent of households in early fourteenth-century Halesowen employed a servant at least occasionally.[26]

The flexible distribution of land in the medieval countryside also supported the establishment of discrete conjugal households. Many children did not have to wait for their parents to die and many siblings did not have to live unmarried in the households of their inheriting brothers because they could obtain small parcels of land from other sources.[27] Rural communities often boasted very active land markets that enabled local households to sell, trade, buy, or lease small properties. Leasing, as long as the term ran for only a few years, was tolerated on virtually all seigneurial estates. And as long as proper forms were observed and fines paid, manorial officers also seldom interfered in the permanent sale or exchange of real estate. Although good lands were scarce in the overpopulated decades before the plague, the land market expanded in many villages not only as some households were forced to sell properties (as during the famine years) but also as many lords, abandoning direct management, leased their demesne lands and ceased to oppose vigorously the fragmentation of tenancies. Since transfers usually involved only small parcels of land, it is likely that most households maintained an inalienable core property (designated for heirs) that was supplemented with alienable small holdings (designated for noninheriting sons and daughters).[28] In Brigstock, for example, at least one or two land transfers were usually noted at each triweekly meeting of the manor court, and their number increased over the course of the early fourteenth century. Most transactions involved a house (*domus*), a curtilage (or yard), a garden plot, or a rod (30 square yards) of arable land. Because of this active market in land, many peasants, like Robert Penifader who granted lands to his daughter Cristina in 1312, 1314, and 1316 and to his son Henry in 1314, were able to obtain small properties for their daughters and sons.[29]

Moreover, a variety of nonagrarian opportunities enabled many conjugal households to survive with very small landholdings.[30] Some regularly supplemented their agricultural incomes by participating in the many by-industries of rural life—dairying, brewing, butchering, baking, thatching, milling, carpentering, and so forth.[31] Others survived on wages earned by working for their lords or neighbors. And still others were active in rural commerce, opening stalls at local markets, transporting goods to nearby towns, and bringing into their villages items to sell to their neighbors. As local markets were established to complement burgeoning regional and international trade, the expansion of commerce into the English countryside in the late thirteenth century allowed more and more households to supplement their agrarian incomes with industrial or commercial work.[32] The records of Brigstock describe peasants not only working as servants, laborers, brewers, and bakers, but also timbering, fishing, collecting peat, selling meat at nearby markets, and even working with cloth.[33]

The large labor market, the brisk trade in small parcels of land, and the diversity of economic opportunity in the countryside worked together to support the economic viability of small, conjugal households. Reacting to these opportunities, the medieval peasantry often encouraged their children to be economically autonomous. At least some young people in the English countryside before the plague acquired separate economic resources while still unmarried. Spending a few years employed as servants or wage-laborers, many worked in areas that historians rarely glimpse. Others possessed lands or pursued occupations that can be traced in court records; half of the young people (both male and female) whose premarital activities could be reconstructed from the Brigstock records exhibited such economic independence before marriage, with most holding small plots of land. These young people, to be sure, were not free of all parental control and still relied heavily on the support of their parents until they married, but they were, nevertheless, slowly acquiring the assets that would allow them to set up independent households after marriage.[34]

The settlements made at the time of marriage completed the process of economic separation from parental households. In some rural societies, each marital partner discretely controls the assets he or she brings to the union, and their separate kin groups retain rights of control and inheritance over these properties. Such arrangements emphasize the importance of lineage and kinship over the conjugal couple. In the medieval English countryside, however, settlements merged the properties of husband and wife into a single conjugal fund to which kin had little access and few rights. Married children doubtless turned to their parents for further assistance in times of special hardship or stress, but the marriage settlements of the medieval peasantry were designed to create economically separate households. When Henry Kroyl junior married Agnes Penifader, for example, they acquired joint rights to the inheritance of a semi-virgate from Henry's father, and Agnes was additionally endowed by Henry with a small house, curtilage, and 6 rods of land. Their case exemplifies the economic separateness of conjugal households; husbands and wives in medieval villages acted as single economic units, bereaved spouses enjoyed considerable rights over conjugal funds, children inherited parental properties, and collateral kin claimed lands only in the absence of direct descendants.[35]

Economic autonomy was matched by social independence. The social separation of married people from their natal families is particularly clear in the actions of young men who, after marriage, attained full membership in their village communities. They became eligible for new levels of public responsibility since, as a rule, only married men could hold local offices. They relied less on kinship and more on friendship in developing larger personal associations within their communities. And they were also newly treated by manorial clerks as independent persons; instead of being known as a dependent son (Henry son of Peter Cocus), a married man needed only his own name for identification (Henry Cocus). On an individual level, this separation could be striking. Henry Kroyl junior, for example, repeatedly relied on his father's assistance during his premarital years of quasi-independence, but after marriage he almost never turned to his father for aid in transacting court business. With marriage, Henry Kroyl junior acquired an independent name, access to village offices, and a wider network of friends and acquaintances that freed him from social reliance upon his father. He became, in short, an independent head of household. The transition differed for women because they moved from one dependent status (daughter) to another (wife), but even women's patterns of court action underscore the importance of conjugality over kinship. After marriage, Henry Kroyl junior's wife Agnes relied almost exclusively on her husband in court, never interacting with either her parents and siblings or her husband's parents. Marriage established Henry Kroyl junior and his wife Agnes as a household separated both economically and socially from their natal families.[36]

Household Size and Structure

The social and economic structures of the pre-plague countryside thus enhanced the independence of conjugal households and downplayed the importance of both kinship and community. Medieval peasants, to be sure, valued both neighborliness and kinship, but neither undermined the essential autonomy of the conjugal household. The size and structure of these households varied widely not only over the course of the household cycle but also in response to economic circumstances.[37] The households of wealthier peasants, for example, were markedly larger than those less advantaged. One probable cause was demographic; poorer households might have suffered lower replacement rates because of both lower fertility and higher mortality. Another likely cause was economic; the fragile economies of poor households promoted contraction rather than expansion because they were unlikely to grow through the hiring of live-in servants and likely to shrink through the early departure of children who had to seek their fortunes elsewhere.[38] Despite such variations, the general patterns of household structure are clear; small in size and simple in form, households were defined as much by residence and function as by kinship.

Demographic evidence for medieval villagers is very sparse, but the low reproductive capacities of preindustrial populations probably limited the expansion of most households. E. A. Wrigley has calculated that in a stationary preindustrial population 20 percent of couples will have no children survive them, 20 percent will be survived by daughters only, and 60 percent will be survived by at least one son.[39] When the population was growing, as throughout much of the twelfth and thirteenth centuries, these ratios probably improved, with fewer couples dying childless or without sons and more couples producing several children to succeed them. In times of demographic stress, as in the early fourteenth century, the proportion of couples with no children or no sons probably increased. The famines and diseases that swept through the English countryside between 1315 and 1322 only aggravated the reproductive difficulties of these years.[40] High mortality and low life expectancy also limited the expandability of rural households. Zvi Razi has estimated that the average male tenant in pre-plague Halesowen could expect, at the age of 20 years, to live another 25 to 28 years.[41] With such low expectations of life, three-generational households were likely rare because few people lived long enough to welcome any grandchildren into the world.

Several thirteenth-century listings from Lincolnshire also suggest that rural households were usually small and simple.[42] Recording each resident's relationship to the head of household, the listings show that most households averaged 4.68 persons and contained only one married couple. These findings are particularly interesting because the Lincolnshire villages practiced partible inheritance, which can promote large, joint-family households that include the marital families of co-inheriting siblings.[43] As a result, the predominance of small, nuclear households in a region of partible inheritance suggests the strong preference of medieval countrypeople for small, simple households. Other estimates of household size, many drawn from areas that practiced impartible inheritance, generally confirm the findings of the Lincolnshire listings. Although much controversy has raged about the proper "multiplier" for estimating population from listings of medieval tenants, the range—from 3.5 to 5.9—has never indicated the possibility of large, extended family households.[44]

Although written records seldom provide direct information about the residential patterns of medieval peasants, excavations of deserted medieval villages support the demographic evidence of small household size.[45] As one might expect, housing varied with socioeconomic status, with the most common structure being the "long house" of the middling tenant. This single building housed both humans and animals, with the byre at one end and living quarters (occasionally with an inner room partitioned off) at the opposite end. Long houses tended to be quite small, with the most common width falling between 4 and 5 meters and length usually running between 8 and 15 meters. Cottars lived in even cruder structures, and farmers of large properties often managed to separate the living area and the byre. Aside from the implication that the small sizes and simple structures of peasant houses accommodated relatively small and simple groups of people, two other archaeological findings reveal further details of household size and structure. First, archaeologists have discovered very few outbuildings on domestic sites or tofts. The main house was often supplemented by a nearby shed, but excavations have yielded little evidence of two contemporary domestic buildings on a single toft. It seems that medieval peasants usually built only one simple domestic structure on each toft and did not often attempt, as in some other rural societies, to house retired parents, a married sibling, or other members of an extended family by constructing either additions to the main building or separate buildings.[46] Second, long houses were continually rebuilt, with completely new orientations and foundations appearing on many excavated tofts at roughly 25-year intervals. Because long houses were often built of flimsy materials—soil, wood, turf—much rebuilding might have been required by simple deterioration. Yet rebuilding was just as frequent when stone foundations and more durable structures were used. It is tempting to interpret this constant rebuilding of domestic structures as having occurred whenever a new household was established on the toft (an interpretation which accords nicely with the 25-year rebuilding interval observed by archaeologists). In any case, the archaeological evidence clearly shows that peasant long houses, constructed neither for large groups nor for permanence, provided ideal accommodation for conjugal households.

The retirement contracts of medieval villagers also suggest the small size and simple structure of rural households. In these "maintenance agreements," an elderly person arranged for retirement by relinquishing property to a person (often, but not invariably, a son) who agreed to support the retired person until death. The person retiring obtained guaranteed maintenance; the second party received permanent property rights. Found in villages that practiced all forms of inheritance, these agreements strongly suggest that most households contained only one married couple. If an extended-family household had been a natural or normal part of the domestic cycle, it seems unlikely that retiring landholders would have required such detailed and complex agreements from their children. Although the sources allow no estimation of what proportion of retiring parents used such enrolled contracts, they never state that such contracts arose from particularly acrimonious relations between parents and children.[47] Instead, it seems likely that maintenance agreements were an accepted method of dealing with the unusual circumstance of a parent living beyond his or her productive years. This point is complemented, of course, by the demographic observation that such survival was probably rare. Moreover, a large number of retiring persons contracted maintenance agreements not with children, but with persons to whom they were apparently unrelated. A recent study of East Anglian retirements found that about half of the retiring persons in the sample did not contract for maintenance with a child.[48] Given the low replacement rates of medieval countrypeople, many elderly people might have had no surviving children, but this was not always the case. It seems that social custom did not require children to care for aged parents and that some children, already established in independent households, saw no advantage to undertaking the care of an elderly parent.

The available information on household size and structure, then, complements evidence of the social and economic autonomy of conjugal units; most households were formed by marriage and included only one nuclear family. Yet rural households cannot be equated with modern nuclear families because, although a conjugal couple and their unmarried children formed its central core, a peasant household regularly included persons who were either unrelated or only distantly related to the head of the house. As a result, kinship cannot be considered as the defining characteristic of pre-plague households. Households remained small and simple in basic structure, but two factors confounded their familial foundations—the ubiquity of live-in servants and the effects of high mortality.

Many rural households included servants. Because servants—like sons or daughters—were dependents whose public identities were subsumed by that of the household head, they are extremely difficult to trace in manorial records. The sources do indicate, however, that servants were both numerous and treated as full household members. One in every two to five rural households before the plague might have included a resident servant who shared fully in the activities of the household—sleeping, working, and eating in common with other members of the domestic unit.[49] The main distinction between the household roles of servant and kin was economic; unlike blood descendants, servants could not hope to share in the final fruits of collective labor through endowment or inheritance. Yet even this distinction was perhaps illusory; a servant had as immediate a stake in household productivity as any other member, and a good servant could even hope for special rewards when employment was terminated. Hugh and Emma Talbot of Brigstock, for example, arranged in 1339 for their female servant to inherit a house and courtyard after their deaths.[50] Because parents exercised considerable discretion in the devolution of property to children, a servant's economic stake in household prosperity approximated that of offspring; both servants and children knew that their daily meals depended on the vitality of the household economy, just as both servants and children could hope to leave the household with some share of the collective wealth. Most likely, servants and dependent children were treated similarly in the public life of their villages. As dependent members of the households in which they were employed, servants were seldom identified by their blood relationships to other households and were seldom pledged by known kin in the village. Instead, servants, like children, were identified by their dependent relationships to their householders and were, when judged guilty of petty crimes, almost invariably pledged by their masters. A servant was, in short, an integral member of the household in which he or she was employed.

The nuclear solidarity of the household was also undermined by death. Faced with the high mortality that prevailed among all age groups in the medieval countryside, the nuclear family of parents and children was a fragile entity. Many couples failed to produce any children who survived them, but even more common was the shattering of a marriage by the early death of a husband or wife. Peter Laslett found that one-third of all children in seventeenth-century Clayworth had lost a natural parent; similar (or worse) rates probably prevailed in rural households before the plague. The remarriages that regularly accompanied such bereavements produced households of stepparents, stepchildren, and stepsiblings. In the presence of such pervasive mortality, only fortunate households could long maintain a biologically discrete nuclear core; instead, even the nuclear family that lay at the heart of the household was often a step-nuclear family, including persons whose familial relationships to one another were remote and indirect.[51]

In the English countryside before the plague, the small conjugal household retained its social importance because it was both economically viable and structurally flexible. Community and kinship were always important to medieval villagers, but neither over-shadowed the rural household; most peasants probably primarily identified themselves not as members of villages or kin groups, but as members of households. As a primary social organization in medieval villages, the conjugal household structured not only private experiences but also public relations. A man's public activities changed as his private status shifted from unmarried son to married householder, just as a woman's public experiences reflected her private status as daughter, wife, or widow. As a result, the small and simple conjugal households of the peasantry profoundly shaped the gender norms of the medieval countryside.

IV

Daughters and Sons

By the time Cristina Penifader married Richard Power in 1317, she was a fairly independent member of Brigstock society. First appearing in the manorial court in 1312, she accumulated extensive property during her unmarried years through gifts from her father; in 1312 he gave her future control of a croft and plot (*placia*) he had purchased, in 1314 he granted her the use of more than a full virgate of meadow, and in 1316 he gave her four butts (or irregularly sized pieces of land) sufficiently valuable to merit the high entry fine of two shillings. When in need of a personal pledge or essoiner during these years, Cristina Penifader turned often to her father, but she was sufficiently independent of his authority to seek such legal assistance usually from other men in the community. She was also, by virtue of her propertied status, a suitor of the Brigstock court, obliged to attend all its meetings unless properly excused.[1]

The experiences of Henry Kroyl junior during his unmarried years were quite similar. In the three years that preceded his marriage to Cristina Penifader's sister in 1319, Henry Kroyl junior also accumulated resources independent from the properties of his father (acquiring small parcels of land in six separate transactions), relied often, but not exclusively, on his father for legal assistance, and paid suit to the Brigstock court. Unlike his future sister-in-law, however,

Henry Kroyl junior also began to acquire the political attributes of an adult man, not only joining a tithing but also assisting others as an essoiner, a personal pledge, and an attorney.[2]

The experiences of Cristina Penifader and Henry Kroyl junior suggest that young people in Brigstock before the plague usually married only after several years of gradual separation from the authority of their parents. Between the dependence of childhood and the independence of married adulthood, at least some young people in the community began to strike out on their own, accruing separate economic resources, expanding social ties beyond the family, and taking on some adult responsibilities. Their experiences also suggest that adolescence, a period of transition between dependent childhood and married adulthood, was known to not only young men but also young women in Brigstock.[3] To be sure, Henry Kroyl junior began to participate during his unmarried years in the political activities from which all women were excluded, but both he and Cristina Penifader acquired prior to marriage many of the economic, social, and legal attributes of full adulthood. If their experiences were typical, daughters and sons in Brigstock shared many common opportunities and responsibilities in the years between childhood and marriage.

Many influences shaped the adolescent experiences of countrypeople in the decades before the plague. Local economies that offered young people easy access to land or employment especially eased the transition from parental authority. In times or places of more limited resources, parents could longer maintain influence over their children by controlling what little land or work was available. Social rank was also important; the sons and daughters of wealthier peasants probably moved more gradually toward autonomy than did the children of those less privileged for whom the transition was probably more abrupt and more difficult. Even birth order affected adolescence not only by designating some children as heirs and others as non-heirs, but also by determining how adolescence coincided with other household circumstances (the transition between childhood and adulthood was probably especially short for younger children whose households were disintegrating through either the marriages of siblings or the deaths of parents). Local economy, social rank, and birth order affected adolescence in important and significant ways, but the activities of young people in Brigstock before the plague suggest that both they and their parents usually anticipated that the years before marriage would be characterized by growing economic, legal, social, and (in the case of males) political autonomy.

Gender and Childhood in the Medieval Countryside

Children, as the most dependent of people, were the least public members of rural society. Children had few legal rights. If their fathers died, minor heirs could claim their inheritances, but they then fell under the control of guardians who not only managed properties but also, if they wished, transferred custody or arranged future marriage. In 1339, for example, William Hayroun went to the Brigstock court and transferred custody of his minor brother John to Thomas Dandelin providing, among other things, for the future marriage of John to Thomas' daughter Emma.[4] Children also had few legal responsibilities. If a child committed an offense, the parent was charged and amerced; in 1337, for example, Katrina Pees of Iver paid two pence because her son had illegally fished in prohibited waters.[5] If a villager sued a child, the suit was either dismissed or delayed until the age of majority. When William Gerveys of Brigstock tried to recover a semi-virgate from Strangia Waleys de Pidentone and her son William in 1303, the court deferred action in the case until William reached maturity (*usque predictus Willelmus habeat etatem ad respondendum*).[6] Children were so completely subsumed into the identity of their householders that clerks often noted them without forename as simply the householder's dependent (*filius/filia*).[7]

Manorial courts seldom specify the precise age at which a child reached legal maturity, but the transition from childhood to adolescence probably occurred between twelve and fourteen years of age. Although estimates of biological maturation are very problematic, most contemporary medical authorities agreed that female sexual maturity was reached between the ages of twelve and fifteen years.[8] Church lawyers roughly concurred, fixing the age of final consent to marriage at twelve years for girls and fourteen years for boys.[9] And local customs usually gave full legal responsibilities to youths of twelve or fourteen years; in many villages minor heirs took control of their properties at such ages, and young men throughout England were obliged to enter tithings at twelve years of age.[10] The coincidence of biological and public maturity was closest at the lowest end of the social scale. The children of sokemen only achieved partial legal stature at fifteen years, and knights' heirs waited until twenty-one years before they could claim their patrimonies. But the children of humble countryfolk—whether free or unfree—began to shoulder adult responsibilities at the age of twelve years.[11]

Prior to reaching maturity, children appeared in the courts of manors like Brigstock only in circumstances that were unusual or unhappy. Bereaved of their fathers, minor heirs briefly appeared in public to claim their properties, but they subsequently withdrew from public view to the control of guardians (usually their mothers).[12] Children also appeared sporadically in the records of courts and coroners as victims or perpetrators of accidents, assaults, and other crimes.[13] Aside from such brief glimpses, the first dozen years of life in the medieval countryside defy historical reconstruction. Despite its limited scope, the extant evidence nevertheless suggests that gender distinctions might have separated the experiences of daughters and sons at an early age in two especially important aspects of life—survival and work.

No rates of infant and child mortality can be calculated for the medieval peasantry, but death rates were certainly high. In his study of Colyton in the sixteenth through eighteenth centuries, E. A. Wrigley found that roughly 12 to 20 percent of children died in infancy and that another 12 to 20 percent failed to reach their fifteenth birthday. Similar rates have been traced for other European populations in the centuries that immediately preceded industrialization. Patterns identified in early modern villages did not necessarily prevail in the medieval countryside, but the economic and demographic stresses precipitated by the overpopulation, famines, and diseases of the early fourteenth century make it very likely that, at best, only about two-thirds to three-fourths of all children born to countrypeople in these decades survived to adulthood—the rest fell victim to illness, accident, or infanticide.[14]

Although the sex ratios of this mortality in infancy and childhood are unknown, it is possible that the odds worked against the survival of female children. Most medieval parents probably loved their children, daughters as well as sons.[15] But peasants often faced difficult circumstances that could force them to favor one child over another; given the high mortality rates of childhood, such partiality, even without outright infanticide, put unfavored children at great risk. All children presented their parents with the burden of support while young and the hope of labor when grown, but boys were also preferred heirs upon whom both family names and family lands would devolve. Rural parents hoped to pass their heritable properties, whether divided between sons or given to only one son, to the next generation in the male line. Even in villages that practiced the preferential inheritance of only one son (primogeniture or ultimogeniture), additional sons had an edge over their sisters because they provided a safeguard against the premature death of the presumed heir. Daughters could inherit in the absence of sons, but the results were less satisfactory because the property was usually fragmented by division among all daughters.

The greater value that inheritance customs gave to male children is reflected in the naming practices of the medieval peasantry. Parents chose forenames for their sons from a limited range of personal names that were reused generation after generation. The repetition of a few names like John, William, Richard, and Robert emphasized the male infant's importance to his family; identified with the forename of his father or grandfather, such a child was designated as a person of consequence to his family's past and future. Less vital to both family and community, female children were named more freely and idiosyncratically. Among females one encounters not only standard names such as Matilda, Agnes, and Alice, but also a large number of unusual names such as Tibia, Lucia, Leticia, Nute, Mariaunt, Ivette, Strangia, and Sibilla. Although these forenames were charming and evocative, they carried no familial importance.[16] Medieval parents might have loved their daughters as much as their sons, but they also expected daughters to contribute less than sons to the family's continuation in the next generation.

Such priorities may have resulted in higher female mortality among children in other places and times, but the evidence for the late medieval English peasantry is equivocal.[17] Lay and ecclesiastical courts rarely prosecuted infanticide and often failed to specify the sex of the murdered child.[18] Accidental deaths reported to coroners show no signs of bias against female children, but instead match modern patterns of childhood mortality.[19] And although the sex ratios of all English listings in the thirteenth and fourteenth centuries are quite skewed, the disproportion of men might as easily result from the clerical underenumeration of women as from the higher mortality of females in childhood.[20] In short, female children probably faced a harder battle for survival than did their brothers, but the demographic information is unable either to confirm or to deny differential childhood mortality. It is most reasonable to conclude that, first, boys were almost certainly not at greater risk than girls and, second, girls were at least possibly more often victims of death from either neglect or abuse.

As members of a rural family economy, children worked as soon as they were able. With visions of workshops and factories, we tend to equate child labor with child abuse, but in the preindustrial countryside the boundaries that distinguished adult from child and work from leisure were relatively undeveloped and fluid. Children worked because everyone worked and because working was living. Barbara Hanawalt's analysis of childhood deaths reported in coroners' rolls has shown that children began to contribute to the support of their households as soon as they were sufficiently mobile; even at about four years of age, when children still spent most of their time at play, they also helped their parents in small ways—watching animals, supervising younger children, completing small domestic chores. By the age of eight, children took responsibility for unsupervised tasks. Some left home to work as servants in other households, some worked as shepherds or industrial helpers, others worked in the fields.[21] A labor ordinance of 1388, reacting to the extreme labor shortage that followed the Black Death, assumed that children were already seasoned workers by the time they reached legal maturity, requiring that any child "which used to labour at the Plough or Cart, or other Labour or Service of Husbandry till they be of Age of Twelve Years, that from thenceforth they shall abide by the same Labour."[22]

In both work and play, children mimicked the gender distinctions of adulthood. Coroners' reports show that, among toddlers, boys died more frequently in accidents outside the home; girls hurt themselves more often playing with pots and cooking utensils. Older boys were accidentally killed in mock battles and working in fields or meadows; older girls roamed about less and died more frequently from accidents in the home or yard. Staying nearer the domestic croft, girls learned early the skills of child care, cooking, and gardening. Boys, wandering farther from home, helped with herding and husbandry.[23]

By the time these children reached adolescence, distinctions of gender were already deeply engrained.

Adolescence

When daughters and sons in Brigstock began to accept the legal responsibilities of adulthood at about the age of twelve years, they also began to separate themselves gradually from the authority of their parents. Often encouraged and supported by their parents, adolescents slowly accrued separate economic resources, developed broader ranges of friends and acquaintances, and assumed the legal obligations of adult villagers. Although slow and often fragmentary, this process began the separation that would ultimately end with the child's establishment of a discrete marital household. At the time that marriage ended adolescence, many young people were still dependent in some measure upon their parents, but they were much less dependent than they had been as young children.

Two problems complicate the study of adolescence in the medieval countryside—defining the chronological scope of adolescence and identifying persons in that stage of life. Adolescence need not necessarily end with marriage (in Renaissance Florence, for example, a man's youth extended to the age of 30, regardless of his marital status). Yet marriage brought such dramatic changes in the public lives of both women and men in Brigstock that it clearly marked the end of adolescence in the medieval countryside.[24] Estimating both the age and incidence of medieval marriage, however, is problematic. Historians have been able to demonstrate that the ambivalent status of an adolescent, who was neither a dependent child nor a married adult, was often either long-lived or even permanent in early modern England. Although marriage rates and ages varied widely, most marriages in the sixteenth and seventeenth centuries were contracted between people in their middle to late twenties, and usually about 10 to 15 percent of the adult population never married. This "European marriage pattern," as it has been called, helped to check population growth throughout northern Europe from the sixteenth through eighteenth centuries, but its origins have yet to be identified firmly because medieval sources yield so little demographic information.[25] Manorial clerks duly recorded the purchases of merchets (or marriage licenses), but they never noted the ages of brides and bridegrooms, and they also did not record all marriages, only those for which licenses were required. As a result, medievalists can only tentatively estimate age at marriage and rates of marriage.

Attempts to gauge the chronological timing of marriage in the medieval countryside must rely on such indirect information that the results are necessarily speculative. Using a series of assumptions based on parental histories, Zvi Razi calculated that peasants on the manor of Halesowen in the early fourteenth century usually married between the ages of 18 and 22 years. Razi argued that a male in the second generation of a Halesowen family usually appeared as a landholder in the court records at 20 years of age and that the marital ages of that man's children could be estimated from the interval between their marriage fines and their father's first appearance as a landholder. For example, Razi claimed that Alice atte Lyche married between the ages of 18 and 21 years because her merchet was paid in 1325, 18 years after her father John atte Lyche first received land from his father. Unfortunately, this method relies not only on a strong correlation among three variables—age, marriage, and first tenure of land—but also on the survival of first-born children to maturity (since children born later will appear to marry at artificially advanced ages). It is also based on possibly unrepresentative data since Razi's calculations involved less than one-third of the merchets recorded (and merchets represent only a fraction of all marriages).[26] Although his final results are tentative, Razi's calculations provide, to date, the only aggregate estimate of marital age in the early fourteenth-century English countryside. Indirect evidence from Brigstock supports his contention of relatively early marriage among the pre-plague peasantry; most young people in Brigstock seem to have married within only a few years of first appearing as mature persons before the manorial court.[27]

Estimating the proportion of adults in medieval villages who lived as spinsters and bachelors is equally difficult. Court rolls are no help in this endeavor because they seldom note the status of being unmarried, but the few extant listings of pre-plague English communities indicate that adult celibacy among the laity, while not unknown, might have been uncommon. If the Lincolnshire surveys analyzed by H. E. Hallam were typical of late thirteenth-century villages, lay celibacy was very rare; households of celibates accounted for less than

4 percent of those surveyed.[28] Many unmarried persons, however, might have escaped the notice of manorial officers because they were landless, mobile, or both. The labor market of the medieval countryside included many landless persons who either never married or only temporarily established unions. The custumals of eastern counties, for example, mention *anilepimen* and *anilepiwymen* (literally translated: single men and single women) who, holding no land of their own, wandered about seeking employment.[29] Because manorial records obscure the activities of such people, their true proportion in the population cannot be estimated. But it seems likely that most villages probably included only a few households of celibates and only a few celibates who lived either temporarily or permanently in the households of others. In the final analysis, information on the marriages and ages of medieval villagers is too incomplete to establish with certainty the demographic characteristics of marriage in the pre-plague countryside. The available evidence suggests that most people not only married but also married by their early twenties, but this evidence is suggestive, not definitive.[30]

Identifying adolescents, especially male adolescents, is as problematic as estimating ages and rates of marriage. The marital statuses of women were usually reliably noted by court clerks. Because a woman moved, in a sense, from one dependent status to another, it was important for the clerks of Brigstock to specify accurately under whose authority she was at any given time. As a result, women cited as daughters were almost invariably unmarried because married women were publicly identified not as their fathers' daughters but as their husbands' wives (Agnes the daughter of Robert Penifader became Agnes the wife of Henry Kroyl junior). To be sure, some women were noted by the clerks without any indication of their domestic status (and have been analyzed in the samples as "women of unknown status"). Most of these were likely widows who, as heads of the households left by their husbands, were less dependent than other women. Others might have been spinsters who, like Cecilia Penifader, spent their adult years free of the authority of both father and husband. Most women, however, were regularly identified by the court clerks as the daughters, wives, or widows of specific men, and these identifications provide reliable guides to household status.

The marital statuses of men are more difficult to ascertain. Clerical identification provides a rough but fallible guide. Once men married and established separate households, they were seldom described by the clerks of Brigstock as dependents of their fathers. Henry Kroyl junior, for example, was identified as either "Henry son of Henry Kroyl" or "Henry Kroyl junior" before his marriage, but used only the latter designation after he married (and when his father died some ten years later, the junior qualification was also dropped). Yet at least some men were sometimes identified as sons of their fathers even after marriage; of the 74 married men (known to be married because they acted jointly with their wives) in the Brigstock samples of civil pleas and land transfers, 9 (12 percent) were identified on at least one occasion by their relationships with their fathers. In some cases, clerks identified married men as their fathers' sons in order to distinguish them from others; when Henry Tulke and his wife Edith obtained future rights to some lands held by Alice Kykhok in 1344, the clerk of Brigstock probably identified Henry as the son of William Tulke in order to distinguish him from another Henry Tulke, son of Radulph, also living in Brigstock during these years.[31] Other married men, however, were identified as their fathers' sons for no apparent reason. So while it is reasonably certain that women identified as daughters were unmarried members of their fathers' households, this certainty is less firm for men identified as sons. The inverse is also problematic; court clerks occasionally cited unmarried men, like Henry Kroyl junior, without any clear indication of their continued dependency on their fathers.

Family reconstitutions cannot adjust for the idiosyncrasies of clerical identification of males because they report on familial relationships, not marital statuses. And the marital histories of men are so poorly reported in manorial courts that only rarely is it possible to ascertain that a man was single, married, or widowed at a specific time. Approximate dates for the marriages of only four males in Brigstock could be determined from the records of the manor. Indeed, the marriages of most men could only be surmised by the appearance of grown children in court (by which time they could have been widowed). Even the appearance of a wife in the court records only briefly identified her husband as certainly married; a few months prior to her appearance, he could have been single, just as he could have been widowed a few months thereafter. As a result, any reliance on clearly traced marital statuses for males not only severely limits the samples but also dramatically skews analyses toward the atypical cases of wealthy (well-documented) males who acted jointly with their wives (thus betraying their marital status).

This conundrum cannot be definitively solved; no method of ascertaining the marital statuses of men cited in manorial courts satisfactorily provides both breadth of coverage and accuracy of attribution. Faced with this dilemma, it has seemed most reasonable to suppose that the clerks who so reliably identified the marital statuses of women also usually reported accurately the marital statuses of men. Unless the context of their action indicated otherwise, men identified as sons by the clerks of Brigstock have been analyzed in the Brigstock samples as adolescent dependents of their fathers. Men whom clerks identified without any statement of household dependency were treated as presumed husbands or householders. This approach certainly introduces some error into the analyses, but other methods are also liable to both error and prejudice. Indeed, the prejudice introduced by this method moves against the main thrust of the findings. Even though this study of male adolescence is based only on the activities of males identified as dependents of their fathers (a method that could skew analyses toward activities that emphasize dependence on parents), this stage of life emerges as a time of considerable independence and autonomy.

The study of adolescence in the medieval countryside presents unusual problems of definition and identification partly because of the social ambivalence of the age. Adolescents were dependents of their householders, but they were also somewhat independent. Perhaps as striking as the social ambivalence of adolescence is the similarity of female and male activities during these years of mixed dependence and independence. In view of their different experiences as children and their different roles as married adults, the public activities of adolescent daughters and sons in Brigstock were remarkably parallel. Distinctions of gender sharply differentiated the political activities of young men and young women, but less strongly shaped the legal, economic, and social experiences of young people before they married.

When childhood ended, young men began to accept political responsibilities from which their sisters were permanently excluded. They entered tithings at the age of twelve years, becoming responsible not only to the tithing but also for the tithing. If an adolescent male committed a crime against the peace, his tithing, not his householder, presented him at the following view of frankpledge, and he was similarly responsible for bringing errant members of his tithing to court. Young men also began to participate in the political networks of their villages by assisting others in court. Because the Brigstock court readily accepted adolescent males as essoiners, personal pledges, and attorneys, young men began to build ties of mutual assistance and obligation with their neighbors. In addition, they became liable for wider duties, although no evidence of the Crown's most notable imposition on male adolescents, conscription, survives in the manorial rolls of Brigstock. The political horizons of men expanded widely during adolescence, but they were barred from direct political authority; only married men were eligible in most rural communities to serve in either village or manorial offices.[32]

In terms of legal competence, the experiences of adolescent sons and daughters were more parallel. The Brigstock court treated adolescents of both sexes as legally responsible adults who could be trusted as landholders, liable as criminals, and competent as suitors. Both young women and young men freely held and disposed of land; both were required, if appropriate, to render suit of court; both personally answered for criminal actions or offenses; and both were eligible to resolve disputes through civil litigation. As shown in Table 4.1, the participation of adolescents in civil pleas followed the general patterns of their gender. Daughters, like all women, tended to come unwillingly to litigation, appearing more often as defendants than plaintiffs, and they ended many suits through judgment or waging law rather than through concords. Sons, like all men, more equally balanced their appearances between plaints and defenses and were especially likely to end cases through concords. Both daughters and sons, however, were disproportionately involved in suits of trespass rather than pleas of contract or debt. Perhaps young people were especially tempted to commit petty thefts and otherwise distress their neighbors, but their preponderance of trespass suits might simply reflect the lowly economic status of adolescence (since many adolescents lacked the resources to conclude agreements of contract or debt). It is also interesting that proportionately more daughters appeared as litigants in the sample than sons, suggesting that adolescence was a time of unusual recourse to civil litigation for women. More sons appeared as litigants than daughters, but sons constituted only 11 percent of all male litigants (39 of 348), as opposed to

TABLE 4.1. Daughters and Sons in the Brigstock Sample of Civil Pleas

Category	Sons		All Males	Daughters		All Females
	Number	Column Percent	Column Percent	Number	Column Percent	Column Percent
Type of Action						
Plaintiff	21	54%	51%	6	35%	38%
Defendant	18	46	49	11	65	62
All actors	39	100	100	17	100	100
Type of plea (if known)						
Plea of trespass	30	83	73	16	100	90
Plea of contract	3	8	5	0	0	2
Plea of debt	3	8	22	0	0	8
All known pleas	36	99	100	16	100	100
Type of resolution (if known)						
Concord	22	85	79	7	58	53
Judgment/law	4	15	21	5	42	47
All known resolutions	26	100	100	12	99	100
Final outcome (if known)						
Actor won	13	50	50	5	42	47
Actor lost	13	50	50	7	58	53
All known outcomes	26	100	100	12	100	100

Note: See Table 2.2 for full information on sexual differentiation in the sample of pleas. Percentages have been rounded to produce integral numbers.

daughters who accounted for 20 percent of female plaintiffs and defendants (17 of 86).[33]

As suggested by the landholding activities of Cristina Penifader and Henry Kroyl junior, gradual separation from the parental household economy was also a characteristic of adolescence in Brigstock. The reconstructed premarital activities of eight young women and four young men show that fully half of these adolescents demonstrated some measure of economic separation before marriage. Cristina Penifader's extensive properties have already been described; Isabella Brother held a small house with a curtilage when she married in 1317; Alice Orgoner inherited lands just prior to her marriage in 1310; Isabella Huet was profiting from commercial brewing and baking three years before her marriage in 1298; Henry Kroyl junior, as described above, first acquired property several years before his 1319 wedding; and Henry Cocus obtained rights to land three years before his marriage in 1304. Parents often assisted their children in these first ventures; Cristina Penifader, Henry Kroyl, and Henry Cocus all received properties as gifts from parents. As a result, the socioeconomic status of parents might have affected their children's access to separate resources (and especially land), but the evidence from Brigstock suggests that differences of rank might have only slightly affected the economic activities of adolescents. In Brigstock, children of both upper-rank and lower-rank villagers attained some measure of economic separateness from their parents. Because officeholders usually came from socially prominent and economically wealthy families, the best guide to socioeconomic rank in Brigstock is officeholding. Of the 7 daughters or sons of officeholders whose premarital activities were traced, 4 acquired lands prior to marriage; of the 5 adolescents whose fathers never held office, the activities of 2 showed evidence of economic autonomy (and one of these was involved in commerce, not landholding).[34]

Because dates of marriage were so seldom reported in the courts of Brigstock, the premarital economic activities of only a few young people can be clearly traced. As a result, the experiences of these few firmly identified adolescents needed to be supplemented with information from a larger and more representative pool—namely, the participation of daughters and sons in the Brigstock sample of land transactions. This sample illustrates how actively young women and men participated in the local land market (Table 4.2). Probably the most

TABLE 4.2. Daughters and Sons in the Brigstock Sample of Land Transactions

Category	Sons		All Males	Daughters		All Females
	Number	Column Percent	Column Percent	Number	Column Percent	Column Percent
Type of action						
Grantor	56	34%	48%	11	26%	60%
Receiver	107	66	52	31	74	40
All actors	163	100	100	42	100	100
Autonomy of actor						
Acted alone	151	93	88	37	88	60
Acted jointly	12	7	12	5	12	40
All actors	163	100	100	42	100	100
Nature of grant						
Not intrafamilial	117	72	83	14	33	63
Intrafamilial	46	28	17	28	67	37
All grants	163	100	100	42	100	100
Size of grant (if known)						
Less than 2 rods	106	88	90	31	86	80
Over 2 rods	15	12	10	5	14	20
All grants of known size	121	100	100	36	100	100

Note: For general information on the breakdown of land transactions according to sex, see Table 2.3. Percentages have been rounded to produce integral numbers.

startling aspect of the land market in Brigstock is the intense involvement of young people; more than one-fourth of those cited in the sampled conveyances of land were identified as sons or daughters of other villagers (205 of the 779 persons trading land in the sample). Indeed, adolescents seem to have been more active in the land market than in other aspects of local life; they constituted only 17 percent of reported criminals and 13 percent of litigants. Without information on the age structure of Brigstock in the early fourteenth century, it is impossible to estimate what proportion of young people traded land during their adolescence, but it seems likely that young people were at least as active in the land market as full adults and very possibly even more active. The sample of land transactions, moreover, suggests again that socioeconomic status only slightly affected access to land; of the 128 adolescent recipients of land whose backgrounds could be traced, 66 were upper rank (with fathers who held local office) and 62 were lower rank (with fathers who never served in official capacities).[35]

Daughters and sons usually controlled freely the properties they obtained on the land market. To be sure, the Brigstock court permitted transfers of properties in which the recipient accepted certain restrictions. In such cases, recipients usually agreed either to enter the property only after a stipulated term or to respect the temporary claims of others to the property. Late entries most often guaranteed the inheritances of sons. On the occasion of their marriage in 1319, for example, Henry Kroyl junior and his new wife received a semivirgate from his parents, but the newlyweds were not to enter the land fully until after both parents died. Such future transfers not only eliminated the risk of later controversy, but also probably ensured that a grandchild would inherit even if a child died prematurely. Other transfers were encumbered by the temporary rights of others; a recipient of land occasionally had to agree to another person's temporary use of the property (often because of a prior lease). Most land transfers, however, involved straightforward conveyances of full and immediate ownership, and most young people held properties that were neither leased, encumbered, nor provisionally granted. Adolescents seldom held properties jointly with their parents, they received properties using the same legal forms employed by adults, and they freely transferred properties without any hindrance. The young people of Brigstock were legally competent to use their lands as they pleased.[36]

Nevertheless, familial considerations figured prominently in the land dealings of adolescents. Logically enough, sons and daughters more often received rather than granted land; just starting out in life, they had little to give and much to accumulate. And, as suggested by the very high proportion of intrafamilial transactions among adolescents, they frequently received such lands from their parents. In the sample, parents granted land directly to 17 daughters and 27 sons (32 percent of all adolescent recipients). It is, moreover, very probable that many other young people received land with parental aid not specifically mentioned in the legal records of property transfers (this is particularly likely for parents who either purchased land for their children from third parties or financially assisted their children in buying land). Because parental expectation and familial custom probably couched land grants to children in terms of preparation for marriage and expansion of family, such grants likely conveyed only an ambivalent independence upon the child. However, they are not without significance, since they provided a separate economic resource for the receiving child and often preceded marriage by several years. Moreover, siblings or parents and children only rarely held parcels of land jointly. The participation of young people in the land market was certainly not homogeneous—some sold or leased properties, others acted jointly with siblings or parents, and still others purchased land from their neighbors. But the Brigstock sample suggests that adolescents characteristically used the land market—often with the help of their parents—to get their first start in life.

In some respects, the land conveyances of adolescent daughters and sons paralleled the general experiences of women and men. Just as women overall constituted only 21 percent of all participants in the Brigstock land market, so only one daughter conveyed or received land for every four sons who did so. Just as women were more likely than men to act jointly or intrafamilially in land transactions, so daughters were more likely than sons to bring partners to their land transfers and to rely on intrafamilial transactions. Moreover, gender directly affected adolescent participation in the Brigstock land market in two specific areas: sons were far more likely than daughters to receive future grants from parents, and daughters relied more heavily than sons on parental gifts of property.[37] The former reflects the preference of sons as heirs (since most future grants were designed to ensure proper inheritance), and the latter suggests that the weakened purchasing power of daughters forced them to lean more heavily on parental generosity than sons.

Nevertheless, the experiences of daughters and sons in the Brigstock land market were similar in many essential features. Adolescents of both sexes were equally represented in the sample; sons constituted 26 percent of all males sampled, and daughters accounted for 26 percent of sampled females. Both appeared disproportionately as receivers of land. Both also were equally likely to receive provisional grants; 26 percent of both sons and daughters received grants that stipulated future access, limited terms, or other encumbrances. And both were perhaps relatively unaffected in their land dealings by socioeconomic background; 43 percent of the daughters who acquired land and 50 percent of sons were of lower rank (with fathers who never held local office).

The active participation of young women and men in Brigstock's land market represents, in a sense, only the tip of the economic iceberg; lying below the surface were other crucial opportunities that fostered the growth of economic autonomy during adolescence. For many young people, the acquisition of land probably marked not the beginning of a separate economic life, but rather its culmination. Many of the adolescents who obtained land through purchases (and not parental gift) must have bought properties with cash accumulated on their own account. Isabella Huet's activities before her marriage suggest that commerce in bread and ale provided possible employment for young people, but she was probably unusual. Brewing and baking required such extensive resources that few unmarried people in Brigstock profited from these industries.[38] Instead, labor was doubtless the most salable resource of most youths, and many adolescents probably hoped to buy land someday by saving money earned as wage-laborers or servants. The proportional importance of both wage labor and service in the medieval countryside is unknown, but both occupations were available to (and perhaps largely filled by) adolescents.[39]

Both lords and villagers hired workers for occasional tasks, skilled and unskilled. Because of their age and inexperience, however, most adolescents probably worked at low-skill tasks, toiling as common laborers, ditchers, hedgers, helpers, and the like. Wages, paid in cash or both cash and food, were calculated by either days worked or tasks completed. When employed, wage-workers could reap profits that exceeded those of servants, but employment was unsteady and often concentrated in certain times of the year. Daughters, like all women, were disadvantaged wage-workers, not only placed in especially low-skill occupations but also paid less than men.[40]

While servants were paid less than wage-laborers, they enjoyed greater stability and protection. By living in their employers' households, servants avoided basic living expenses. And because they often worked for a year or more in the same household, they not only were protected from seasonal unemployment but also sometimes profited from the generosity of their employers. Agnes Waleys of Weldon, for example, worked in the Brigstock household of Hugh and Emma Talbot for at least five years and possibly eight years or more. Probably the servant (*ancilla*) of the Talbots mentioned in 1336, she was given a house and courtyard by her employers in 1339 that she was to obtain after their deaths. Five years later, the Talbots gave her immediate use of a garden plot. Her experience, while probably not common, was certainly not unique.[41] Servants are so poorly reported in medieval records that many questions about their experiences are matters of speculation rather than proof: children from poor or large households were probably especially likely to seek employment as servants; the work required of them likely replicated the work they had done for their parents; they probably kept the bulk of their annual wages rather than sending profits back to their parents; and for most servants, the occupation was temporary, not permanent. Both daughters and sons found employment as servants, but young women might have been especially active in service since, of the 32 servants identified in Brigstock, 19 (or 59 percent) were female. Just as women were paid lower wages than men, so they also received lower salaries as servants.[42]

Although information about both wage work and service in the medieval countryside is very limited, the gender distinctions of adolescent landholding clearly applied just as well to the working experiences of young people. Both daughters and sons attempted to establish separate economic reserves by saving money earned as workers or servants, but sons were more successful than daughters. One result might have been the greater eagerness of daughters to leave their villages to seek better opportunities elsewhere. Faced with disadvantageous inheritance customs, landholding practices, and working conditions, many young women might have moved to towns that offered more female employment.[43] Many others, however, stayed in the villages of their birth, where they, like sons (although less successfully than sons), slowly accumulated economic reserves separate from those of their parents.

As reflected in activities reported in the Brigstock court, the social transition from childhood to adulthood was strongly shaped and supervised by parents. Before he married Agnes Penifader in 1319, Henry Kroyl junior built a modest network of court associations which revolved around his father. Although he interacted in court on 30 occasions with 20 different people, he dealt more than once with only three people—nine times with his father and twice each with two villagers to whom he was not related. His father was both quantitatively dominant and qualitatively important; the only multiplex relationship (involving more than one *type* of contact) in Henry Kroyl Junior's premarital network was with his father. In addition to these direct contacts, Henry Kroyl junior also depended indirectly on his father's social influence; many of the people in his network also had independent associations with his father. Henry Kroyl junior's ambivalent independence was not peculiar to the male sex. Cristina Penifader's experiences before her marriage closely paralleled those of her future brother-in-law; her adolescent network was small, her father stood out both quantitatively and qualitatively, and most of her associates were also friends of her father.[44]

Pledging patterns illustrate how the mingling of dependence and independence in the premarital networks of Henry Kroyl junior and Cristina Penifader characterized the social experiences of many adolescents in Brigstock (see Table 4.3). Young women and men were no longer children, completely subsumed under the authority of their householders, but neither were they thoroughly independent. Whether appearing as parties to land conveyances, as alleged criminals, or as litigants, young people were much more likely than full adults to turn to family members for assistance in meeting their court obligations. Indeed, they often used familial pledges twice as frequently as did full adults. In most cases, adolescents were aided by their fathers or heads of household. The 38 familial pledges used by young offenders in the sample of crimes, for example, included 30

TABLE 4.3. Familial Pledging of Adolescents in the Brigstock Samples

Category	Sons	All Males	Daughters	All Females
Sample of land transactions				
Number of familial pledges	38	57	15	18
Percentage of all pledges	35%	18%	52%	29%
Sample of crimes				
Number of familial pledges	23	67	15	66
Percentage of all pledges	47%	23%	56%	46%
Sample of civil pleas				
Number of litigants assisted by family	11	36	5	15
Percentage of all litigants assisted	39%	13%	33%	24%

Note: Familial pledges include all pledges who either were of a specified relationship to the subject or shared a reliable surname with the subject. Analysis of the sample of civil pleas differed from analyses of the other samples in two respects. First, the information in the sample of civil pleas includes not only pledging but also other forms of assistance (i.e., essoining, acting as an attorney). Second, the information on assistors in the sample of civil pleas is based not on each instance of assistance (i.e., each pledge or essoiner), but on the overall configuration of each litigant's assistance (i.e., whether a litigant used family members for assistance never, sometimes, or always during the course of the case). Percentages have been rounded to produce integral numbers.

instances of pledging by householders.[45] Since familial pledges seldom accounted for much more than half of the assistors used by adolescents, however, young people were not thoroughly dependent, but the process of building social contacts and obligations in the village proceeded slowly. As young people expanded their social horizons, they remained protected and guided by their parents.

Distinctions of gender certainly influenced the adolescent blending of dependence and independence in social activity. Just as all women were pledged more frequently than men by relatives, so familial pledging of daughters usually exceeded that of sons. Just as the court networks of all women tended to be small, so Cristina Penifader's network was only about one-half the size of Henry Kroyl junior's. But the social experiences of daughters and sons were fundamentally similar. First, children of both sexes struck out on their own during adolescence; neither daughters nor sons remained during these years completely dependent socially on their parents. Second, the process of social separation was incomplete for both sexes; daughters remained more dependent than sons, but adolescent males nevertheless retained important ties of dependence with their parents.

From a somewhat different perspective, crime presentments also reflect the peculiar social circumstances of adolescents in Brigstock (see Table 4.4). Daughters and sons generally conformed to the reported criminal patterns of their sex; daughters committed proportionally more antisocial crimes, and sons were guilty of more crimes perpetrated against specific persons. Although sons were amerced about twice as frequently as daughters for crimes, they both constituted about the same proportion of criminals reported for their sex; roughly one of every five or six reported criminals was an adolescent.[46] The reported crimes of young people, however, also reflected their ambivalent social status. Misbehavior in the fields, for example, accounted for an exceptionally large proportion of crimes reported against sons. Because the sorts of offenses covered by such presentments (gleaning badly, pilfering hay, and the like) were usually associated with household dependents (especially women), the importance of such conduct in the criminality of sons underscores their continued dependence in the households of their fathers. The stronger familial orientation of adolescents might also be indicated in their propensity for intrafamilial crime; of the eight persons cited in the sample for offenses perpetrated against members of their families, four were adolescents. Moreover, although sons were cited for more householder crimes (building purprestures, receiving strangers, pasturing illegally) than daughters, adolescents of both sexes were guilty of fewer such offenses than were older villagers. The reported criminality of young people of both sexes, then, reflects the semi-independence of youth, but even here, young men seem to have achieved a greater measure of independence than young women.[47]

In Brigstock before the plague, adolescent daughters and sons edged in fundamentally similar ways toward adult independence. Sons began to acquire political privileges denied to all women, but young people of both sexes moved—legally, economically, and socially—away from the control of their parents. Even though this period of semi-independence made more sense for sons (who were heading toward the full independence of married householders) than for daughters (who could anticipate renewed dependence when they married), both sexes slowly became less dependent on their parents

TABLE 4.4. Daughters and Sons in the Brigstock Sample of Crimes

Category	Sons		All Males	Daughters		All Females
	Number	Column Percent	Column Percent	Number	Column Percent	Column Percent
Crimes against the community						
Illegal pasturing	1	2%	3%	0	0%	1%
Misconduct in fields	12	19	9	13	38	38
Property damage	6	10	12	1	3	10
Insolence to officers	0	0	1	0	0	1
Rescue of seized property	6	10	5	0	0	2
Harboring strangers	3	5	8	0	0	3
Behavior that caused hue	10	16	18	7	21	15
Unjust raising of hue	1	2	2	3	9	9
Miscellaneous	1	2	3	6	18	6
Subtotal	40	65	62	30	88	83
Crimes against persons						
Attacks (and threatened attacks)	18	29	31	3	9	13
Hamsokens (housebreakings)	4	6	7	1	3	4
Subtotal	22	35	38	4	12	17
Total: All crimes	62	100	100	34	100	100

Note: See Table 2.4 for full information on sexual differentiation in reported crimes. Percentages have been rounded to produce integral numbers.

in the years that preceded marriage. Although all parents were certainly not unequivocally delighted with the growing independence of their children, most probably accepted its inevitability. Parental grants of land might epitomize the attitudes of most fathers and mothers; although seldom large, the gifts did help children to set out on their own. Perhaps if substantial villagers like Robert Penifader were willing to give properties to their children, others less fortunate were willing to let their offspring work outside the household and keep part or all of their wages. Yet the ambivalent independence of adolescence must have created misunderstandings between even the best-intentioned parents and their children. Legal rights aside, many parents might have expected to control the landholdings and movable goods of their children; their children probably often thought otherwise. In such circumstances, parental authority remained dominant. When Margery the daughter of Richard Prille tried to take two calves from his household, an inquisition ordered by the Brigstock court immediately buttressed parental authority by affirming her father's ownership of the beasts.[48] Still subject to the authority of a parent or householder until they married, adolescents like Margery Prille were not yet full adults.

How typical was the semi-independence of adolescents in Brigstock before the plague? What circumstances facilitated a gradual transition from dependent childhood to independent adulthood? With the knowledge now at hand, answers to such questions must necessarily be tentative and speculative, but information on adolescence in Iver and Houghton-cum-Wyton suggests that young people elsewhere also achieved some measure of independence from their parents before they married. According to two separate measures, young people in Iver during the early fourteenth century were just as economically separate as their counterparts in Brigstock. First, of the 29 persons whose premarital careers could be traced, 9 held lands and 2 were involved in other economic pursuits; roughly 2 of every 5 traced adolescents controlled discrete resources before marriage. Second, daughters or their prospective husbands frequently paid their own marriage license fines (merchets), suggesting that they had accumulated sufficient independent savings to meet this seigneurial imposition on their own (in most known cases, the father of the bride was still alive). As in Brigstock, this adolescent independence was both incomplete and nurtured by parents; many of Iver's young land-holders had received their properties from their parents, and many children (even among those who held lands) still relied on their parents for further assistance at the time of marriage.[49]

The evidence of adolescent autonomy in Houghton-cum-Wyton is more equivocal. Daughters regularly paid their own merchets in Houghton-cum-Wyton, indicating independent accumulation prior to marriage. Yet only 2 of the 19 young people whose premarital careers were traced displayed any economic independence before marriage. And evidence presented in a suit in 1308 raises the possi-bility that at least some young people in Houghton-cum-Wyton re-mained dependent on their parents even after marriage. The suit centered around the marriage settlement of Andrew Prepositus' daughter Agnes and Stephen Prepositus' son Stephen. According to the court,

> the aforesaid Stephen [the father] should have maintained Agnes the daughter of the said Andrew and should have housed her in his home or in a suitable dwelling in his courtyard, providing her with all the necessities of life. . . . Afterwards, Stephen, in violation of the agreement, expelled Agnes from his home.

This statement suggests that Agnes and Stephen junior did not estab-lish an independent conjugal home when they married, but instead remained subject to the goodwill of Stephen's father, residing either in his home or within his courtyard. They were also so dependent that both the marriage contract and the resultant suit involved not them, but their parents. On balance, the evidence on adolescence in Houghton-cum-Wyton is too insubstantial for certainty, but it does seem likely that young people in that community were less indepen-dent of their parents than in either of the other two manors.[50]

The comparative experiences of adolescents in Brigstock, Iver, and Houghton-cum-Wyton suggest that economic conditions profoundly shaped adolescence in the medieval countryside. In situations where land was plentiful or alternative employment was available, youths were probably better able to move away from parental authority. If resources, however, were limited, parents—by controlling the distribu-tion of both land and employment—retained influence over their chil-dren's lives for longer periods. Both Brigstock and Iver, in contrast to Houghton-cum-Wyton, boasted active land markets that provided young people with relatively easy access to the most vital resource of their society. The flexible economies of these two manors—one located in a forest and the other a pastoral community—probably also offered more opportunities for youthful employment than the farming economy of Houghton-cum-Wyton. As a result, young people in both Brigstock and Iver likely enjoyed many more opportunities for independent accumulation than did their counterparts in Houghton-cum-Wyton.

In the same way that it fostered regional variations in parent-child relations, economic circumstance also probably framed the adolescent experiences of privileged villagers, setting them apart from the youths of those less fortunate. Sons and daughters of relatively wealthy families like the Penifaders and the Kroyls were able to move slowly toward adulthood under the tutelage and generosity of their parents, but the transition was probably less easy for the offspring of the less privileged. Even though the Brigstock sample of land transactions revealed many parents of modest resources endowing their children with property, they did so somewhat less frequently and less amply than did parents of more privileged status. Parents of lower rank also probably more often urged their children either to emigrate in search of better opportunities or to enter service at very early ages.[51]

Adolescent experiences, then, were shaped not only by gender but also by local economy and social status. Birth order was also important. Both the timing and the nature of premarital experiences were probably influenced profoundly by a child's birth rank. The adolescence of a presumed heir must have often differed from those of noninheriting siblings; if nothing else, the heir knew that properties received in youth would be enlarged via inheritance, whereas other children faced adulthood equipped with only their adolescent portions. Moreover, the breakup of a household likely affected younger children more dramatically than their elder siblings. The marriage of a child or the death of a parent was a turning point in most households that redounded upon all children; children still at home often quickly married or left the household with independent portions. As a result, younger children probably knew less of an adolescent transition than did their elder siblings. Agnes Penifader, for example, as the last to appear in the court records, was probably the youngest of her siblings. Unlike her sisters Cristina and Cecilia, who both received lands from their father during adolescence, Agnes first appeared in the court on the day of her marriage settlement. And she was married within a year of the death of her father.[52]

The Act of Marriage

Although the adolescent experiences of medieval villagers were shaped by many forces, the probable ideal—as illustrated by the histories of privileged families like the Penifaders and Kroyls in flexible economies like that of early fourteenth-century Brigstock—was for children of both sexes to move gradually toward independence from their parents in the years before they married. As this slow transition from childhood to adulthood was coming to an end, adolescents usually faced the most momentous events of their lives—choice of spouse, marriage, and the establishment of a conjugal household. When young men and women contemplated marriage in the medieval countryside, they needed to placate a formidable host of authorities interested in limiting or even dictating their marital choices. Because marriage transferred properties, forged alliances, and created new households, the process interested manor, Church, village, and family. Lords supervised marriage to regulate the flow of personnel in and out of their manors and to tax the transfers of chattels or land in marriage settlements.[53] Priests hastened to assure that the sacrament of marriage was not sullied by improper procedures, consanguinity, or other impediments. Neighbors and parents sought marriages that neither threatened community harmony nor thwarted familial ambition. Marriage joined two individuals, but it was an event of immense public concern and interest.

The theoretical task of mediating between these diverse interests fell to the Church, which by the thirteenth century acknowledged the primacy of personal choice over the interests of lords, neighbors, parents, and even priests. Alexander III's decree that a valid marriage was made by the free exchange of consent by the principals in words of the present tense defined the medieval requirements for marriage. Vows made under coercion or vows couched in terms of future consent were insufficient, but proper vows alone sufficed to make a marriage binding.[54] The Church heartily acknowledged the desirability of parental approval, ecclesiastical supervision, and seigneurial consent; persons who avoided public marriage were subject to both discipline and penance. But the Church also recognized that public marriage was unnecessary; a man and a woman could contract a valid marriage by simply exchanging binding vows of consent in complete privacy. While consistent in doctrine, the Church's teachings on marriage were confusing in practice. On the one hand, priests urged their parishioners to marry formally and publicly. Persons contemplating marriage were urged to obtain the assent of their lords, friends, and families and to assure the absence of impediments through the publication of three sets of banns prior to the wedding date. The actual wedding ideally included not only the freely given consent of the bride and groom, but also the sanctification of religious ceremony and the acknowledgment of communal celebration. On the other hand, priests recognized that all this was technically unnecessary. If a couple chose to marry clandestinely without the involvement or consent of others, they could do so. Priests frowned on clandestine marriages (and occasionally punished couples guilty of such contracts), but nevertheless accepted them as indissoluble unions sanctified by God.

In the best of circumstances, such equivocal teachings would have led to much confusion. Even the most devout parishioners faced two options when marrying—the one approved and requested, the other disapproved but sufficient. In the medieval countryside, where the Church's control over the daily lives of the peasantry was so limited, this confusion led to extensive nonconformity. Cases brought before Church courts do not fully report the extent of noncompliance (because they cover only those marriages which had not only broken down but also come to official notice); they do, however, show that almost every aspect of the Church's teaching on marriage was regularly abrogated by the laity. Although clandestine marriages accounted for the bulk of marriage litigation, bigamy, desertion, adulterous liaisons, consanguineous unions, and coerced vows also figured in the agenda of medieval ecclesiastical courts. Medieval peasants probably knew the Church's teachings about the proper mode of marrying, but it was an ideal to which they did not fully subscribe.[55]

As a result, although the Church theoretically controlled the marriage process, the practical task of arbitrating between the various groups interested in marriage fell to the peasants themselves. Writing about a generation after the plague, the author of *Piers Plowman* described the contract of marriage as follows:[56]

And thus was wedlock wrought   with a middle person
First by the fathers' will   and the friends' council
And then by the assent of themselves   as they two might accord
And thus wedlock was wrought   and God himself it made
In earth its heaven is   himself was the witness.

These lines recognized the canonical importance of God's sanctification of marital vows, but few other aspects of the Church's teachings were mentioned; no lords agreed to the match, no banns checked for impediments, no priests presided over the exchange of vows, and no mass celebrated the union. Instead, the process was much more communal and informal; fathers agreed to the match, consulted their neighbors, and sought the concurrence of the principals. As glimpsed through occasional citations in court rolls, rustic marriage incorporated these elements into a three-stage process—the marriage settlement, the exchange of vows, and the public celebration.

The marriage settlement required complex and elaborate negotiations that might have been often aided, as described in *Piers Plowman,* by a "middle person" or matchmaker. Parents, neighbors, and children all participated in the final contract. Primary responsibility fell upon the parents who often agreed to contribute goods and properties to the establishment of the new conjugal household. In Brigstock, for example, Beatrice Helkok's parents agreed to supply the newlyweds with an unspecified amount of cash, a cow (valued at 10 shillings), and some clothing (valued at 13 shillings, 4 pence). Her husband brought to the marriage a guarantee by his parents that he would inherit a semi-virgate.[57] In addition to the conjugal settlement of property, the marriage contract could also provide for the other expenses of marriage—the payment of the merchet (if required) and the costs of the wedding feast. Friends acted as advisors and witnesses to the negotiations; the Helkok settlement was witnessed by Peter Avice and Richard Aylward, neither of whom was related to the families involved. The principals themselves not only were probably consulted early about their needs and preferences but also retained the important right to accept or to reject the final arrangements. Without their consent, no marriage was valid.[58] The ideal marriage contract, then, involved the generosity of parents, the advice of friends, and the agreement of the principals.

The exchange of vows was the essential part of marriage, but it seems to have been a remarkably simple and straightforward affair. Trothplight involved the joining of hands, the gift of a ring by the husband to the wife (as a symbol of her dower) and the statement in words of the present tense that each accepted the other as a spouse. Although no priest was present and no blessings offered, this ceremony alone sufficed, in the eyes of both the medieval Church and the peasantry, to create a valid marriage. Some couples may have chosen to follow the trothplight with a formal wedding at the parish church, which made the marriage licit as well as valid and also assured beyond a doubt the dower of the widow and the legitimacy of children. Many peasants, however, likely married without a Church wedding because it was both costly and not strictly required.[59]

The final part of the marriage process was, of course, the public celebration that incorporated the new couple into the community. Marriage celebrations acknowledged the validity of a private agreement through public feasting and drinking. Few people might have witnessed the marriage settlement or the exchange of vows, but many participated in the celebrations that accepted the new couple and their household into the village. Revels also, by bringing together all those interested in the marriage, helped to bury any animosities that might have arisen during the earlier stages of planning and negotiation. On some manors, the invitation of lords or their servants was explicitly required, and priests almost certainly attended.[60] The details of these feasts are largely unrecorded in the records, but their cost illustrates their importance; Beatrice Helkok's father paid 20 shillings for her *convivium die nuptiarum,* a sum almost equal to the value of the chattels with which he endowed her.[61]

All marriages, to be sure, did not follow this orderly progression. Some overbearing parents attempted to force their children's consent to marriage; some young people bypassed all formalities by exchanging private vows; and others skipped vows altogether and simply cohabited. More than likely, economic circumstances shaped the extent to which a given marriage conformed to the norms of rural society. Because young people from privileged families could hope for substantial endowments from their parents, they probably most nearly adhered to the proper forms. If they married secretly or co-habited, they had much to lose. Adolescents from poorer households, however, were less restricted; to them, marriage must have sometimes seemed both unnecessary and prohibitively expensive. Yet most marriages probably included some variation of the three stages of settlement, vows, and celebration. All marriages, no matter how informal, also potentially required the involvement of manor, Church, and community.

Because marriage could require not only proper vows but also complex negotiations, formal settlements, and expensive celebrations, many young people were thrown back, at the end of adolescence, upon the guidance and generosity of their parents. The preceding years of growing economic, social, and legal autonomy prepared young people not for the independent contracting of marriage, but rather for independent households after marriage. The actual business of arranging a marriage was often far too complex for young people to handle on their own. On the one hand, marriage required the balancing of numerous demands and authorities. No other event in life so attracted the attention of others; lords, priests, neighbors, and friends all had priorities and interests to be considered. Young people contemplating marriage were less experienced than their parents in coping with these groups, so they probably especially relied upon parental guidance and resources to satisfy such interests. On the other hand, because marriage established a separate household, it required economic resources that exceeded those of most adolescents. As a result, young people, even those previously endowed by their parents with land, often looked to their parents for financial assistance in the marriage settlement. Sons and daughters married as young adults, not children, but they were nevertheless still reliant on their parents.

Despite their dependence on parental aid in the negotiations and settlements that preceded marriage, young people were seldom forced into marriages against their will. Canon law stated unequivocally that principals could refuse proposed matches, and contemporary literature also reflects a social disapproval of coerced unions. But aside from the right to refuse, young people likely also had considerable say in choosing their marital partner. The very experience of adolescence, an experience apparently supported and encouraged by most parents, ensured that marriages were usually contracted by fairly mature and sophisticated persons. The extant records illuminate only the most public aspects of these years—the landholdings of youths, their employment in the households of other villagers, their expanding social networks, their legal obligations. But these years also provided many informal opportunities for young people to weigh the complex issues of marriage and to meet potential spouses. As they worked in the fields or labored in the houses of their neighbors, they observed good and bad marriages and learned to identify the factors most important to a successful union. As they walked about their villages, traveled to nearby markets, and celebrated the feasts of each year, they also got to know potential mates. Indeed, the numerous amercements in some manorial courts for both fornication (leyrwite) and illegitimate birth (childwite) suggest that some young people got to know candidates for marriage quite well.[62] Adolescence, in short, ensured that young people were mature enough to choose their own spouses; instead of being barely more than children, they were young adults on the threshold of full majority.

Moreover, the social effects of marriage simply were not extensive enough to warrant much familial coercion. Because marriage created a new household, it profoundly affected the principals, but redounded only indirectly and mildly upon their families. The social options of parents, brothers, and sisters were little changed by marriage. The union of Agnes Penifader and Henry Kroyl junior, for example, tremendously changed their lives, but much less strongly touched their families. Although some of their siblings exploited the new ties with in-laws created by the union, others ignored them. The use of kin related through marriage was always simple and direct; Agnes Penifader's brothers and sisters dealt occasionally with her husband, but seldom with her husband's brothers or parents. Most interestingly, the parents of Agnes Penifader and Henry Kroyl junior virtually never used the in-law connections created by their marriage; the union was, in a sense, completely irrelevant to the social experiences of their parents (as reflected in court interactions). It is hard to escape the conclusion that neither parents nor siblings benefited enough from this marriage to merit their excessive interference in its planning. Since marriage joined together two individuals, not their families, choice might well have rested primarily with the prospective bride and bridegroom.[63]

The variability of social distinctions in the medieval countryside also might have enhanced the ability of young people to choose their own spouses. Familial status was so subject to the vagaries of economy and demography that marriages between persons of different socioeconomic strata were quite common, and no strict set of criteria governed the choice of marriage partner in the medieval countryside. Of the marriages traced in Brigstock and Iver before the plague, over one-third united an upper-rank person with a spouse of lower rank.[64] Villages were also so integrated into regional networks that many persons married partners from other communities. Possibly as many as one-third of all marriages in the medieval countryside were geographically exogamous.[65] If rural social structures had been clearly defined and closed, parents and friends would have had to enforce rigid standards in the choosing of spouses; the wishes of children are especially likely to be ignored in societies either separated into closed classes or isolated from outside influence. In such conditions, socially or geographically exogamous marriages are so intolerable that the wishes of children are more likely to be superseded by social requirements. But the rural society of England in the later Middle Ages was so variable and fluid that the range of acceptable marital choices was relatively flexible. As a result, the personal preferences of children were less likely to clash with social or parental expectations.

Although adolescents probably had considerable voice in the selection of their marital partners, the entire issue of "freedom to choose" is somewhat moot. In most marriages, the interests of parents and child doubtless coincided—both sought a good match that would settle the child permanently, securely, and happily in a marital household. Not surprisingly, adolescents commonly shared their parents' values in such decisions; even with today's emphasis on individualism and romance, most people eventually marry partners who conform closely to the expectations of their families. Indeed, parents in manors like Brigstock were so confident of this unity of interest that they nurtured and encouraged the adolescent independence of their offspring even though such independence increased the possibility of controversy in marital decision-making. Marriage was a weighty business, requiring the balancing of personal, economic, and social considerations. Although parents and children might have weighed these factors differently, they probably recognized the importance of each element as well as the importance of compromise. Given the gravity of the occasion and the complexity of its issues, conflicts were inevitable, but such tensions did not usually overshadow the consensus that characterized the making of most marriages. Working together in both agreement and disagreement, parents and children selected appropriate partners, negotiated settlements, and pacified all interests.

The act of marriage was the most crucial transition in the lives of both men and women, but it is very poorly described in historical records. Since manor and parish only superficially regulated rustic marriages, the extant sources—manorial records of marriage licenses and ecclesiastical records of marital disputes—permit only brief glimpses of the local customs and expectations that governed marriage. The most elusive aspect of this puzzle is the question of how gender shaped the experience of contracting a marriage. In most respects, only speculation is possible. Almost certainly, courtship customs dictated different roles for men and women. And very likely prospective husbands (as future householders) were more closely consulted in marriage negotiations than were their prospective wives. The rites and festivals of marriage probably also emphasized the different responsibilities of the new husband and wife.

On the issue of marriage settlements, however, the evidence is clearer; as a rule, men brought land to marriage and women brought movable goods. The Helkok settlement described above was quite typical; Beatrice Helkok's parents provided chattels (cash, a cow, clothing, and the marriage feast), and her husband contributed his widowed mother's guarantee that he would inherit a semi-virgate. Indeed, a few cases suggest that women who held land during adolescence even returned such properties to their natal families when they married. In 1337, for example, Cristina in le More transferred control of two properties in Iver to her brother in the same court at which her father purchased her marriage license. And in 1319, Elicia le Shephirde of Brigstock, who had jointly held land with her sister (a gift from their mother) for several years before she married Richard Aylward, granted full ownership of the property to her sister. To be sure, some women merged properties acquired during adolescence into their conjugal holdings and some landless men married propertied women, but the marriage settlement was usually divided along gender lines with men contributing land and women contributing chattels. Such arrangements matched well the property customs of the medieval countryside. Men, as preferred heirs, enjoyed easier access to land. Women not only less frequently acquired land through either inheritance or parental gift, but also lost control of property when they married; many parents might have been reluctant to endow a daughter with lands that her husband would control.[66]

When young people came to the business of marrying, their experiences reflected both the ambivalent independence of adolescence and the adult responsibilities of married life. A contract entered neither dependently nor independently, marriage epitomized the equivocal autonomy of adolescence. Each aspect of the marriage process—the choice of spouse, the negotiations, the formal rituals, and the public celebrations—was usually a cooperative undertaking of parents and children. The parental role was one of guidance, not command. After years of slow separation, their children were embarking on a fully independent venture; parents helped establish the new conjugal household, but they could not autocratically dictate its nature. As well as marking the final ambivalence of adolescence, the marriage contract also foreshadowed the adult status created by conjugality. The need to pacify lords, priest, and neighbors reflected the public importance of a new household's creation, just as the gender differences of marriage settlements reflected the different roles that awaited husbands and wives. For marriage abruptly ended the common experiences of the sexes during adolescence; men and women who had faced many similar options as youths encountered dissimilar opportunities as husbands and wives. Dictating a larger measure of dependence for daughters, gender certainly shaped the lives of adolescents, but the basic pattern of gradual separation from parental authority was shared by both young women and young men. The common path of adolescence, however, branched with marriage toward full independence for men and a new kind of dependence for women.

V

Wives and Husbands

By establishing independent households at marriage, daughters and sons ended the gradual loosening of parental ties that had characterized their adolescent years; as wives and husbands, they would live apart from their parents. The married state, however, brought different opportunities for the two sexes. Husbands, once freed from parental supervision, were subject to no further domestic authority. But wives, also freed from parental control, found themselves under a new authority—that of their husbands. When married adults looked back on their adolescent years, husbands likely recalled the slow growth of an independence which had fully blossomed at marriage, whereas wives likely remembered a modest measure of public opportunity which they no longer possessed. The semi-autonomy of adolescence eased the transition from parental to conjugal household for young people of both sexes, but the final destination brought independence for men and dependence for women.

Marriages in the medieval countryside were neither particularly stable nor enduring. On the one hand, medieval peasants sometimes dissolved their marriages. Unions contracted with property settlements, formal vows, and public celebrations probably carried such public approbation that they were difficult to terminate, but more informal arrangements were easily abolished. Although the Church

100

always insisted firmly on the indissolubility of marital vows, it could only minimally enforce permanence because its lawyers could not even ascertain in many cases whether a valid marriage had actually occurred. Cohabitation, de facto divorce, and bigamy were all part of life in the medieval countryside.[1] On the other hand, death cut short many other marriages. Wives faced the rigors of childbirth, husbands encountered the dangers of plowing and carting, and both fell victim to common diseases and accidents. Of the Brigstock marriages whose duration could be estimated, one lasted 2 years and another 42 years, but the average union was ended by death after 15 to 17 years. Short marriages, however, were matched by short life expectancies. Although few unions endured for more than two decades uninterrupted by death, few people lived as long as three decades after reaching marriageable age. The frequency of remarriage also assured that many of those prematurely widowed found new partners. Marriage was an often temporary and fragile institution, but most adults in communities like Brigstock spent most of their adult years joined to another in marriage.[2]

Historians of modern families, seeking to distinguish the private experiences of people in "traditional" Europe from those of people in modern Europe, have often claimed that neither love nor sexual enjoyment was common in premodern marriages. Contrasting the economic concerns of medieval marriage with the romantic concerns of modern marriage, they have argued that marriages in past times were practical, not pleasurable.[3] Yet medieval villagers probably expected to find both emotional and sexual satisfaction in marriage. Fourteenth-century peasants had almost certainly not absorbed the ideals of romantic love that were becoming so popular among their social superiors, but they surely valued the companionable love of wife and husband. Although the medieval peasantry have left neither rustic love poetry nor family letters, other sources illustrate the comfortable affection that medieval countryfolk expected from their partners. To begin with, personal incompatibility was a common reason for marital dissolution; cases adjudicated in Church courts often arose because of one partner's displeasure with the other and desire to be free to seek a more appealing companion. Just as high divorce rates in modern society arise in part from high standards of marital love, so the flexibility of medieval marriage customs reflected a concern with the quality of conjugal relations. Indeed, some peasants fought against considerable opposition to end marriages in which they were unhappy. Agnes Pole of Houghton, for example, continued an adulterous affair with Stephen Note for several years despite the vigorous objections of her neighbors. Fined for adultery in 1308, the lovers were not at all cowed by public disapproval; they not only continued the liaison, but also freely harassed Agnes' husband. By 1310, the situation had deteriorated so badly that the court stepped in, forcing Agnes to pay an uncommonly large amercement of 40 pence, to return to her husband, and to promise her future goodwill toward him. After this forced reconciliation, Agnes and Stephen disappeared from the manor court; perhaps they finally obeyed the dictates of their neighbors, but they also might have left the manor to seek unencumbered happiness elsewhere. Although the Church opposed those whose personal dissatisfactions prompted adultery, divorce, and the like, it also reinforced the expectation that marriage would include both affection and compatability. Elaborating on the Augustinian teaching that *fides* was one of the three vital components of marriage, churchmen consistently emphasized the importance of marital companionship.[4]

The high quality of marital relations was also often witnessed by dying husbands who appointed their wives as either executors or co-executors of their wills. In Brigstock in the early 1340s, for example, Agnes the widow of John Hirdman, acting with Henry Hirdman as her husband's co-executor, pursued a series of cases in the manor court involving debts owed to or by her husband. Appointments of wives as executors were unnecessary (widows could claim dowers without being executors) and possibly impractical (since wives, although familiar with the familial holdings, were less experienced than most men in the legal matters that plagued many estates). But husbands, it seems, turned to their wives for this final task because they knew that the conjugal enterprise, although theoretically controlled by themselves, was actually a joint affair which their wives could be confidently trusted to bring to a close.[5] Occasional glimpses from the taciturn records of manorial administrators also testify to the affections of wives and husbands; the love shared by Richard and Elicia Aylward, for example, was apparently clear to all their neighbors in Brigstock—one of their younger sons was nicknamed Treuelove.[6]

Although medieval records seldom illuminate the sexual experiences of rural dwellers, no contemporary sources lend any credence to the view that preindustrial sexual relations were either uncreative or particularly unpleasurable for women. Medical literature indirectly suggests that medieval women often found considerable sexual satisfaction; most authors of medical treatises in the Middle Ages agreed not only that women were more sexual than men, but also that a woman could not conceive unless she experienced orgasm during sexual intercourse.[7] Religious treatises similarly indicate that sexual play was neither dull nor instrumental; penitentials directed priests to inquire subtly about their parishioners' use of a variety of proscribed sexual practices.[8] Manorial fines for illicit sexual intercourse and illegitimate births also testify to both the extent of sexual activity and the pleasure of women; with so many births in the countryside attributed to unmarried women, it is hard to suppose that most women viewed sexual intercourse as an unpleasant marital obligation.[9] Only rarely can medievalists read directly about the sexual joys of countrypeople, but most evidence indirectly suggests that English peasants, like the inhabitants of Montaillou, took considerable pleasure from sexual play.[10]

It would be foolish to imagine that all medieval marriages were both companionable and sexually satisfying. Medieval people thought of conjugality as a hierarchy headed by a husband who not only controlled his wife's financial assets and public behavior, but also freely enforced his will through physical violence. Wife-beating, as featured in both popular and sacred literature, was considered to be a normal part of marriage.[11] But the extensive patriarchal authority given to husbands must have often lapsed under the banalities of everyday domestic life. Theoretically powerful, husbands probably often shared domestic decisions with their wives. Anthropologists have commented on how the exigencies of the rural family economy often promote a mutual respect between wives and husbands; such might well have been the case for many married couples in the medieval countryside.[12] Indeed, medieval peasants, not handicapped by the unrealistic ideals of romantic love, might have more often found a modest contentment in marriage than do modern wives and husbands. Certainly, it seems they were less often violently disappointed; medieval rates of spousal homicide were comparatively low.[13]

Beyond the general surmise that many countrypeople in the Middle Ages probably hoped to obtain both emotional and sexual satisfaction from marriage, little is known about the private aspects of married life in medieval villages. Manorial records extant for manors like Brigstock, however, illustrate clearly how marriage affected the public activities of women and men—their legal stature, their economic opportunities, their networks of acquaintance and friendship. These public actions show that, although spouses might have often shared a great deal in their private lives, their public personalities were profoundly dissimilar. As at no other time of life, the public opportunities of women and men were most distinct when they lived together as wives and husbands.

The Political and Legal Stature of Wives and Husbands

Marriage widened the political gap between women and men in medieval villages. During adolescence, sons, by joining tithings and by assisting others in court as personal pledges and the like, enjoyed political associations unavailable to daughters. These opportunities expanded with marriage because men, through marriage, gained access to local office. Two unspoken requirements determined the eligibility of males for official service in medieval villages: offices were normally restricted, first, to the economically privileged and, second, to married householders. As a rule, only married men participated in the management of community affairs as jurors, affeerors, reeves, tithingmen, and aletasters. All married men did not serve in local offices, but only married men were eligible to do so. Henry Kroyl junior, for example, embarked on a distinguished career of official service almost immediately after his marriage. Active in the courts of Brigstock since 1316, he did not first serve as an officer until September 1319, just a few months after his marriage to Agnes Penifader. During the following three decades, he not only occasionally worked as a bailiff and juror, but also virtually controlled the supervision of the ale industry in Stanion by acting continuously as one of the aletasters for the settlement. As adolescents, young men participated in the basic political organizations of Brigstock; as married householders, they gained the additional opportunity of controlling political processes through local offices.[14]

The legal treatment of women and men also diverged with marriage. Unmarried sons and daughters were often accorded equivalent responsibilities by the Brigstock court; they were trusted as landholders, responsible for their own actions as criminals, competent to seek or to offer redress as litigants, and expected, if appropriate, to render court suit by attending each triweekly meeting of the court. This rough equality ended with marriage. On the one hand, the legal responsibilities of men expanded because, as husbands, they were deemed responsible not just for their personal actions, but also for the actions of their households and dependents. On the other hand, the legal obligations of women contracted because wives were legally covered in many respects by their husbands. Neither sex was particularly advantaged by these changes. Husbands participated more actively in the legal affairs of Brigstock, but they also accrued the onerous legal responsibilities of householders. Wives ceased to be treated by the court as legally competent adults, but they also enjoyed the shelter of their husband's authority. Yet, despite the equivocal effect of the legal changes occasioned by marriage, their main intent was clear; the customary law of communities like Brigstock treated husbands as householders and wives as their dependents.

As householders, husbands were often held personally responsible for the corporate actions of their domestic groups. Male householders paid most of the fines levied in the Brigstock court for crimes perpetrated by households rather than individuals—for illegal use of pastures, for building purprestures, obstructing roads, or otherwise misusing property, and for harboring strangers beyond the permitted few days (see Table 5.1). These were economic crimes arising from

TABLE 5.1. Householder Crimes in the Brigstock Sample of Crimes

	Illegal Pasturing		Property Damage[a]		Harboring Strangers	
Category	Number	Column Percent	Number	Column Percent	Number	Column Percent
Presumed male householders	11	79%	41	64%	27	77%
Sons	1	7	6	9	3	9
All women	2	14	17	27	5	14
All criminals	14	100	64	100	35	100

[a] Property damage includes illegal purprestures, obstructions placed in the road, illegal piles of dung, and broken hedges. Women were particularly prominent among those cited for breaking hedges (7 females and 6 males). Percentages have been rounded to produce integral numbers.

the exigencies of the rural family economy. Households overburdened the pastures because they needed the income from animal husbandry, households secretly took in purprestures or moved boundary stones because they needed to increase their harvest yields, and households offered shelter to strangers in order to use their labor. Everyone in a household benefited from such offenses, but husbands, who as householders theoretically controlled all corporate decisions, had to accept responsibility for those decisions that went awry.

The responsibilities of householders in Brigstock even extended to the independent actions of their dependents. Most adults in Brigstock were adjudged personally responsible for their own actions and paid their own criminal amercements or civil liabilities. Occasionally, however, the court waived the principle of personal accountability, and in such cases the penalty fell upon the subject's householder. Some husbands were required to answer for the crimes of their dependents; in 1300, John Brum was placed in mercy by the Brigstock court because his wife had illegally damaged hedges in the forest, and in 1331, William Cissor paid a fine to the court because his wife had sold ale with false measures. Others were ordered to guarantee that their dependents would behave properly in the future; in 1317, William Kut had to find pledges to assure the court of Brigstock that not only he but also his wife and children would cause no further trouble in the community. Still others were impleaded for the actions of their wives; in 1325, Galfridus ad Solarium sued both Margery Golle and her husband William alleging that Margery alone had slandered him.[15] Some of these cases of householder liability probably arose from the economic nature of the offense; since the actions of the dependent benefited the whole household, the normal principle of individual responsibility was superseded by the principle of householder responsibility for all economic matters. But the economic activities of dependents were only rarely covered in such a fashion by their householders; most dependents who broke hedges or sold ale improperly paid their own fines.[16] Other instances of householder liability, moreover, had no economic basis. It seems, in short, that countrypeople like those in Brigstock might have invoked the principle of householder responsibility whenever they wished to solve a problem swiftly and conclusively. Although the principle was rarely applied, all householders probably knew that they were potentially liable in the courts for the actions of their dependents.

In contrast to the experiences of men whose legal responsibilities expanded after marriage beyond accountability for their own personal actions, the legal competence of women deteriorated when they became wives. As suitors, criminals, and litigants, wives were treated by the Brigstock court in ways that distinguished them from all other adults, regardless of age, sex, or marital status. Probably the most telling evidence of the legal status of wives is that they were the only adult landholders not obliged to attend all meetings of the Brigstock court. When a female landholder married, her obligation to attend court lapsed, and her husband paid suit for her. As an unmarried landholder, for example, Cristina Penifader attended all court sessions or obtained an excuse for her absence. Last appearing as a suitor at the court of 16 June 1317, she married Richard Power in the following month, and he assumed all subsequent obligations for court attendance. In contrast, her spinster sister Cecilia Penifader continued throughout her life to owe suit of court. The practice of husbands doing suit for their wives is evident in the records of every court session; the list of suitors excused from attendance never included wives, but regularly included landholding daughters and widows. The principle was clearly stated in an inheritance inquisition held in 1326; the jurors stated that the property in question was to be divided among the three daughters of Robert le Northerne and that court suit was to be paid only by the husband of the eldest daughter. This practice in Brigstock not only typified the custom of most manorial courts but also corresponded closely to the common law under which husbands assumed all the legal obligations associated with the landed properties of their wives.[17]

The Brigstock court also sometimes treated misbehaving wives differently from other criminals. Most wives in Brigstock, like all other adults in the community, personally paid the amercements levied for their own offenses, yet a few wives escaped personal liability, leaving their husbands to answer for them. As illustrated by the experiences of William Cissor and John Brum, male householders in Brigstock were sometimes liable not just for the illegal activities of their dependent children but also for the offenses of their wives. These instances were rare, but telling. No fathers were deemed responsible for the crimes of their adolescent daughters; no sons of widows paid their mothers' amercements; and no wives ever accepted liability for their husbands' offenses. The Brigstock court waived the principle of personal culpability only if the criminal was a minor child or a wife. Again, practices in Brigstock exemplify the normal treatment of errant wives under both customary and common law; wives were generally deemed responsible for their own offenses, but occasionally escaped punishment. The most outstanding instance in the common law courts was cited by Bracton who described the different punishments of a husband and wife jointly guilty of producing a forged charter; he was hanged, but she was freed because she acted under her husband's authority (*quia fuit sub virga viri sui*).[18]

Wives who settled disputes through court litigation encountered unusual opportunities and problems that also illustrate their peculiar legal status. From adolescence on, adults of both sexes independently pleaded cases in the Brigstock court and answered suits brought against them. The only regular exceptions to autonomous litigation were wives of whom almost two-thirds pursued pleas accompanied by their husbands (see Table 5.2). Some joint pleas arose from joint grievances; persons harmed together would seek redress together, and persons guilty of harming another would be jointly sued for damages. Joint offenses did not, however, necessitate joint pleas; in 1303, for example, John Carectarius and his wife Alice were separately (and successfully) impleaded for their com-

TABLE 5.2.   Joint Litigation in the Brigstock Sample of Civil Pleas

Category	Number Acting Jointly	All Actors	Percentage of Joint Actors
Women			
Wives	23	35	66%
Widows	2	12	17
Daughters	1	17	6
Women of unknown status	1	22	5
All women	27	86	31
Men			
Presumed male householders	39	309	13
Sons	1	39	3
All men	40	348	11
All litigants	67	434	15

Note: Percentages have been rounded to produce integral numbers.

bined attack on his sister Emma.[19] Instead of originating mainly in joint complaints, joint pleas seem to have been a legal option often available only to wives. Women did not lose their competency as litigants when they married; a full one-third of the wives in the Brigstock sample pursued claims unaccompanied by their husbands. Yet a wife could choose to bring her husband with her to answer a plea in which he was not personally concerned. The involvement described above of William Golle in his wife's slander suit is a case in point. Such joint actions offered wives not only the benefit of their husbands' more extensive legal expertise, but also an enhanced ability to delay prosecution (because joint actions doubled the number of permitted essoins).

Although joint litigation gave certain advantages to wives, the option was rooted in their legal dependency. No other adults were permitted to bring an otherwise disinterested party with them to a court suit; even husbands could not reverse the process and add their wives to their own personal disputes. Wives alone were able to bring their husbands to litigation because they alone were dependent adults. This ambivalent status of mature dependency seems to have profoundly confused the treatment of wives in joint litigation. In some cases, the Brigstock court insisted that both husband and wife had to be present for a joint plea to proceed. In 1314, for example, Walter Helkok and his wife Emma successfully postponed their case against William Hayroun by Emma's essoin; the court determined that Walter could not respond in Emma's absence. In another court of the same year, Sarah the wife of Hugh ad Crucem lost her case against Richard Westwode and his wife Godwyne because she inadvertently dropped Godwyne from the plea. But in other cases, the court was completely indifferent to the participation of wives in joint pleas. When Robert Molendinarius sued Richard Aukyn and his wife Margery in 1343, he dropped Margery after the first statement of complaint, and the case proceeded as if Margery had never been involved. In 1331, Emma the wife of Richard Suig essoined in their joint plea against Egidius le Faber, but her husband concorded the case despite her absence.[20] In short, sometimes the court treated wives as full litigants, insisting on their participation for a case to proceed, but in other instances, the court treated wives like dependents, assuming that their husbands could act alone in their joint interest. Needless to say, the inverse never applied; in the absence of her husband, a wife never pursued a joint plea. As with the treatment of wives as suitors and criminals by the Brigstock court, their peculiar status as litigants was paralleled in the common law which expected a husband to be liable "for debts incurred or wrongs committed by his wife."[21] The Brigstock court, like common law courts, treated wives as dependents under the guardianship of their husbands.

The Conjugal Economy: Property

Under English common law, no community of goods between a husband and wife existed; instead, the husband largely controlled, for the duration of the marriage, all of the properties owned by either his wife or himself. He could freely alienate, without his wife's consent, properties of which he was seised, so long as he did not undermine her right to claim dower lands designated for her maintenance during widowhood. He could similarly alienate his wife's properties, although such grants could not endure after the marriage unless his wife had freely assented to the sale. Her free assent, however, was difficult to ascertain since she was subjected to her husband's will as long as he lived (*cui ipsa in vita sua contradicere non potuit*). A husband also totally controlled all the chattels of the conjugal household, and his wife had no claim upon them beyond the usual allowance made for her necessary clothing and *paraphernalia*.[22] The proprietal rights of husbands in Brigstock roughly emulated the common law. For the duration of a marriage in Brigstock, the public right to control all assets of the household pertained either to the husband alone or to the husband acting jointly with his wife. Although wives retained some minimal powers of assent or dissent, the conjugal fund during the time of marriage was, in practical terms, the husband's estate.

The husband's control over movable goods was apparently unlimited. Just as the right of serfs to disperse their chattels by will was often disputed (since all their goods theoretically belonged to their lords), so wives had no testamentary powers (since all conjugal goods pertained to their husbands).[23] Precisely because the authority of husbands in this area was so straightforward and unchallenged, rules about the dispersal of chattels seldom surface in the records of manors like Brigstock, but everyday practices underscore the husband's complete control of all conjugal goods. Brigstock customs show, for example, that although wives often brought chattels to their marriage settlements, they immediately lost any public interest in them. When Beatrice Helkok's father failed to deliver all the goods promised in her marriage contract, she took no part in the ensuing suit between her husband and her father because a bride's chattels became not the joint concern of the wife and husband, but rather the sole concern of the husband. Similarly, wives, during the years of marriage, could not independently dispose of any household goods whether brought to the marriage or acquired during marriage. As a result, no married women appeared alone in the Brigstock sample of civil pleas as parties to pleas of debt or broken contract because wives could not independently contract to loan or to sell goods they did not legally own. Even after marriage ended, a former wife's claims to the movable portion of the conjugal fund were very limited; the Brigstock custumal of 1391 stated that a widow could sell household goods, but only in cases of necessity; otherwise, she was required simply to use the goods and to leave them to the proper heir of her husband.[24] In other villages, widows were sometimes allowed full possession of some portion of their conjugal goods (usually one-third), yet even in death the bulk of movable properties pertained to the husband rather than to the joint ownership of husband and wife.[25]

Husbands also essentially controlled all the real properties of their households. Some properties they held jointly with their wives. Core family holdings—expected to sustain the conjugal family, to provide for the wife during widowhood, and to pass intact to the next generation—were usually jointly held.[26] Lands acquired by wives either before or during marriage also fell under joint ownership. Joint ownership, however, did not imply equal control; peasant wives are best described as subordinate co-tenants with their husbands who acted as guardians of the property. Given a husband's private and public authority over his wife, he would have been able to exert considerable pressure to gain his will about the disposal of joint properties. The Brigstock courts are silent on this subject, but the court rolls of other manors report the practice of examining wives apart from their husbands (*sola examinata*) to assure their full assent to sales of joint properties. The authority of husbands, however, was so pervasive that joint properties were sometimes alienated over the vigorous protests of wives. Ada Elizabeth Levett described a conveyance of land completed with the wife sobbing in court (*lacrimentem in pleno halimoto*); the transfer was later voided (after the husband's death) because of the wife's protests, but its initial acceptance by the court illustrates the proprietal powers of husbands.[27] Husbands, moreover, autonomously managed properties they independently acquired through either inheritance or purchase. In villages with active land markets like Brigstock, the most vigorous conveyors of land were husbands who freely traded, sold, or leased properties such as these without seeking the formal concurrence of their wives.[28]

When a woman married, then, she lost all independent control over properties she either had acquired or would acquire in the future; such lands automatically became the joint holding of husband and wife. To be sure, husbands could not dispose of these lands without the consent of their wives, but wives also could not convey such properties unaccompanied by their husbands. Husbands, in contrast to their wives, often retained independent control over properties they had separately acquired. The results of this asymmetry are seen clearly in the participation of husbands and wives in the Brigstock land market (see Table 5.3). Male householders comprised the core of the manor's traders of land, accounting for 58 percent of all persons involved in land deals; the rest were sons or women of various marital statuses. Furthermore, almost nine out of every ten husbands in the sample transacted their land deals without the agreement of their wives. Coming frequently to court, trading in small parcels of land, and dealing with neighbors rather than kin, husbands acting alone were the most common participants in the village's land market. The business in real property was, in a sense, the business of husbands.

Wives, in contrast, traded land only infrequently and seldom autonomously. Their participation accounted for less than 8 percent of those sampled. Of the 40 wives who granted land in the sample, all but 3 acted jointly with their husbands: 2 of these conveyed land to their husbands, and the third, a remarried widow, granted properties of her first husband to their son. As a rule, wives never granted land without their husbands because, quite simply, they were not permitted to do so; when Quena the wife of William ad Crucem tried to convey her inherited lands without her husband in 1315, the jurors unhesitatingly voided the sale.[29] Although a wife's independent re-

TABLE 5.3. Wives and Husbands in the Brigstock Sample of Land Transactions

Category	Presumed Male Householders		Wives		All Females
	Number	Column Percent	Number	Column Percent	Column Percent
Type of action					
Grantor	243	54%	40	67%	60%
Receiver	211	46	20	33	40
All actors	454	100	60	100	100
Autonomy of actor					
Acted alone	395	87	11	18	60
Acted jointly	59	13	49	82	40
All actors	454	100	60	100	100
Nature of grant					
Not intrafamilial	395	87	51	85	63
Intrafamilial	59	13	9	15	37
All grants	454	100	60	100	100
Size of grant (if known)					
Less than 2 rods	340	91	35	74	80
Over 2 rods	35	9	12	26	20
All grants of known size	375	100	47	100	100

Note: Percentages have been rounded to produce integral numbers.

ceipt of land did not threaten her husband's claim to the property, most wives also received land jointly with their husbands. Prescribed by customary restrictions, the joint activity of wives in the land market was characteristic of them alone; no other adults, male or female, faced such limitations on their ability to convey landed property.

In addition, wives often traded land under unusual circumstances. They were more likely than most other women or any men to grant rather than to receive land. Husbands used the land market to reshuffle their expendable parcels of land, and adolescents took advantage of land sales to accumulate properties in anticipation of marriage. Yet wives usually joined their husbands in granting away land over which they had some claim. Unlike other women, wives also seldom participated in intrafamilial transactions. Women who acted autonomously in the land market often either granted or received land from kin, but wives, who usually acted jointly with their husbands, conformed to the male pattern of few intrafamilial transactions. Finally, wives dealt quite frequently in large parcels of property. Men most often used the land market to trade small pieces of land; wives, however, were most likely to accompany their husbands when large properties were being conveyed outside the family. The Brigstock land market, as a forum for the frequent and autonomous exchange of small parcels of land between villagers, was primarily available to husbands and virtually closed to wives.

Because the Brigstock market in land was unusually active for a rural community in the early fourteenth century, the proprietal rights of wives and husbands in Brigstock do not necessarily exemplify the customs of other contemporary manors. Although many lords in the late thirteenth and early fourteenth centuries increasingly countenanced land conveyances on their manors, tenants subject to close seigneurial control, like those on the manor of Houghton-cum-Wyton, traded relatively few properties in the decades before the plague. The possibility that continued seigneurial supervision of landholding might have worked to the advantage of women merits further inquiry, but the proprietal rights of wives and husbands in Brigstock verify Maitland's observation that "in England the law for the great becomes the law for all."[30] When seigneurial controls eased so much that peasants were able to manage freely their own properties, they closely followed the common law in granting husbands extensive control over all conjugal properties.

The Conjugal Economy: Work

Just as the conjugal fund was not equally controlled by husbands and wives, but was instead basically administered by husbands acting as heads of households, so the working lives of husbands and wives were not strictly parallel. Both worked with equal vigor to support the household and both relied with equal intensity on the other's labor, but both did not share equally in either the control or the profits of work. First, women's work, reacting constantly to the labor demands of men's tasks, tended to be less autonomous and less focused; wives provided their households with an extremely flexible source of labor that was continuously reassigned to match the more specialized work of their husbands. Second, women's work was more profoundly submerged into the communal household economy. Both sexes worked primarily for corporate rather than individual gain; yet, as was the case with conjugal property, husbands exercised more personal control over the fruits of this corporate labor than did wives.

Little is known about the one area of work exclusively controlled by women, reproduction. If, however, the reproductive activities of medieval countrywomen matched those of women in sixteenth- and seventeenth-century England, they spent most of their adult years either pregnant or nursing an infant child. Nevertheless, the life-time fertility of women was probably low. First, infertility likely limited the reproductive capacities of many women; some women never conceived, some became barren through accident or disease, and others temporarily suffered from amenorrhea due to poor health or poor diet.[31] Second, nursing often effectively delayed conception for over a year; when mothers nursed their children in early modern England, the usual uncontrolled interval between births was about 2.5 years.[32] Third, women almost certainly attempted, with varying degrees of success, to limit births through either contraceptive techniques or self-induced abortions. Such private matters are notoriously difficult to trace, but medieval sources tell us not only that techniques of birth control were known, but also that Church officials were very concerned about discouraging their use. Probably the most common technique was simple abstinence; a thirteenth-century sermon about the sins of peasants specifically attacked "those men who abstain from knowing their wives lest children should be born."[33] Fourth, many pregnancies must have ended inadvertently with either miscarriages or stillbirths. Working hard and eating poorly, medieval countrywomen probably often failed to carry even desired pregnancies to full term. Under ideal circumstances in early modern England, a nursing mother was likely to produce about eight children over the course of a twenty-year marriage. The economic stresses and famines of the early fourteenth century likely assured that medieval countrywomen conceived less frequently, carried fewer conceptions to successful births, and then buried between one-fourth to one-third of their children before they reached maturity.[34]

Aside from reproductive work, the sexual division of labor in the medieval countryside was clear, but relatively undeveloped. Men tended to be responsible for heavier work that took them away from the domestic croft—plowing fields, carting goods, felling trees, herding animals. Women often joined men in the fields as planters, weeders, and gleaners, but they also completed many lighter jobs centered near the household—gardening, dairying, raising poultry. In the late medieval "Ballad of a Tyrannical Husband," the husband spent his days plowing, while the wife worked around the home, watching children, cleaning house, preparing meals, brewing, baking, caring for poultry and dairy animals, making butter and cheese, and working wool and flax into cloth.[35] On a given working day, most men on a manor like Brigstock probably worked in outlying fields, pastures, and woodlands, while most women worked in the immediate vicinity of the settlement. Yet these broad distinctions were not rigidly enforced. No records directly report how the peasant household distributed its labor resources; however, manorial bailiffs sometimes hired women to do work usually assigned to men (even plowing), and men were similarly employed for traditionally female jobs (e.g., dairying, gleaning). Although many tasks were loosely associated with either men or women, few were actually proscribed for one sex.[36]

Within the peasant household, the tasks of husband and wife were symbiotic, but flexible. The distribution of work responded to the demands of the agricultural year. At agricultural peaks such as during harvesting or planting, women joined their husbands more frequently in the fields, but when the winter months brought little agrarian work, men more often joined their wives around the croft. An effective domestic economy needed the productive efforts of both husband and wife; households that lacked either had to hire laborers or servants to fill the gap. Nevertheless, although both men and women relied on the other's labor, women's work seems to have always ranked second to the more primary tasks of men, as seen by their participation in production for use, hired labor, and trade.

Wives probably spent little of their time at the tasks associated with modern housewifery; child care was a much less time-consuming matter than in more recent centuries, household possessions were minimal and required little upkeep, and food preparation was relatively simple and fast. By the early fourteenth century, wives also probably spent less time in basic production than in previous centuries because the growth of a market economy encouraged the purchase of such commodities as bread, ale, and cloth.[37] All these domestic concerns certainly consumed some measure of each woman's working day (the classic literary image of a rural wife remained that of a spinning woman), but most time was spent in the direct production of food in the immediate vicinity of the croft. Although no peasant account books or domestic memoirs survive to describe the productivity of such work, there is every reason to suppose that the wife's work within the croft was just as crucial as her husband's labor in outlying fields and pastures. Often as large as an acre or two, the croft had two special advantages (aside from its proximity) over other familial properties; it was not subject to any regulation by the village community, and it was very easily fertilized with household waste. As a result, the domestic croft offered the household both flexibility and productivity. Piers Plowman expected to harvest beans, peas, leeks, parsley, turnips, onions, pot-herbs, and cherries from his croft. In addition to cultivating fruit trees and growing herbs, edible vegetables, hemp, and flax, wives also used crofts to raise pigs, chickens, and other small animals.[38]

The commodities produced by wives within the domestic croft complemented their husbands' more specialized production of grain. The medieval peasant diet would have been incomplete without either the grains produced in the fields or the fruits, vegetables, and herbs produced in the crofts, but the latter, in a sense, supplemented the former.[39] As a result, a wife's labor supplemented that of her husband. When field work demanded additional laborers, wives left their tasks around the croft and joined their husbands in the fields. Because they always expected to work intermittently in the fields, wives had to ensure that their other tasks, whether in crofts or elsewhere, were flexible enough to accommodate this primary demand, and because the productive work of wives was necessarily so flexible, it was also less specialized. At the same time that wives juggled the many tasks around the croft, they also undertook work in the fields where the most skilled jobs were, logically enough, left to men; while men plowed and hedged and mowed, their wives weeded, broke clods, and collected stubble. When William Langland described the working lives of impoverished peasants, he depicted the husband as a plowman and the wife as not only helping her husband by goading the ox, but also working around the croft, caring for children, carding, combing and spinning wool, preparing food, laying rushes, and the like.[40] Not peculiar to medieval peasants, these male/female patterns of production for use are well matched to the economic circumstances of rural life by providing both stability (in male work) and adaptability (in female work); indeed, such patterns are characteristic of most societies that rely on plow agriculture.[41] One result was that the work of a husband was both more regular and more focused than that of his wife. Another result, as reported in medieval literature, was that a wife's work was never ending. The unappreciated wife of the tyrannical husband replied to his complaints that "I have mor to doo then I doo may" and described the many ways in which she looked "to owr good withowt and withyn."[42] A sympathetic poet of the early sixteenth century agreed, saying

> A woman is a worthy wight:
> She serveth a man both day and night;
> Therto she putteth all her might;
> And yet she hath but care and wo.[43]

Aside from production for use, both husbands and wives (especially in poorer households) supplemented the domestic economy by hiring out their labor. Wives, however, were disadvantaged in the labor market because women regularly received lower wages than men. Manorial accounts, our only records for rural wage rates, show that women's jobs were constantly undervalued and that women and men employed for the same tasks were often paid at different rates.[44] Medieval accountants were not unaware of the advantages that wage differentials offered to employers; the anonymous author of the thirteenth-century treatise on estate management *Husbandry* advised bailiffs to hire a woman for certain jobs because she would work "for much less money than a man would take."[45] Under such circumstances, many households in need of income from wages probably chose to hire out husbands to do specialized paid work and to keep wives working at the diverse tasks of direct production for use. Manorial accounts show that while women hired out their labor during seasonal peaks of demand for workers (when they might have been able to bargain more effectively for high wages), men more often worked as hired laborers on a regular daily basis throughout the year.[46]

Similarly, households that sought to generate income through trade or specialized services were more likely to assign such activities to husbands than to wives. Although the food trades of medieval villages often included many females, most other aspects of rural trade were dominated by men. Women were seldom found among the many specialized occupations of the medieval countryside; carpenters, thatchers, and smiths were almost invariably male.[47] Women also seldom traded commodities other than foodstuffs at local markets; often prominent among those selling poultry, dairy products, and vegetables, women rarely worked as traders of cloth, tools, or bulk grain.[48] The trading activities of wives, moreover, were more limited than those of other women because, as wives, they could not conclude contracts without legally implicating their husbands. Wives of burgesses could trade autonomously by becoming *femmes soles,* but it is unlikely that rural wives, trading at local markets, often obtained this legal exemption from *couverture.* As a result, rural wives competed most effectively in commercial markets that were localized, nonspecialized, and small scale.

Information about the daily production, wage labor, and local trade of rural households, although often indirect and inferential, clearly indicates that husbands and wives undertook very different economic responsibilities. The labor of both partners was essential to the well-being of the household, but the husband's work took on primary importance; the wife's work both supplemented and conformed to the demands of the primary activity as defined by the husband's tasks. The work of husbands was more public (whether in fields regulated by community ordinance, in laboring for others, or in markets), more specialized (whether, again, in direct production, paid labor, or trade), and more esteemed (as shown most directly by wage rates) than the work of their wives.

The rural ale industry of medieval England offers an opportunity to trace all of these trends more clearly and more fully. The market for ale in the medieval countryside was both vast and well regulated. Although most rural households occasionally produced their own ale, the process was so time-consuming and the final product soured so quickly that most households simply could not meet their needs by domestic production alone. Until hops were introduced from the continent in the late fourteenth century (producing a new beverage called beer), English ale soured within only a few days. Since ale was virtually the only liquid consumed by medieval peasants (water was, probably justly, considered to be unhealthy), each household required a large and steady supply of this perishable item. The solution for most households was to alternate producing ale with buying ale, creating a large and ready market for rural ale-sellers.[49]

In the decades before the plague, the regulation of the ale industry in England was based on the thirteenth-century Assize of Bread and Ale which imposed national standards of measurement, quality, and pricing to which all commercial brewers were subject. Weights and measures were to be checked for accuracy, quality was to be carefully monitored, and prices were to be determined by a sliding scale based on fluctuations in the cost of grains. Within only a few decades, however, the assize was used to license as well as to supervise; on manors like Brigstock, ale-sellers who sold at exorbitant prices, with false measures, or without adequate quality control, paid especially heavy, punitive amercements, but all vendors of ale were liable for amercement. At every triweekly meeting of the court, the aletasters of Brigstock identified and amerced (for "breaking the assize") all persons who had sold ale in the interval since the last court meeting, thus generating the extensive records that survive for the historical study of this rural industry.[50]

These records show that ale-selling was the most common activity that brought peasant women before their manorial courts. The actual numbers of female brewers varied widely from manor to manor. In Brigstock virtually all ale citations were made against women, in Houghton-cum-Wyton women accounted for about nine out of every ten such entries, and in Iver only about one-fourth of ale amerce-

TABLE 5.4. Ale Citations of Women and Men in Brigstock,
Iver, and Houghton-cum-Wyton

	Males		Females		Both Sexes	
Manor	*Number*	*Row Percent*	*Number*	*Row Percent*	*Number*	*Row Percent*
Brigstock	47	1%	3,797	99%	3,844	100%
Iver	1,127	73	425	27	1,552	100
Houghton-cum-Wyton	20	11	168	89	188	100

Note: Percentages have been rounded to produce integral numbers.

ments were paid by women (see Table 5.4). But on all three manors
brewing was the single most common reason for legal notice of
women, accounting for one-third to one-half of all female appearances before their local tribunals.[51] Indeed, the ability to produce ale
seems to have been a skill acquired by most women; since about one-
third of the women identified in Brigstock were cited for selling ale,
probably all women on the manor were knowledgeable about producing ale (even if many never sold their ale for profit).[52]
The brewing process took many days and much labor. The grain,
usually barley, had to be soaked for several days, then drained of excess water and carefully germinated to create malt. After the malt
was dried and ground, the brewer added it to hot water for fermenta-
tion. From this mixture, the brewer drained off the wort and sometimes added herbs or yeast as a final touch.[53] Although the necessary
supplies were extensive, they were readily available in most households; large pots, vats, ladles, and straining cloths were found in the
principalia of even the poorest households.[54] Commercial brewing, in
short, offered no insurmountable obstacles to women; the skills were
familiar, the equipment was available, and the market was ready.
Few women, however, concentrated their labors on the ale industry. Most of Brigstock's brewers sold ale rarely and sporadically, and
only a few dozen women showed any genuine commitment to the ale
trade. Brigstock's commercial brewing industry operated simultaneously on two levels. Accounting for 88 percent of the village's identified female brewers, 273 women sold ale only infrequently; over the
course of their lives, most acquired less than 10 ale amercements and

none acquired more than 29. More than likely, most of the women on this first tier sold ale to make an occasional profit from a household task; when these women brewed for domestic consumption, they sometimes brewed larger amounts than necessary and sold the excess to their neighbors. Although minor female brewers collectively accounted for over one-third of the manor's ale trade, their market activity, on an individual level, was fairly insignificant; on the average, each paid only about 5 ale amercements during the course of her career. For most of these women, moreover, ale citations were distributed haphazardly over many years. Emma Pote, for example, accumulated 22 ale amercements over a 22-year period. On the second tier, worked a small elite group of 38 brewers, each of whom acquired 30 or more citations. These few dozen women controlled almost 60 percent of the ale market. Steadily meeting the needs of the village's ale-buyers, they regularly supplemented their household economies through ale sales; they were, in a sense, the true ale-wives of the community.[55]

Who were these ale-wives? Commercial brewing was not a preserve of the privileged, nor was it abandoned to the poor (see Table 5.5). The households of some ale-wives were headed by males who wielded considerable political and economic influence in Brigstock, but many other ale-wives were less fortunate and came from households headed by men of more modest influence. The distribution of ale-wives between officeholding and nonofficeholding households roughly paralleled the overall pattern in the community; of the 277 surnames identified in Brigstock, 35 percent were associated with officeholding.

TABLE 5.5. The Social Backgrounds of Brigstock's Ale-Wives

Category	Number	Percent
Socioeconomic status		
Husband held local office	13	34%
Husband never held local office	22	58
Unknown	3	8
Longevity of Residence		
Identified by permanent surname	23	61
Identified by impermanent surname	13	34
Unknown	2	5

Note: Percentages have been rounded to produce integral numbers.

Although socioeconomic position was relatively unimportant, long residence in the community was vital. Only 32 percent of Brigstock's surnames betrayed permanency of residence (appearing in the records throughout the period surveyed), but almost two-thirds of Brigstock's ale-wives were members of such long-resident families. Neither itinerants nor newcomers (of whom there were many in Brigstock) could hope to turn a tidy profit in the ale business.

The most distinctive characteristic of ale-wives, however, was that they were, just as their title implied, not daughters, not widows, but wives. Although Brigstock's professional brewers included a few widows, all such women had begun selling ale before their husbands died, and several withdrew from the ale market within a few years of widowhood. Similarly, no spinsters or adolescent daughters have been identified among the ale-wives of the village. As a result, brewing represents one of the few known public arenas that was actually opened to women by marriage. Insofar as evidence is available, it also suggests that wives were particularly active in commercial brewing during the middle years of married life; between the special requirements of the early years of marriage and the lessened obligations of old age, these women responded to the needs of their growing families by obtaining ancillary income through ale sales.[56]

As suggested by the preponderance of wives, brewing seems to have been too complex and costly a business to be pursued by women who lacked the support of a full household. Instead, it was usually a corporate business organized and supervised by wives. The ale-wife's position as supervisor of a household activity is best seen in the brewing histories of single households that often included not only the wife, but also occasionally the husband or daughter. Alice the wife of Richard Coleman, for example, accumulated 70 ale citations in Brigstock between 1299 and 1325. On one occasion, in November 1313 (when Alice was perhaps ill or otherwise incapacitated), her husband Richard paid the ale amercement. When Alice stopped commercial brewing a little over a decade later, her daughter Emma took over the business for a brief period. During these decades, the Coleman household was clearly committed to commercial brewing; the household's wife usually paid the ale amercement, but other family members replaced her whenever necessary. Alice Coleman did not work independently at a lucrative trade, but instead supervised a corporate, household activity.[57]

The brewing history of Richard and Alice Coleman's household was also typical in its relationship to other brewing households in the community. As a rule, most ale-wives were related to other women active in the ale trade. At the same time that Alice Coleman and her household were producing and selling ale, the wives of Richard Coleman's two brothers were also active in the ale market. Alice Coleman might have exchanged supplies, tools, and techniques with her sisters-in-law, but these women did not sell ale in common. Instead, they competed in the ale market, offering their products for sale simultaneously. In Brigstock, the conjugal household was the basic unit of the brewing business.[58]

Although ale-wives spent many active years in the industry, their market activity was neither steady nor predictable. On the average, ale-wives worked in commercial brewing for about two decades, yet during that period they brewed irregularly and often stopped brewing for considerable lengths of time. Usually an ale-wife sold ale on only about one-third of the occasions available to her.[59] The wife of Richard Gilbert, for example, accumulated 58 ale citations between 1328 and 1345. In some years, her market activity approached saturation, but in other years, her participation dropped to negligible levels, and for five years in the midst of her brewing career, she ceased brewing altogether.[60] Her career was typical; the average ale-wife in Brigstock accumulated a large number of amercements not because she brewed regularly, but because she brewed intermittently over long periods.

Female brewing in Brigstock, then, exemplifies the working habits of wives in other sectors. First, brewing—because it involved common female skills, tools available in many households, and occasional attention over long periods of time—appealed to wives who sought simple ways of supplementing their family economies. Second, the localized and small-scale ale market suited wives who competed poorly in larger markets and who simply wanted to make quick profits without infringing on their other duties. Third, women, whether sporadic brewers or more professional ale-wives, treated the industry not as a primary occupation, but rather as an occasional means of supplementing the main economic activities of their households.

The Brigstock ale-wife was, insofar as information is available, fairly typical. In both Iver and Houghton-cum-Wyton female brewers were most often married women who sought sporadically to enhance their familial incomes through ale sales.[61] But ale-wives in Brigstock did differ from other rural brewers in one important respect; they faced almost no significant male competition. Only a few dozen ale amercements were assessed against Brigstock males, and all such men were married to women already active in the ale market. In most villages, however, women did not enjoy such control of the ale industry. In Houghton-cum-Wyton during the same decades, 11 percent of all brewing fines were levied against men, and in Iver males accounted for 73 percent of all brewing fines (see Table 5.4). These vastly different levels of male and female brewing do not reflect broad variations in the organization of the ale industry in these three villages. As in Brigstock, brewing activity in both Houghton-cum-Wyton and Iver was dispersed among households of diverse socioeconomic status, but was especially pursued by families in long residence. Similarly, the distribution of casual and committed brewers did not vary significantly; in all three villages, a large proportion of amercements were paid by very occasional brewers. Insofar as the economic viability of the ale industry can be judged by patterns in ale amercements (both total number levied and average amount assessed), it also does not correlate with shifts in the numbers of men and women involved in the trade. Except for their widely divergent sex ratios, the ale industries of Brigstock, Houghton-cum-Wyton, and Iver were remarkably similar.

The explanation for these different levels of male and female brewing lies less with industrial organization than with the internal dynamics of the family economy and the flexibility characteristic of the working lives of wives. Every rural household had to decide how best, in view of local economic circumstances, to distribute its labor resources. In some environments, it made sense to leave commercial brewing to wives, but in other settings husbands had both the time and the inclination to get involved in commercial ale production. Iver's villagers supported themselves primarily through stock-raising and fishing. Because these activities were not particularly labor intensive, Iver's males got involved in brewing and dominated this industry in their village. Houghton-cum-Wyton was a classic open-field farming community, and the yearly cycle of plowing, sowing, and harvesting left considerably fewer males free to engage in commercial brewing. In the forest village of Brigstock, however, males not only worked in the village's open fields, but also were diverted from brewing by their activities in the surrounding woodlands (hunting, assarting, etc.). It appears, in short, that different levels of male and female brewing reflect regional variations in the allocation of labor within the peasant household; wives were most likely to supervise the brewing businesses of their households when their husband's primary work obligations were arduous and time-consuming.

This hypothesis is further strengthened by another feature common to the food markets of all three villages. Despite the widely different sex ratios of brewing in Iver, Houghton-cum-Wyton, and Brigstock, the relative number of women involved in commerce on all three manors steadily increased through the early decades of the fourteenth century. There were, in other words, proportionally more females selling foodstuffs in the 1340s than in earlier decades.[62] The best explanation for this common trend lies in changing economic circumstances that, in turn, altered the distribution of work within the rural family economy; the economic problems of the decades that preceded the plague probably drew male attention away from secondary pursuits like commercial brewing. Because brewing was an almost universal female skill that confined workers to the household area, families faced with economic hardship could most easily relegate commercial brewing to its female members and, hence, release males to seek economic relief in other sectors. Thus the internal dynamics of the rural household economy best explain fluctuations, both regionally and chronologically, in levels of female commercial brewing. Wives only dominated the brewing industries of their villages when the economic energies of their husbands were diverted elsewhere.

The rural ale industry, then, exemplifies the subordination characteristic of the working lives of rural wives. As dependent members of households headed by their husbands, ale-wives accommodated their commercial activities to the work of their husbands. Moreover, although the structures of the household economy necessitated the variability and adaptability of wives' work, rural society reinforced these working patterns by offering women no public advantages from their labor. Because the records are largely silent on the issue, it is difficult to assess the personal importance of these commercial activities to the ale-wives themselves. No personal diaries, no observers' reports, no letters survive to illuminate the private satisfactions of rural ale-wives or the subtle ways in which commercial brewing might have enhanced a woman's stature in the eyes of relatives, friends, and neighbors. Because an ale-wife brought cash into the peasant household, her efforts might have helped to equalize her relationship with her husband. Because her sales of ale helped to maintain or even to enhance her family's socioeconomic status, she might have gained personal prestige as a clever household manager among her friends and neighbors. And because her commercial work brought her into contact with many other villagers, she might have enjoyed a breadth of social acquaintance that distinguished her from other women. Such benefits, however possible, cannot be verified.[63]

Instead, the extant records demonstrate quite clearly that ale-wives, despite their public activity in the ale market, did not derive any special public benefits from their work. They did not, of course, publicly control the income generated by their trade; profits were immediately submerged into the conjugal fund legally controlled by their husbands. They also were as publicly inactive as other wives, subsumed into the personalities of their husbands. Consider Brigstock's 10 most active ale-wives (who each accrued 70 or more citations for ale sales). These women seldom came to court except to pay ale amercements, and they were almost invariably accompanied or assisted by their husbands.[64] Margery the wife of William Golle was the exception who proves the rule. For a woman, she was unusually active in the manor court, paying 119 ale amercements and appearing in Brigstock's court on numerous other occasions (including 11 court cases against other villagers). She was sued several times by persons who claimed that she had unjustly slandered them in the community. In every litigious appearance, Margery Golle pleaded jointly with her husband (even when the dispute arose from Margery's misconduct alone), and on several occasions, she refused to answer an accusation because her husband was not present.[65] Margery Golle's market activities doubtless brought her into contact with numerous persons in the Brigstock community, but she went to the court of Brigstock shadowed and protected by her husband. Needless to say, Brigstock's ale-wives, despite their proven public reliability as ale-sellers, could not serve as personal pledges, and they were not, despite their obvious qualifications, elected to serve as aletasters. In the eyes of one of the most important institutions in medieval rural life—the triweekly gathering of tenants at the manor court—an ale-wife was, quite simply, just another dependent wife.

Comparisons between manors also suggest that commercial brewing did not alter the public options of women. One might have anticipated that strong contrasts in the public opportunity and visibility of women would have distinguished manors where women were commercially active from manors in which most commerce in foodstuffs was controlled by men. But this contrast has not been found; Brigstock women, who thoroughly controlled their manor's ale trade, enjoyed no special rights or legal perquisites that were denied the women of manors like Iver where men dominated the ale industry.

The fact that an ale-wife's public activity in the ale market did not translate into behavioral changes in the public life of her village is not necessarily remarkable. Yet the full implications of this can best be seen by adding two contrasting perspectives to this picture of public immobility. First, commercial activity and court responsibilities were not invariably separate, but could be closely tied *if* the brewer was male.[66] If Iver was typical of other villages whose ale markets were dominated by males, brewing was a major route to public advancement and authority for males. Male brewers in Iver were twice as likely as nonbrewing males to wield political clout through public office. Indeed, most officers were also brewers.[67] Unlike female brewers whose public careers were undifferentiated from those of nonbrewing women, male brewers distinguished themselves from other men in the public life of Iver. For men, commercial brewing and public power were closely linked; the wall that separated commercial success and public authority obstructed only women. The second perspective complements the first. Although ale-wives failed to penetrate the public institutions of their society, other women did so. Adolescent daughters enjoyed a legal and economic autonomy that eluded all wives, and widows also distinguished themselves from wives by their greater independence of public action. Women changed their political, legal, economic, and social opportunities not through work but through household position.

The economic unit created by marriage was founded on the mutual dependency of husband and wife. Both brought properties or goods to the conjugal fund, both worked (albeit at different tasks) to support the household during the years of marriage, and both hoped to share, when the marriage ended, in the final dispersal of the conjugal fund. In the medieval countryside, as in most rural societies, the household economy relied on the contributions of both wives and husbands. It was this notion of mutual reliance and contribution that led the tyrannical husband to acknowledge to his wife that "the good we have is halfe dele thyn."[68] But despite this symbiosis, the economic experiences of married women and married men moved in different directions. For men, marriage brought both economic opportunities and economic control; as heads of households, they assumed almost full authority over the domestic economy. For women, marriage brought economic subordination; at the same time that they lost independent control of chattels and lands, they also accommodated their work to match the larger needs of their households. It was this notion that the domestic economy belonged to the husband that led the goodwife to admonish her daughter to "make not thy husband poor" and the anonymous author of an antifeminist song to berate wives who went to ale-houses "to sspende ther husbondes money."[69] The conjugal economy was a joint economy, but whenever personal autonomy or personal advancement transgressed upon the notion of corporation, the independent person was a husband.

Wives and Husbands in Village Society

Since marriage so dramatically limited the legal and economic options of women, it is not surprising that it also decreed fundamentally different social roles for wives and husbands. During adolescence, as we have seen, young people of both sexes slowly became more active members of Brigstock society while nevertheless retaining close ties with their parents. But the basic similarity in the social experiences of daughters and sons changed with marriage when wives and husbands, instead of sharing fundamentally similar social opportunities, developed court networks of radically distinct size, content, and structure. Husbands, as heads of households, acquired the social attributes of full adulthood, developing numerous and complex associations with other householders in the area. Wives, as dependents of their husbands, withdrew into their conjugal households, abandoning even the underdeveloped social autonomy of adolescence. These changes are clearly illustrated in the different public associations formed by Henry Kroyl junior and his wife Agnes Penifader-Kroyl.[70]

After his marriage to Agnes Penifader in 1319, Henry Kroyl junior's social independence expanded quickly. Although his limited public contacts during his premarital years had been strongly centered on his father, this paternal influence declined sharply as Henry Kroyl junior's court network grew after his marriage to include a much more diverse collection of cognatic, affinal, and nonfamilial associations.[71] After accumulating nine contacts in the courts between 1316 and 1319, father and son interacted only twice in public during the ten years after the marriage. Although the elder Henry Kroyl remained economically and politically active during this decade, his married son proceeded to construct an exclusive set of public associations. Yet Henry Kroyl junior, as a married man, moved away only from his father's authority, not from his family, for he continued to find his most important and enduring associations from among his natal kin; his brother John Kroyl quickly became the single most important person in his rapidly expanding network. Henry Kroyl junior's brother was also, in a sense, his best friend.[72] Marriage, then, eliminated paternal influence over the public associations of Henry Kroyl junior without altering the general importance of natal family in his social life.

At the same time, Henry Kroyl junior's court network was growing rapidly. His premarital network had boasted only 30 interactions with 20 people and only one multiplex relationship that involved more than one type of interaction (with, predictably, his father). But during his married years, his network grew to include 21 multiplex relationships among his 322 contacts in court with 156 people. As an influential and powerful man in Brigstock, Henry Kroyl junior cultivated many friends and associates. His cognatic relatives, with whom his public contacts remained exceptionally frequent, varied, and multiplex, always constituted the most important segment of his social life. Yet his horizons expanded to include not only modest associations with his wife's siblings, but also a vast array of associations with persons in the community to whom he was not related (see Tables 5.6 and 5.7).

Henry Kroyl junior enjoyed an unusually broad range of public contacts, but the basic features of his court network typified that of other married men. None of the other Kroyl or Penifader brothers relied heavily on their fathers after they married, and several, like Henry Kroyl junior, cultivated important adult relationships with brothers.[73] Henry Cocus, the only other new husband in early fourteenth-century Brigstock whose court network could be traced both before and after marriage, experienced changes quite similar to those

TABLE 5.6. Quantitative Breakdown of Henry Kroyl Junior's Postmarital Network

Category	Number of Persons	Number of Contacts	Number of Multiplex Relationships	Average Number of Contacts per Person	Percent of Total Persons	Percent of Total Contacts	Percent of Multiplex Relationships within Category
Cognates	5	33	3	6.6	3%	10.0%	60.0%
Affines	9	27	1	3.0	6	8.5	11.0
Nonrelatives	142	262	17	1.8	91	81.5	12.0
Total	156	322	21	2.0	100	100.0	13.5

Note: Percentages have been rounded to produce integral numbers.

TABLE 5.7. Qualitative Breakdown of Henry Kroyl Junior's Postmarital Network

Type of Interaction	Cognates		Affines		Nonrelatives		Total	
	Number	Column Percent	Number	Column Percent	Number	Column Percent	Number	Column Percent
Assistance received	6	18%	0	0%	18	7%	24	7.5%
Assistance given	11	34	26	96	199	76	236	73.0
Joint action	10	30	1	4	15	6	26	8.0
Land received	2	6	0	0	4	1	6	2.0
Land given	3	9	0	0	3	1	6	2.0
Dispute	1	3	0	0	23	9	24	7.5
Total	33	100	27	100	262	100	322	100.0

Note: When possible, percentages have been rounded to produce integral numbers.

of Henry Kroyl junior. In the years before he married Beatrice Helkok in 1304, Henry Cocus leaned heavily on the assistance of his father Peter (who died prior to his son's marriage). After his marriage, Henry Cocus, like Henry Kroyl junior, developed an important post-marital relationship with a male sibling; his court contacts with his brother William were almost unsurpassed by his other public associations.[74]

The patterns seen in these individual cases also emerge in aggregate trends of court assistance (see Table 5.8). When sons needed pledges, they frequently turned to family members and more often than not such assistors were fathers. But when married men needed pledges, they much less frequently used familial pledges and rarely used their fathers (although some fathers, like Peter Cocus, died before their sons married, many others, like Henry Kroyl senior, lived well beyond the marriages of their sons). Indeed, since brothers probably accounted for most of the pledges of presumed, but unspecified relationship shown in Table 5.8, brothers essentially replaced fathers as the favored familial pledges of husbands. Confirming the typicality of Henry Kroyl junior's personal network, these aggregate trends show that men's social experiences changed in two fundamental ways after marriage. First, their public horizons expanded rapidly, and as they accumulated larger networks of friends and acquaintances, they increasingly relied less on familial ties for support in their court dealings. Second, paternal influence waned after a man's marriage and was often, although not necessarily, replaced by a more egalitarian, sustaining relationship with a brother.

The changes experienced by wives were equally momentous, but qualitatively different. The shift in status from adolescent daughter to wife was accompanied in most cases by a change in surname; Agnes the daughter of Robert Penifader became Agnes the wife of Henry Kroyl junior. This change in public stature reflected a new set of personal allegiances and dependencies. For Agnes Penifader-Kroyl, marriage precipitated a totally new familial orientation rather than merely (as for her husband) a rearrangement of ties with natal kin. As a married woman, Agnes Penifader-Kroyl abandoned any public or formal association with her original family. Her unmarried sister and her married brothers continued throughout their lives to associate with each other in court, but Agnes Penifader-Kroyl never again dealt publicly with her siblings. She did not, to be sure, completely forsake

TABLE 5.8. Familial Pledging of Men in the Brigstock Samples of Crimes and Land Transactions

Category	Presumed Male Householders		Sons		All Men	
	Number	Column Percent	Number	Column Percent	Number	Column Percent
Total nonfamilial pledges	392	86%	96	61%	488	80%
Total familial pledges	63	14	61	39	124	20
Relationship of familial pledge						
Father/other householder	7	11	47	77	54	44
Brother	5	8	8	13	13	10
Other known relationship	5	8	1	2	6	5
Unspecified relationship	46	73	5	8	51	41

Note: Pledges from the sample of pleas were not included because each litigant could accumulate many pledges. Householders include all men cited independently, without any dependent relationship specified to another householder in the village. Because clerks only noted sibling ties in exceptional cases, it is very likely that many pledges of unspecified relationship were, in fact, brothers. Percentages have been rounded to produce integral numbers.

134

all contact with her natal family after marriage; because her husband interacted in the court with all her siblings, she enjoyed a continuing, albeit indirect exchange with the members of the household in which she had been raised. But it is significant that her court network—her record of public alliances and allegiances—never included members of her family of origin. Her public name, public status, and public dependence shifted irrevocably with marriage away from her parents and siblings.

But Agnes Penifader-Kroyl, rather than being freed from all familial influence after marriage, simply redirected and even intensified the familial content of her public experiences. Her very small court network (31 contacts with 11 people) was centered strongly around her new marital commitment; she boasted multiple contacts with only three people—her husband, his brother John Kroyl, and their close friend William Werketon.[75] Despite the new familial orientation occasioned by her marriage, Agnes Penifader-Kroyl relied so heavily on this new family that familial contacts accounted for 61 percent of all her recorded associations (the comparable figure for her husband was only 18 percent). Thus Agnes Penifader-Kroyl sharply redefined her family of orientation at the same time that she intensified her dependency on that new family in her public dealings.

Agnes Penifader-Kroyl's public break with her natal family was not unusual; it exemplified the experiences of other married women. Of the eight other Brigstock women whose postmarital activities could be precisely traced, four wives also never interacted in the village courts with their families of origin.[76] The other four women associated only minimally with blood kin after their marriages. Beatrice Helkok-Cocus was pledged once by her father (just seven months after her marriage), but she had no subsequent contacts with any Helkoks, relying instead on her husband, his family, and other nonrelated villagers. Cecilia Breche, who had married Alan Koyk by 1306, exchanged lands with her brother Radulph Breche in 1311, but usually interacted in the courts with either her husband or persons to whom she was not related. Emma Kyde, the wife of Simon Tappe, was once pledged by her uncle Henry Kyde in 1329, but this single natal contact was only a small part of her total court network at 20 contacts.[77] Cristina Penifader-Power's postmarital behavior was complicated by her marriage to Richard Power of Cranford and subsequent residence outside of Brigstock. When she did sporadically return to the Brigstock courts to pursue various land claims, however, she never relied on her brothers for assistance. Of her 19 court transactions after marriage, she interacted 7 times with her husband (all joint actions), appeared in property disputes against nieces or nephews 5 times, once received pledging aid from her brother-in-law Henry Kroyl junior, and interacted with 6 nonrelatives. This pattern contrasts sharply with Cristina Penifader's premarital network in which eight of her fifteen transactions were with natal kin (either her father or her brother Henry). Even women who did enjoy contact with their families of origin after marriage, then, had very few formal interactions with their natal relatives and usually focused their social energies on their husbands and their husbands' families.

Pledging patterns taken from the Brigstock sample of crimes confirm that most married women, like Agnes Penifader-Kroyl, relied heavily on members of their marital families in their public dealings (see Table 5.9). As a general rule, women always called more on family members when they came to court than did men, but wives were more likely than women of any other marital status to depend on persons to whom they were related. Moreover, wives usually turned not to any relative, but specifically to their husbands. While wives guilty of crimes sometimes sought assistance in pledging from neighbors, when they looked to a family member for such assistance they invariably used their husbands as pledges. The firm break that marriage brought in the social experiences of women is best illustrated in the contrasting experiences of Agnes Penifader-Kroyl and her unmarried sister Cecilia Penifader. Both sisters appeared in the Brigstock court with roughly equal frequency, but Cecilia Penifader built a much larger personal network (45 contacts with 22 people) than did her sister. Cecilia Penifader also never relied as heavily as did her sister on family members, and she, again unlike her sister, never severed her public ties with her parents and siblings. Cecilia Penifader, as a spinster, carried into adulthood the basic configurations of a female adolescent's social network; throughout her life she relied heavily, but not exclusively, on her natal kin. Her sister Agnes Penifader-Kroyl, with her small court network almost exclusively focused on conjugal kin, represents the married alternative.

Two main characteristics, then, distinguished the social experiences of husbands and wives. First, husbands' networks expanded far beyond the familial base of adolescence to incorporate many associa-

TABLE 5.9. Familial Pledging of Women in the Brigstock Sample of Crimes

Category	Wives		Daughters		Widows/Women of Unknown Status		All Women	
	Number	Column Percent	Number	Column Percent	Number	Column Percent	Number	Column Percent
Total nonfamilial pledges	13	25%	12	44%	52	81%	77	54%
Total familial pledges	39	75	15	56	12	19	66	46
Relationship of pledge								
Father/other householder	0	0	11	73	1	8	12	18
Husband	39	100	0	0	0	0	39	59
Other known relationship	0	0	0	0	3	25	3	5
Unspecified relationship	0	0	4	27	8	67	12	18

Note: Data on the pledging of women in the sample of land transactions were not used because the pledging patterns of wives in land conveyances were skewed by their propensity to act jointly in such matters with their husbands. Percentages have been rounded to produce integral numbers.

tions with persons to whom they were not related. In direct contrast, wives intensified the familial content of their social lives and narrowed the breadth of their acquaintances. Second, married men usually maintained contact with their siblings, whereas married women only rarely interacted publicly with their natal kin. Husbands' social experiences logically developed from the semi-autonomy of adolescence; as they grew older, they simply realigned natal ties and slowly expanded their associations with neighbors and friends. But wives' social experiences represented an abrupt shift from adolescence; severing their reliance on natal kin, wives narrowed, rather than expanded, their social options. In summarizing the main characteristics of the adult networks of the Penifader siblings, Table 5.10 shows how both

TABLE 5.10.   The Court Networks of the Penifader Siblings

Gender/Household Position	Network Configuration		Familial Content		
	Number of Persons	Number of Contacts	Number of Familial Contacts	Percent of All Contacts	Number of Siblings Contacted
Married women					
Cristina Penifader-Power	11	19	12	63%	1
Agnes Penifader-Kroyl	11	31	19	61	0
Spinster					
Cecilia Penifader	22	45	21	47	4
Married men					
Robert II Penifader	36	64	25	39	4
Henry Penifader	44	69	21	30	4
William Penifader	42	118	36	31	5

Note: The data for Cristina Penifader-Power include only her postmarital court contacts. Because the marriage dates of the Penifader brothers are unknown, all of their associations are included in these calculations. The two Penifader sisters only partially traced in the courts (Alice II and Emma) have been excluded. Familial contacts include all kin contacts—natal, marital, and affinal. In calculating the number of siblings contacted, an interaction with a sibling's spouse has been treated as if it were a direct contact with that sibling. Percentages have been rounded to produce integral numbers.

gender and household position affected the social experiences of adults in Brigstock before the plague. The networks of married women, represented by the postmarital associations of the sisters Cristina and Agnes, were very small, heavily oriented toward family, and largely exclusive of sibling contacts. The networks of married men, as shown by the experiences of the Penifader brothers, were larger, less dependent on family, and inclusive of sibling ties. Midway between these two patterns were the experiences of adolescents and lifelong celibates; moderate in both size and familial content, Cecilia Penifader's network always retained its youthful focus on natal kin.

When young women and young men married, their common conjugal status offered few common experiences in the public life of Brigstock. In the eyes of the law, husbands were responsible householders capable of governing not only themselves but also their families and their communities; wives were dependents of their husbands capable of few independent actions. In the regulation of the household economy, husbands again enjoyed pride of place; they controlled all the goods and properties of the household, they set the patterns of work to which other members of the household conformed, and they derived the most public benefit from the improving economic state of their households. In the social life of Brigstock, husbands also achieved full autonomy, developing networks of mutual aid and dependency with their neighbors and fellow villagers; their wives seemingly retreated into their homes, rarely associating in formal, public ways with persons outside their households. Only men, in a sense, achieved the public independence promised in adolescence; women became independent of their parents only to face renewed dependence in their marital households.

These public changes do not, of course, tell the full story of how marriage altered the experiences of women and men in Brigstock. Although publicly dependent, a wife also likely obtained many private advantages from her married status. Because marriage was expected, she received social approval through marrying. Because the conjugal household was a highly effective economic unit, she could hope to achieve greater economic security by marrying. Because marriage completed the adolescent transition away from parental authority, she gained full independence from her parents when she married. Because men were both physically and publicly powerful, she enjoyed, as a wife, the protection offered by her husband. Most important of all, a wife knew that she was vital to the functioning of her household, a *domina domus* so skilled at household affairs that she could, if necessary, manage domestic matters alone in widowhood.[78] Producing children, working in the croft and fields, bringing in wages from her hired labor, and profiting from sales of foodstuffs or other goods, wives almost certainly derived considerable satisfaction from their contributions to the household economy.

Private satisfaction, however, did not necessarily confer esteem. Although we shall never know how much the low public status of wives might have been balanced by private experiences, we should beware of assuming that modern estimations of marriage and motherhood prevailed in the medieval countryside. Didactic writers promoted the ideal of a wife who was both productive and submissive, but wives were more often satirized than idealized in medieval literature. The *fabliaux* taught, for example, that "No man marries without regretting it," depicting wives as either so industrious and clever that they dominated their husbands or so lazy and wasteful that they brought ruin.[79] Perhaps medieval wives, asked to be not only economically vital but also publicly submissive, seldom reached a balance between activity and passivity that satisfied their male contemporaries. Their maternal functions also brought limited prestige; because motherhood and child care were much less valued than they would be in later centuries, medieval writers little noticed or praised the mothering activities of wives.[80] At best, the medieval peasant wife was an object of pity, not esteem; William Langland ended his description of the work of a peasant wife by saying, "ruth is to read or in rime to show the woe of those women that woneth in cots."[81]

Whatever the private ramifications of marriage might have been, the records of the Brigstock court leave little doubt that marriage brought public independence for men and a new kind of dependence for women. Moreover, since most peasants in the early fourteenth century spent most of their adult years married, the autonomy of husbands and dependence of wives shaped profoundly the gender norms of the countryside. When medieval people talked of wives or husbands, they sometimes specifically meant married women or married men, but sometimes they were simply describing adults of either sex, especially adults of low social status. Adulthood and marriage were inextricably intertwined. But, although femaleness was largely defined by the submissiveness expected of wives, wifely subordination was not necessarily permanent. Women who outlived their husbands faced public opportunities that often exceeded even the semi-independence of adolescent daughters.

VI

Widows

Alice the wife of Peter Avice typified the public reticence of wives in
Brigstock. She seldom brought business before the local court and
relied often in such matters on her husband. Acting on her own, she
paid six amercements for selling ale, she used the court to settle four
disputes, and she once incurred censure for her disrespectful behavior toward the bailiff. Five other matters brought her to court
accompanied by her husband; in 1292, they paid jointly for admit-
tance to a quarter-virgate, and between 1295 and 1301, they together
pursued four cases against other villagers. Over the course of her 24
years as a wife, Alice Avice accumulated a small court network of
only 22 contacts with 14 people. She interacted in court most frequently with her husband (8 contacts), who far outweighed in importance any of the other associations reflected in her court actions.[1]

After Peter Avice died, however, Alice's public reticence was replaced by public assertion. Usually coming to court unaccompanied
by others, she paid rent on her holding, she purchased and sold
lands, she answered for various offenses associated with property
ownership, she brought or responded to six complaints against other
villagers, and she even acted on three occasions as a legal surety,
guaranteeing that others would meet their legal obligations. During a widowhood that lasted eight years less than her marriage,

Alice Avice developed a much larger court network than she had known as a wife: 34 contacts with 25 people. Her associations as a widow, moreover, were notable for their diversity rather than for their reliance on a single person. The records of the Brigstock court leave little doubt that the death of Peter Avice in 1316, no matter how personally distressing it might have been to his widow, left her in a new position of public authority. She accepted the responsibilities of a householder, she vigorously and effectively administered her holdings, and she actively participated in the social community of Brigstock.[2]

Many medieval countrywomen, like Alice Avice, faced years of widowhood at the end of their lives. The absence of marriage or death records makes it impossible to calculate precisely the usual duration of marriage on manors like Brigstock, but most marriages probably endured for little more than two decades. Of the 53 widows in Brigstock whose marital histories could be partially reconstructed from activities noted in the manor court, the gap between first citation as a wife and first mention of bereavement stretched from as little as 2 years to as much as 42 years, but the median of 15 years was quite close to the average of 17 years. Because these calculations underestimate the actual duration of marriage, most marriages in Brigstock likely ended with the death of a spouse after the passage of about two decades.[3] Although very rough, these estimates match Razi's calculations for Halesowen, which suggest that marriages on that manor before the plague usually lasted about 23 to 26 years.[4] Moreover, an average marital duration of about 20 years likely characterized English rural communities throughout the preindustrial period; analyses of the information found in registers of early modern English communities suggest that most marriages in the sixteenth and seventeenth centuries also ended with the death of a spouse after about two decades.[5]

Were women more likely to be widowed than men? Although at least 12 percent of the women identified in the courts of Brigstock before the plague survived their husbands, no comparable figures for men are available because manorial records never mention male widowhood.[6] It is highly likely, however, that widowhood was a more temporary status for males than for females; studies of preindustrial European communities have shown that widowed men remarried more frequently and also more quickly than did widowed women.[7]

Mortality rates dictated whether more men or more women were deprived of their spouses, but social custom invariably assured that more women than men remained alone. In Brigstock, widows often survived their husbands for considerable lengths of time. Of the 53 unremarried widows whose court activities could be reconstructed, the gap between first citation as a widow and last court appearance stretched from 1 to 37 years, and the median of 5 years fell significantly below the average of 9 years. Although experiences varied widely (doubtless reflecting the age at which a woman lost her husband), most widows in the community probably survived their husbands for at least several years and possibly as much as a decade or more.

As suggested by the public activities of the widowed Alice Avice, widowhood brought medieval countrywomen new responsibilities and opportunities. Because rural households were built around the conjugal unity of husband and wife, bereaved wives necessarily assumed many of the functions of their dead husbands. Widows whose sons were too young to claim their inheritances usually took custody of minor heirs and controlled their conjugal estates until the heirs' maturity.[8] In addition, widows enjoyed dower rights that superseded the claims of heirs, whether minor or mature. Under the common law, a widow's dower extended over only one-third of her husband's property, but customary law often granted to widows as their "free bench" from one-half to all of their husbands' lands. As a rule, rural custom gave widows only the use of free bench lands, dictating that they were not to alienate such properties without the consent of their husbands' heirs; this right of use, however, often endured throughout the widow's life, regardless of either remarriage or the maturation of heirs.[9] As a result, widows controlled significant proportions of land in the medieval countryside; in many villages, 10 to 15 percent of all holdings were in the hands of women, most of whom were widows.[10]

Precisely because of the enhanced public stature that widowhood offered women, their experiences are especially difficult to trace in the records of manors like Brigstock. Wives and adolescent daughters, as dependents of householders, were regularly and reliably cited in manorial records by their dependency status, but widows, as independent householders, were often cited with no indication of marital status. Matilda Manning, for example, was invariably identified as "Matilda the wife of John Manning" during her married years (10 citations), but after her husband died, the manorial clerk usually identified her simply as "Matilda Manning" (9 citations) instead of indicating her widowed state by calling her "Matilda the widow of John Manning" (2 citations).[11] Indeed, some widows, like Alice Goldhop the widow of Hugh Helkok, resumed their former names after the deaths of their husbands. Unless the records have included some indication of widowed status (a clerical identification, a payment of relief or heriot, a transfer of free bench lands), the marital condition of such women cannot be precisely determined. If the record of Alice Goldhop's payment of heriot in 1322 had not survived, for example, historical reconstruction of her widowed status would have been impossible because she was never again specifically identified by the court clerk as a widow.[12]

As a result, many widows are doubtless hidden among the "women of unknown marital status" found in the reconstructed population of Brigstock. Some of these women were probably spinsters who grew beyond the authority of their fathers without ever coming under the authority of husbands. The experiences of those who remained perpetually unmarried are, with a few exceptional cases such as that of Cecilia Penifader, notoriously difficult to trace. But most "women of unknown status" were likely widows for whom bereavement brought new responsibilities and opportunities. Certainly, these women— whether spinsters or widows—were distinguished by their breadth and independence of public action from wives and adolescent daughters in the Brigstock samples.[13] To offset the obstacles posed not only by the obfuscation of widowhood in the extant records but also by the small numbers of cited widows found in the Brigstock samples, widowhood in Brigstock is best studied from a total reconstruction rather than a sampling. Some widows have doubtless remained untraced, but all of the criminal, litigious, and proprietal transactions of the 106 widows identified in Brigstock before the plague have been fully considered.

If all the women of Brigstock had reacted to widowhood with the vigor and independence of Alice Avice, our picture of the intersection of household status and female experience would be neatly completed: semiautonomous daughters, dependent wives, autonomous widows. Yet the realities of widows' lives were more complex and varied. Some women, like Alice Avice, assertively responded to the responsibilities of widowhood; others, however, seem to have taken

little part in public affairs. Alice Avice's counterpart was Alice Penifader who reacted to the death of her husband Robert in 1318 by
withdrawal, not assertion; the Brigstock records note only her many
excused absences from meetings of the court. Widowhood was an
exceptionally varied status, with not only personality but also locale,
socioeconomic standing, and age affecting each woman's response to
the death of her husband.[14]

Locale profoundly shaped one of the most important decisions
faced by rural widows—the choice either to remarry or to remain
single. In villages where land was scarce, remarriage was frequent,
but when land was readily available, widows remarried only rarely.
With the economic diversity offered by its forest location and the
ready access to property provided by the local market in land, Brigstock offered few economic incentives for remarrying. As a result,
most widows remained single, only about one of every thirteen marrying a second time. Iver's pastoral economy similarly discouraged
remarriage.[15] But in other contemporary villages, remarriage was
such a crucial means of redistributing resources that most widows
married again. In early fourteenth-century Halesowen, for example,
six of every ten widows remarried.[16] Although the connection between land availability and remarriage in the medieval countryside is
clear, motivations are less certain. Perhaps widows were usually
eager to remarry, but could only bargain successfully for new husbands when they controlled lands valued by prospective suitors.[17]
Or perhaps few widows wished to remarry, but those in land-hungry
villages were compelled to do so because of their extensive proprietal
rights.[18] In either case, the very existence of the widowed state varied
widely from village to village. In some communities, remarriage was
so common that few women acted for long as widowed heads of
household; when they remarried, they essentially resumed their prior
status as wives. Other villages boasted many widows who, instead of
remarrying, spent many years administering the households and properties left by their husbands.

Within a given village, the experience of widowhood varied dramatically according to the solvency of the household left by the husband. Widows of wealthier husbands who had planned carefully for
their bereavement faced secure and settled prospects, but widows of
poorer husbands often struggled with great difficulty for their basic
livelihood. The effect of socioeconomic standing is clearly seen in the

Brigstock records; just as male heads of lower-rank households generally came less frequently before the court, so lower-rank widows generated less court notice than widows of more privileged status. Two-thirds of officeholders' widows were noticeably active in the Brigstock court, compared to only one-third of the widows of men who never held local office. Publicly active widows were, more often than not, widows of wealthy and influential men.[19]

The varied experiences wrought by socioeconomic status were compounded by age, since women widowed early in life faced more opportunities than those widowed in their later years. A widow's age strongly affected her likelihood of remarriage. Young widows, responsible for young children and all the economic resources left by their husbands, were more likely not only to be expected to remarry (placing their households again under the normative control of a male) but also to desire the emotional comfort offered by a second spouse. Older widows, whose grown children had already established separate homes, likely faced less pressure to remarry (because they controlled only small households) and also possibly were less interested in obtaining new partners. Remarriage in Brigstock was very rare, but most of the women who sought second husbands had apparently lost their first husbands prematurely.[20]

Age also probably affected the public presence of widows as reported in manorial courts. The ages of persons traced in the courts of Brigstock cannot be precisely calculated, but Table 6.1 illustrates how men slowly withdrew from public life as they aged; each of the five men studied participated less in the basic political networks of Brigstock—acting as pledges, essoining friends from court attendance, serving as officers—during his later decades than he had done earlier. Henry Kroyl senior's life provides a particularly good example of this phenomenon because the marriage of his son Henry junior in 1319 clearly marked the beginning of his retirement. He had served his community as an officer (usually a juror or an affeeror) on 23 occasions in the ten years prior to his son's marriage; although he lived for a decade after the marriage, he never again took on official responsibilities. His three land conveyances in the 1309–1319 decade similarly contrast with the single transfer of property accomplished in his last ten years, as do the three disputes that went to litigation in the former period as opposed to only one in the latter. Although Henry Kroyl senior remained an independent householder until his death in

Table 6.1. The Effect of Aging on Male Public Activity in Brigstock

Individual	First Decade of Court Activity	Second Decade of Court Activity	Third Decade of Court Activity	Fourth Decade of Court Activity	Fifth Decade of Court Activity
Richard Aylward, 1292–1335					
Pledger/essoiner	3	16	32	17	
Officer	0	4	22	13	
Total	3	20	54	30	
Henry Cade, 1295–1336					
Pledger/essoiner	3	16	17	4	
Officer	0	1	3	6	
Total	3	17	20	10	
William Durant, 1297–1337					
Pledger/essoiner	2	1	18	16	
Officer	0	0	16	6	
Total	2	1	34	22	
Gilbert Son of Galfridus, 1287–1335					
Pledger/essoiner	11	28	28	31	3
Officer	0	9	23	21	7
Total	11	37	51	52	10
John Hirdman, 1303–1340					
Pledger/essoiner	7	100	11	12	
Officer	0	1	2	1	
Total	7	101	13	13	

1329, as he aged, he slowly withdrew from the public life of Brigstock. The same circumstances that encouraged his lessening interest in public matters also doubtless affected many widows, ensuring that elderly widows were less active than younger widows in community life.[21]

Because aging adversely affected economic productivity, elderly persons also numbered heavily among the poor of preindustrial communities. Both villagers and lords were concerned with care of those for whom age brought either poverty or disability. By restricting gleaning to the poor, local bylaws assured that such persons would receive basic sustenance. Seigneurial policies that replaced incompetent tenants certainly did not hurt manorial revenues, but they also provided secure maintenance for those unable to provide for themselves. The link between aging and poverty suggests that many of the apparent disabilities of widowhood (as seen in retirement contracts, work defaults, requests to be excused from court, and the like) were more often caused by age than by widowhood itself. One of the ironies of widowhood in the medieval countryside is the mingling of old age with access to new responsibilities and privileges.[22]

As a result of the forces exerted by locale, socioeconomic status, and age, each new widow faced a unique situation. As long as she remained unremarried, however, she shared with all other widows the status of a female endowed with extensive public authority; thus widows fit awkwardly into the social hierarchy of the medieval world. In a society of male householders, they were female heads of households. In a legal system that so often distinguished clearly between the public rights of males and females, they took on some of the public attributes of men. In an economy that most valued landholding, their peculiar land claims threatened the proper devolution of assets from father to son. Because of the conjugal basis of the rural household, the death of a husband required that his wife replace him; their household was usually too discrete from kin to find his replacement among brothers, cousins, or even sons (for whom the attainment of householder status was associated with marriage, not inheritance). But when a widow assumed her husband's responsibilities, she became an anomaly—a householder who was not male. All widows in Brigstock did not fully utilize the public opportunities presented by their ambivalent status. Some asserted both domestic and public authority, others managed their households without much involvement in public matters, and still others might have retired from active management of their households. Few widows, however, totally eschewed the public opportunities of their new stature, and the overall patterns of their public activities were unlike those of either male householders or other women. Widows were never as publicly active and autonomous as male householders, but the breadth of their public actions as householders, as landholders, and as villagers clearly surpassed the more limited political, legal, economic, and social options of wives and adolescent daughters.

Widows as Householders

The last two chapters have shown how the political and legal activities of men in Brigstock expanded when they became married heads of households. Adolescent males were politically active both as members of tithings and as essoiners, attorneys, and pledges; married males could additionally participate in the official hierarchy of Brigstock by serving as bailiffs, affeerors, aletasters, and the like. Similarly, adolescent males accepted legal responsibility for their own affairs, paying fines, answering or bringing suits, attending court if required to do so; married male householders shouldered further responsibilities not only for the corporate actions of their households but also occasionally for the independent offenses of their wives and children. When widows in Brigstock took over the households left by their husbands, they seldom retired meekly from all domestic duties. They did not, however, fully assume their husbands' privileges and obligations. Located awkwardly on the public spectrum between the expansive authority of male householders and the dependency of wives and children, widows took over many of the functions once completed by their husbands. Yet they acquired more responsibilities than privileges.

Because of the conjugal basis of the peasant household, widows' households were exceptionally diverse and unstable. The size and structure of all households varied with socioeconomic circumstances and age of head, but households headed by widows, ipso facto in the later stages of the household cycle, were especially variable. More often than not, widows either had married offspring established in separate households or else soon supervised the leaving of their children. Alice the widow of John Popelin of Iver might have been typical; one daughter had married a few years before John's death, and another daughter and a son married shortly thereafter.[23] Low replacement rates ensured that the households of many other widows were especially small; of every five widows, probably one had no living children and another had no living sons.[24]

Although widows lived in households that were often small and disintegrating, their public position was clear. On the one hand, they resumed all the legal options they had known when unmarried; widows, like adolescent daughters (but unlike some wives), owed suit to the court of Brigstock, answered for their own crimes and offenses, resolved disputes through litigation usually unaccompanied by others, and freely concluded contracts or other agreements with their fellow villagers. On the other hand, widows also assumed control of their newly shattered conjugal households. Because households were formed at marriage and shaped around the conjugal unity of husband and wife, no other option was automatically available; sons, who established discrete households upon marriage, could not readily step into their fathers' places. When William Popelin married a few years after the death of his father John, for example, he did not assume domestic authority over his widowed mother, but instead lived separately from her.[25] Studies of the household structures of English villagers in the sixteenth through eighteenth centuries have shown that most widows remained in their marital households and did not retire into the households of married children.[26] The public activities of widows in early fourteenth-century Brigstock suggest that they, like their counterparts in early modern villages, normally took over the domestic responsibilities of their husbands.

Of the 101 unremarried widows in the community whose careers have been reconstructed, the public actions of only 10 betrayed an unwillingness to meet their responsibilities as householders and, in most cases, the evidence of disability is quite minimal.[27] Three widows made arrangements for retirement, concluding maintenance agreements in which they granted property in return for guaranteed support. Matilda Cocus tried to arrange a pension with her son, but resumed control of her holding when the agreement soured; in 1311, an inquisition determined that she (widowed since 1302) could reclaim her land from her son because he had failed to provide her with the food and clothing he had promised. She was still managing the land herself several years later.[28] Emma Sephirde, after 17 years of widowhood, divided some property (*placia*) between her sons in 1319, specifying that they were to give her a cartload of hay each year for the holding. Yet she continued to manage other lands on her own and six years later arranged for one son to enter the residue of her holdings after her death.[29] Emma With retired after her second husband died not to her son's home but rather jointly with her son; in 1331, they both, acknowledging their poverty and inability to do services, granted their land away in return for an annual rent.[30] None of these widows successfully retired under the protection of a son, and all three seem to have been quite advanced in age at the time they began to make provision for retirement. Aside from these three equivocal cases, no other hints of retirements appear in the reconstructed histories of Brigstock's widows.

Evidence of economic disability on the part of widows is also rare. Both Emma With (who claimed poverty in transferring her lands for an annual rent) and Matilda Cocus (who was cited after the maintenance dispute with her son for failing to find a servant for herding and plowing) might have been prompted to think of retirement because of problems managing their holdings. But the public activities of only one other widow betrayed any evidence of economic difficulties; Edith the widow of Gilbert Cocus claimed poverty in a plea she entered some nine years after the death of her husband. As with retirements, the evidence of economic disability is not only sparse but also ambivalent; claims of poverty accompanied the court actions of some demonstrably wealthy suitors, and male householders were also occasionally cited for work defaults.[31]

Another indicator of disability, the seeking of relief from the obligation of attending court, involved only six widows. Emma Werketon, whose son replaced her as court suitor, might have wished to withdraw permanently from public life. Five other widows paid fines to relax court suit temporarily (never more than one year), without specifying replacements. Fines to avoid court attendance, however, are uncertain indicators of public withdrawal since men frequently avoided attending court without jeopardizing their public status. Henry Cade, for example, fined once to relax suit of court for a full year and frequently proffered excuses for not attending specific meetings; nevertheless he served on several local juries during the course of his adult life.[32]

In contrast to the limited evidence suggesting that widows in Brigstock were unwilling or unable to assume the responsibilities of householders, the Brigstock records contain abundant examples of widows publicly acting as heads of households. For every one widow who betrayed any difficulty managing her household, roughly three widows in the community capably assumed the duties of householders. As their husbands had done before them, many widows in Brigstock accepted responsibility for the actions of their dependents and their households. Only one widow paid an amercement for a misdemeanor committed by a member of her household, but many widows paid amercements for crimes associated with householding (see Table 6.2).[33] The overall pattern of the reported criminality of widows generally follows the female norm in the crime sample; most citations against widows involved antisocial actions rather than personal attacks or thefts. Yet widows deviated from the expected pat-

TABLE 6.2. The Reported Criminality of Widows in Brigstock

Category	Widows		Female Norm (from sample)	Male Norm (from sample)
	Number	Percent		
Crimes against the community				
Illegal pasturing	1	2.0%	1%	3%
Misconduct in fields	5	11.0	38	9
Property damage	15	33.0	10	12
Insolence to officers	0	0.0	1	1
Rescue of seized property	3	6.5	2	5
Harboring strangers	10	22.0	3	8
Behavior that caused hue	2	4.0	15	18
Unjust raising of hue	3	6.5	9	2
Miscellaneous	0	0.0	6	3
Subtotal	39	85.0	83	62
Crimes against persons				
Attacks (and threats)	4	8.5	13	31
Hamsokens (housebreaking)	3	6.5	4	7
Subtotal	7	15.0	17	38
Total: All crimes	46	100.0	100	100

Note: To provide the best comparison with the sample of crimes, only crimes reported against widows in the views of frankpledge have been considered. When possible, percentages have been rounded to produce integral numbers.

tern for females by the preponderance of amercements they paid for household offenses—for improper use of pastures, for misuse of their holdings or other property damage, and for allowing strangers to tarry overlong in their homes. Indeed, because widows seem to have been notably less criminal than other adults, over half of their criminal amercements covered such household offenses. All told, sixteen widows in Brigstock paid sums in the court for either the offenses of their dependents or crimes associated with householding. Another five widows similarly betrayed their householding responsibilities by paying rents noted in the one listing of rents extant for the manor.[34]

Moreover, other widows acted in court in a capacity that was unusual for women, but common for householders; they pledged for their dependents. Of the thousands of sureties recorded in the Brigstock court between 1287 and 1348, only 46 were offered by females and most of these were widows pledging for the petty crimes of their sons and daughters (see Table 6.3). Of the 24 women accepted by the court as pledges, at least 14 were widows, and the unknown marital status of 9 other female pledges raises the strong possibility that they were also widowed heads of household. Only 1 woman who acted as a pledge was cited as being married, and the dating of that instance in 1348 (the year the plague arrived in England) lends doubt to this attribution that cannot be verified (because the 1348 courts are the last extant for Brigstock for several decades). The major criterion for acceptance of a female pledge was widowhood; women from various social strata (as shown by the official activities of either their husbands or other males of presumed relationship to them) acted in this capacity. Most of the recipients of female pledging were the dependents of their pledges; 26 of the 46 cases (57 percent) explicitly involved a mother pledging for her child, and 1 case involved a probable, but unverified, mother-son tie. The rate of familial pledging by these widows was, in fact, probably much higher; in 3 other cases, the pledger and pledgee shared a surname, and other women might well have been pledging for servants. Finally, these widows usually only acted as sureties for the payment of the small amercements levied for petty crimes (38 cases) or baking activities (2 cases). The few women who served as pledges in other sorts of legal transactions were personally involved in other aspects of the case. Emma Pote, Alice Avice, and Strangia Tulke were the original holders of the lands whose acquisition by another prompted their pledging activities, and Alice Somonor was a joint party with her son in the court plea that generated her pledge for his future appearance. Clearly, widows were accepted as pledges not because the court wished to extend to them a legal privilege usually reserved to males, but because the court expected them, as householders, to accept responsibility for their dependents.[35]

Counting widows, not incidents, Table 6.4 summarizes the extant evidence on how the widows of Brigstock met their householding responsibilities. Even when indicators of retirement or disability are defined as broadly as possible, only 10 of the 101 widows in Brigstock betrayed an unwillingness to fulfill the duties of their deceased husbands. In contrast, almost one-third of the widows in the community demonstrably acted as heads of the households vacated by their husbands. This one-third, moreover, represents a minimum, since many widows quietly managed their households through many years without ever meriting notice by the Brigstock court. Consider, for example, Agnes the widow of Hugh Heyr who paid her husband's heriot in 1306 and next appeared before the court in 1311 when she was excused from attending a single session; although she had been attending court during the five years after 1306 and presumably resumed regular attendance after her single essoin in 1311, her reliable fulfillment of the obligation to attend court was not noted by the clerk of the manor court.[36] The predilection of manorial courts to record incapacity rather than competency suggests that most widows not cited for retirements or derelictions were, in fact, quietly meeting their householding responsibilities. Because the items considered in Table 6.4 represent only brief incidents in the public careers of these widows, their full implications can best be seen in the reported activities of the three widows in Brigstock whose court citations have provided evidence of both disability and capability.

Paying her husband's heriot in 1302, Matilda Cocus first brought substantial business before the court in 1304. In that year, she pledged for a daughter guilty of trespass, she successfully defended (joined by her sons Walter and Henry, and Henry's wife Beatrice) a land claim brought by Cristina ad Fontem, and she raised a just hue against her son Henry. Her difficult relationship with Henry came to a head six years later in the failed maintenance agreement of 1311. After resuming control of her lands, she probably used servants to maintain her lands (one was noted in 1313), and encountered no

TABLE 6.3. Female Pledges in Brigstock

Case No.	Pledge's Name	Marital Status	Rank[a]	Year of Entry	Relationship of Pledgee to Pledger	Transaction Requiring Pledge
1 a	Alice widow of Peter Avice	Widow	Upper	1316	Unknown (son?)	Land transaction
b				1317	Daughters	Land transaction
c				1328	Unknown	Petty crime
2 a	Elicia widow of Peter Aylward	Widow	Upper	1335	Son	Petty crime
b				1336	Son	Petty crime
c				1337	Son	Petty crime
d				1340	Son	Petty crime
e				1340	Son	Petty crime
3 a	Matilda Baker	Widow	Upper	1340	Son	Petty crime
b				1340	Son	Petty crime
c				1340	Son	Petty crime
d				1343	Unknown	Petty crime
e				1343	Unknown	Petty crime
f				1343	Daughter	Petty crime
g				1345	Unknown	Petty crime
4 a	Matilda Bate	Unknown	(Upper)	1337	Unknown	Petty crime
b				1344	Unknown	Petty crime
5 a	Margery Cocus	Unknown	(Upper)	1343	Unknown	Petty crime
b				1343	Unknown	Petty crime
c				1344	Unknown	Baking fine
d				1344	Unknown	Petty crime
6	Matilda widow of Peter Cocus	Widow	Upper	1304	Daughter	Petty crime
7	Margery Fory	Unknown	(Lower)	1345	Daughter	Petty crime

156

8	Margery widow of William Golle	Widow	Upper	1343	Daughter	Baking fine
9	Alice (Goldhop) widow of Hugh Helkok	Widow	Upper	1322	Unknown	Petty crime
10	Alice widow of William Hem	Widow	Lower	1344	Unknown	Petty crime
11	Alice wife of Robert Kroyl	Wife (?)	Lower	1348	Child	Petty crime
12	Margery Laynde	Unknown	(Upper)	1335	Unknown	Petty crime
13	Alice Leche	Unknown	(Upper)	1343	Son	Petty crime
14	Emma Page	Unknown	(Lower)	1344	Unknown	Petty crime
15	Alice widow of Henry Pidenton	Widow	Upper	1337	Son	Petty crime
16 a	Emma widow of Thomas Pote	Widow	Lower	1320	Son	Petty crime
b				1320	Son	Land transaction
c				1321	Son	Land transaction
17	Unnamed mother of Emma Robin	Unknown	(Lower)	1331	Daughter	Petty crime
18 a	Alice Robin	Unknown	(Lower)	1339	Unknown	Petty crime
b				1340	Unknown	Petty crime
19	Alice widow of Robert Somonor	Widow	Lower	1317	Son	Plea
20 a	Matilda widow of Hugh Tubbe	Widow	Lower	1344	Daughter	Petty crime
b				1345	Unknown	Petty crime
c				1345	Daughter	Petty crime
21	Strangia widow of Henry Tulke	Widow	Upper	1344	Son	Land transaction
22 a	Margery widow of John Werketon	Widow	Lower	1340	Daughter	Petty crime
b				1340	Unknown	Petty crime
23	Alice *relicta* . . .	Widow	Indiv.	1340	Unknown	Petty crime
24	Matilda Honie	Unknown	Indiv.	1344	Daughter	Petty crime

a All rankings have been derived from the official activity of the pledge's husband, except those placed in parentheses (for which no precise data were available).

TABLE 6.4.   Widows as Householders in Brigstock

Categories	Number	Percent of All Unremarried Widows
Evidence of disability		
Retirements	3	3%
Economic problems	1	1
Avoidance of court suit	6	6
Total	10	10
Evidence of capability		
Paid fine for dependent	1	1
Paid fine for householder crime	15	15
Paid rent	5	5
Acted as a pledge	10	10
Total	31	31

Note: This table includes data only on the 101 unremarried widows reconstructed from the identified surnames of the manor (one widow who acted as a pledge was incompletely identified and is not counted here). This table excludes from subsequent subcategories a widow counted in a prior subcategory (i.e., a woman noted for both evidence of retirement and economic problems was counted in the retirement subcategory). Percentages have been rounded to produce integral numbers.

further difficulties until 1314 when she was cited for failing to provide a servant to do plowing and herding. In her last year of court activity (1315), she pursued cases against two villagers (one concluded successfully, the other's resolution unknown), and transferred a half rod of land to her son Henry. Although Matilda Cocus certainly encountered some difficulties during her more than dozen years of widowhood, her last court appearances show her to be still in control of her free bench lands and still independent of her sons (she never once, for example, sought pledging assistance from them).[37]

After her husband Peter Swetman died in 1302, Emma Sephirde resumed her own name, but retained clear authority over her offspring by virtue of her proprietal rights. In the first year of her widowhood, she transferred future rights in a *placia* with a curtilage and two rods from her free bench to her son Henry who promptly transferred the property to his brother Peter. Twelve years later, she gave a small house to her daughters Elicia and Agnes. Five years thereafter, she made the possible retirement provisions described above, dividing a croft between Henry and Peter with the stipulation that they provide her with a cartload of hay each year in return for tenure of the property. In 1319, she still, however, held sufficient land to be included in the partial rental for that year, paying 12 pence (the normal rent for a quarter-virgate). In her last court appearance in 1325, she granted ownership of the residue of her properties to her son Henry, to be entered after her death. Throughout her long widowhood, she also intermittently sold ale (10 amercements) and bread (6 amercements). Emma Sephirde never paid amercements for her children, or pledged for their crimes, or answered for the collective misdemeanors of her household, but there can be little doubt that she remained, throughout her long widowhood, not only independent of her children but also somewhat dominant over them.[38]

Alice Somonor's life as a widow was more difficult, and of the three, she was probably the least economically privileged (her husband never held local office). After her husband died in 1316, she had to be distrained for payment of heriot, and she and her son John (as co-executors of the estate) faced three pleas of debt. During the course of one case, she pledged once for John's future appearance. Acting on her own, she also pursued (and lost) another plea. In December 1318, she paid 3 pence to be excused from court suit until the following Michaelmas, but she retained her landholdings (paying rent of 2 shillings in 1319) and presumably resumed attending court after her exemption expired in September 1319. She also dispersed small properties through her children to third parties. In 1322, she transferred a *placia* and a *domus* from her free bench to her son Robert who immediately conveyed the property to another person, and ten years later she gave a tenement from her free bench to her son Henry who similarly transferred the property outside the family. Like Matilda Cocus, Alice Somonor encountered some problems during her public life as a widow, but she nevertheless retained her independence throughout her last appearances in the extant records.[39]

Most widows in Brigstock, then, probably remained independent heads of household until they died. Few remarried, few retired, few failed to meet their legal obligations. But the widow as householder was both publicly and privately anomalous. On the public level, male control of the political structures of Brigstock was based on the assumption that all females were dependents of a male householder;

women did not, for example, need to be inducted into tithings because they were presumed to be always under the authority of a
father or husband. A widow, however, not only lived independently,
but also, as a householder, met one of the prime prerequisites for
attaining official responsibilities. Yet widows neither joined tithings
nor served as officers. Even the pledging of widows was so restricted
that it offered few opportunities for building networks of mutual
assistance and cooperation within the manor. More influenced by
gender than by household position, politics remained a male affair.

On the private level, the assumption that households would be
headed by males meant that widows were never more than substitutes
for their husbands. Created at marriage, households were permanently identified with the husband whose authority extended, in some
matters, even beyond death. As illustrated by the widow's use, not full
control, of free bench lands, widows acted as their husbands' surro-
gates, but they could not fully emulate their husbands' authority.
Moreover, their households were probably often smaller and poorer
than they had been during the lifetimes of their husbands; heirs ma-
tured and claimed their portions of the familiar property, and other
children married and sought endowments. The tensions created by the
widow's ambivalent authority during these years of household disintegration seem to have been quite considerable in Brigstock. Intrafamilial conflicts were rarely recorded in the Brigstock courts, accounting for less than 2 percent of all criminals studied and only
3 percent of litigants sampled. Widows, however, often came into
formal conflict with family; 10 percent of all widows in Brigstock encountered at least one problem with children or kin that could not be
resolved without court intervention (see Table 6.5). Most of these
disputes involved the disposition of land.

Widows as Landholders

In Brigstock, a widow's primary asset was her landed property. It
has been suggested that widows and spinsters in some preindustrial
villages were particularly active as moneylenders, but this was not the
case in Brigstock; most of the widows involved in debt litigation
before the manor court were defendants, not plaintiffs.[40] In medieval
towns, widows often supported themselves by selling ale and other

TABLE 6.5. The Intrafamilial Conflicts of Widows in Brigstock

Widow	Nature of Conflict
1. Elicia the widow of Richard Aylward	Raised hue against her daughter (26/9/1338); suffered a housebreaking (hamsoken) committed by her son's wife (11/10/1342).
2. Mablia the widow of Adam Carpenter	Sued John and Richard Carpenter (relation unknown) to get her one-third of property (7/1/1328).
3. Edith the widow of Gilbert Cocus	Boundaries had to be placed between her land and that of her daughter (25/1/1301).
4. Matilda the widow of Peter Cocus	Raised a hue against her son Henry (17/9/1304); reclaimed land when Henry failed to fulfill a maintenance contract (15/7/1311).
5. Mablia the widow of Radulph Coleman	Simon Coleman (relation unknown) disputed her attempt to transfer land (28/1/1328).
6. Margery the widow of William Geffray	Daughter tried to claim her inheritance prematurely (6/7/1341 and 16/2/1343).
7. Agnes the widow of Hugh Gilbe	Paid for an inquisition to determine whether a certain property belonged to her or her son (3/6/1322).
8. Elicia the widow of William Helkok	Son prevented her attempt to sell free bench (17/8/1302).
9. Alice the widow of Gilbert le Heyr	Argued with nephew over land (2/11/1318).
10. Emma the widow of Thomas Pote	Boundaries had to be placed between her land and that of Richard son of John Pote (relation unknown) (4/4/1321).
11. Matilda the widow of Hugh Tubbe	Raised a hue against her daughter (25/9/1343); attacked her son's wife (25/9/1343).
12. Alice the widow of Radulph Tulke	Cheated by son on two-step transfer of land (20/3/1315).

foodstuffs or by running the businesses of their deceased husbands, but commercial activity was less common among the widows of Brigstock. Both aging and widowhood seem to have discouraged commercial involvement. Most of Brigstock's ale-wives abandoned brewing for profit as they grew older, and few were still selling ale when their husbands died. Several of these quickly ceased brewing for profit when their husbands died, and only three women brewed with any regularity for profit as widows. Similarly, only five widows, accounting for 11 of 233 baking amercements, baked bread for profit. Perhaps the small, truncated households of widows not only required less income from food sales but also were less capable of sustaining commercial enterprises.[41] Widows were most active in the economy of Brigstock not as traders or sellers or moneylenders, but as landholders.

Insofar as husbands and wives shared a community of property, it was a community of assets, not authority. Both spouses contributed their property and labor to the venture, but only the husband effectively controlled the conjugal economy. A wife was, at best, her husband's subordinate partner in the control of their household's movable goods, landholdings, and labor resources. The inequality of this partnership was probably most apparent at the husband's death when conjugal assets were divided and dispersed, rather than delivered intact to the bereaved wife. A wife's death had no such effect on the continuation of the conjugal estate, but because a husband authoritatively controlled the household economy, its unity ceased when he died. Two basic principles guided the dispersal of a male householder's property in the medieval countryside: his widow had to be provided with a secure holding from the conjugal property sufficient to ensure her continued well-being (her free bench), and his heirs had to claim their inheritances as straightforwardly and as quickly as possible. The next generation was, in short, to move into ownership without threatening the maintenance of the *relicta,* the woman left behind.

These simple objectives were difficult to achieve. On the one hand, a widow provided with secure and ample tenure undermined the rights of her husband's heirs. If her ownership was complete, she could alienate lands or sell assets that her husband had intended for his heirs. If her settlement was too generous, she could delay for many years the devolution of substantial properties to the heirs of her husband. On the other hand, an heir who immediately entered the properties of the deceased also undermined the widow's security; no wise husband wished to leave his wife dependent solely on the goodwill of his heirs. Because no single system provided a foolproof solution to the dilemma posed by the legitimate, but contrary, claims of widows and heirs, the tenurial rights of widows varied enormously from village to village. The widow's free bench could include one-third, one-half, or all of the conjugal holding. Most widows claimed their portions without paying entry fines (indicating their status as co-tenants with their husbands), but widows on some manors were fined *pro introitu* (indicating that they were considered to be not co-tenants, but heirs). Some widows held their free bench for life, but in other villages widows relinquished free bench holdings when they remarried or when heirs reached maturity. If a widow did keep her free bench after remarriage, her second husband sometimes could and sometimes could not claim the property if she predeceased him. The variability of custom, however, should not obscure the essential features of provision for widows. First, in all villages, widows of landholders were provided with properties separate from the claims of heirs; details varied over time and place, but the customs of all rural communities ensured that widows were not wholly dependent on the generosity of heirs. Second, most widows were custodians, not full owners of the lands designated for their maintenance; their rights of use could sometimes be passed to their second husbands or leased to others, but widows were not supposed to sell or otherwise to alienate their settlements.[42]

In Brigstock before the plague, the proprietal claims of widows provided them with more extensive landholdings than those available to other women. Wives, of course, could not independently control personal properties, and although adolescent daughters and spinsters managed their lands freely, these properties tended to be small parcels obtained through gift or purchase. Some heiresses obtained larger properties, but they usually married quickly. Widows, however, often enjoyed extensive control over extensive properties. First, widows resumed management of all personal properties that had been previously merged into the conjugal fund; a woman who independently acquired land (through purchase, gift, or inheritance) forfeited control of that land to her husband during her marriage, but regained full ownership when widowed. Second, widows also claimed free bench from their husbands' lands. The customs that governed the settlement of free bench in Brigstock, however, defy full reconstruction. Some widows paid heriots (a tax on the chattels left by the deceased), others paid reliefs (entry fines to the property), and still others were subject to no fines whatsoever. Some widows apparently claimed as free bench all of the heritable property of their youngest sons, but others claimed a third of the conjugal estate.[43] Nevertheless, all widows in Brigstock held their free bench for life, relinquishing such properties neither at remarriage nor at the maturation of their heirs. As a consequence of the claims of widows not only to resume full control of properties obtained in their own right but also to exercise temporary control over part or all of the conjugal estate, most female holders of large properties in Brigstock were widows. Of the 60 people listed in the partial rental that survives for Brigstock from 1319, 11 (18 percent) were women, of whom at least 6 were widows (and the unknown marital statuses of the remaining 5 women suggest that they, too, might have been widowed).[44]

Widows in Brigstock assertively managed the properties that fell under their control. Dying husbands probably hoped that their widows would quietly maintain the lands provided for them, eventually passing the property intact to their heirs. In Brigstock, such hopes were not always realized; half of the widows in the community brought some of their properties to the local land market (and half of their transfers explicitly identified the conveyed property as free bench land). Dying husbands also likely hoped that their wives would supervise the devolution of resources among their children, assuring that noninheriting offspring were provided with adequate portions or endowments. Although many widows in Brigstock went to court to grant properties to their children, others used the land market to their own advantage, buying, selling, and trading with their neighbors; well over half of the transfers initiated by widows conveyed land outside of the family.[45] To wield such control over their properties, widows in Brigstock devised four methods of circumventing the custodial restrictions of free bench tenure.

Although widows could not permanently alienate their free bench lands, they were free to lease them. Some leases specified terms, as when Margery the widow of John in Cimiterio, joined by her daughter Custancia, leased one acre to Robert Malin for a six-year term. Other leases were set to expire at the widow's death; in 1343, for example, Cristina the widow of Peter Tubbe leased one rod from her free bench to Walter ad Stagnum, specifying that he was to hold it until she died (*ad terminum vite sue sine alique contradictione aliter hominis heredis vel alterius*). Although only a few such leases were recorded in the courts of Brigstock, many more agreements were probably never noted in the legal records of the manor because short-term leases required no enrollment. Leasing not only enabled widows to realize at least temporarily the capital value of their properties but also permitted them to profit from the upswing in land values in the late thirteenth and early fourteenth centuries. Widows, more likely than most to hold disposable lands that they could lease for a few seasons, might have been especially advantaged by rising land values in the half-century before the plague.[46]

Some widows in Brigstock also probably sold free bench lands, despite the customary restriction on such sales. Such efforts were eased in Brigstock by some confusion about the validity of sales of free bench; although a jury in 1297 had accepted a widow's sale, another inquisition five years later determined that widows could not sell any part of their settlements.[47] Only one widow in Brigstock clearly alienated part of her free bench; in 1335, Alice the widow of Gilbert le Heyr transferred a *placia* from her free bench to John Hirdman. Other widows, however, clearly attempted to do so; Elicia Helkok's son had to pay for court inquisition to prevent his mother from selling free bench lands, and both Mablia Coleman and Leticia Chapman endured similar challenges to their land conveyances. It is perhaps telling that about half of the transfers effected by widows in Brigstock made no mention of either free bench or the rights of heirs.[48] Some of these lands were properties that widows held in their own right and were free to alienate, but others might well have been free bench properties being transferred under the guise of normal conveyance.

In other cases, widows secured the right to alienate free bench lands from the eventual heirs of the properties. Because widows and heirs were sequential, not joint, owners of free bench properties, they seldom conveyed land jointly; heirs could, however, forfeit their future claims, leaving widows with unencumbered control of their free bench lands. Usually, the widow granted the free bench to the heir and received it back in full ownership. In 1317, for example, Isabella Leche gave two rods from her free bench to her son who immediately returned the property to her; she then sold part of the land to a neighbor.[49]

Finally, many widows who wished to convey free bench lands obtained the concurrence of the heir through two-step transfers that conveyed the property to a third party via the heir. In 1340, for example, Alice the widow of Henry son of Peter gave a tenement from her free bench to her son and heir John, who immediately transferred it to John Wolf. This method of circumventing free bench restrictions was especially popular in Brigstock; of the 106 grants made by widows, 37 (35 percent) thus conveyed free bench through the heir to a third party. These two-step transfers ensured that conveyances of free bench could not be later challenged by angry heirs, but they were not without danger. In 1315, Alice Tulke wanted to endow her daughter with a tenement from her free bench, but when she gave the property to her son Henry he vilely (*viliter*) kept the tenement rather than passing it along to his sister. Alice Tulke's appeals to the court failed to bring her son to justice; because she had fully conveyed the property to him, he retained control of the holding.[50]

Widows, of course, freely managed any properties they held in their own right, but these four options—leases, surreptitious sales, receipts of full ownership from the heir, and two-step conveyances through the heir—also allowed them to use their free bench lands much like other landholders, independently disposing of small parcels at advantageous moments. Few acted precipitously. Of the 22 widows for whom the timing of transfers could be established, only 5 conveyed any land within the first year of bereavement; the average interval between the beginning of widowhood and the first transfer of land was about seven years.[51] Few sold or gave their entire property. At most, only 13 widows might have conveyed their entire holdings, but 8 of these arranged to retain use of the property for the duration of their lives. Few also came to the land market solely to arrange for the endowments of children. Only 16 widows used land conveyances exclusively to grant holdings to their sons or daughters. Nevertheless, although widows seem to have been as eager as other landholders to control their properties fully, their land conveyances also betray the particular familial circumstances of their status.

As heads of disintegrating households, widows so often used the land market to provide for their children that their overall patterns of land conveyance are distinguished clearly from those of other

TABLE 6.6. Widows in the Brigstock Land Market

Category	Widows Number	Widows Percent	Female Norm (from sample)	Male Norm (from sample)
Type of action				
Grantor	106	87%	60%	48%
Receiver	16	13	40	52
All actors	122	100	100	100
Autonomy of actor				
Acted alone	65	53	60	88
Acted alone in two-step transfer	37	30	—	—
Acted jointly	20	16	40	12
All actors	122	99	100	100
Nature of grant				
Not intrafamilial	49	40	63	83
Intrafamilial	73	60	37	17
All grants	122	100	100	100
Size of grant (if known)				
Less than 2 rods	79	78	80	90
Over 2 rods	22	22	20	10
All grants of known size	101	100	100	100

Note: Percentages have been rounded to produce integral numbers.

traders (see Table 6.6). Widows figured disproportionately as sellers or givers of land, but their prominence in this capacity does not suggest poverty or disability as much as the responsibilities of widows in the developmental cycle of the rural household. Managing households undergoing disintegration, widows were more interested in dispersing familial properties than in accumulation. Most often, widows granted such properties not to neighbors or friends, but to children. Some of these grants were the first steps of the two-step conveyances that transferred free bench through heirs to nonrelatives (29 grants), but most went either directly or indirectly to the widow's heir or other children (39 grants; the remaining 5 intrafamilial transfers represent receipts of land by widows). And grants by widows, likely to come more often from large conjugal holdings, were more substantial than the usual small parcels transferred in Brigstock (although it should be emphasized that many of these larger grants provided for the widow's continued use of the property until her death). To a large extent, the widows of Brigstock adequately fulfilled the expectation that they would distribute resources among their children; of the 54 widows active in the land market, 41 (76 percent) conveyed at least some land to their children.[52] As exemplified by Emma Sephirde's grants to two sons and two daughters, many provided for noninheriting children as well as allowing designated heirs to gain early access to some of their properties.

Yet the image of the altruistic widow dispersing properties among her children, though accurate, is incomplete. Because they supervised households undergoing disintegration, widows were especially active in intrafamilial conveyances, but such domestic concerns comprised only a part of their participation in the local land market. Thirteen widows transferred land directly to unrelated persons, and another 21 conveyed property outside the family using the two-step process involving the heir.[53] Widows often provided for their children, but they also often used land to their own advantage. The counterpoint to Emma Sephirde might be Margery the widow of John in Cimiterio who repeatedly alienated properties from her family. In 1332, she transferred first a rod and then (joined by her daughter) one-half rod to John Broyer; in 1333, she transferred to Cecilia Penifader two half-rods and, later in the same court, a selion (or strip); and accompanied by her daughter in 1335, she sold one and a half rods to Robert Malin and one rod to Cecilia Penifader, and then leased an acre to Robert Malin for six years.[54]

As landholders, then, widows demonstrated the same ambiguities seen in their householding activities. Although widows were not passive custodians of their lands, they also did not use their properties as freely and as autonomously as did male landholders. Men in Brigstock used the land market primarily to alter the size or configuration of their holdings. By consolidating properties, selling small parcels, and offering short-term leases, men constantly adjusted their needs and their resources. Widows similarly traded land to their own advantage, but they were also more bound than others by familial responsibilities. Just as widows were partial householders, so they were partial landholders. Restricted by both the tenurial limitations of free bench and the familial obligations inherent to their status, widows nevertheless managed their estates as vigorously and as independently as their circumstances allowed.

Widows as Villagers

Both daughters and wives were less active in the social circles of Brigstock than were men of comparable status. It is difficult to trace social relations in court records, but the legal associations of women suggest that they were considerably more oriented toward family than were men; when a woman in Brigstock came to court to resolve a dispute, to transfer land, to answer for a crime, or to conclude any type of legal business, she was much more likely than a man either to deal with relatives in these transactions or to rely on a relative for legal assistance. Reported crimes also show that women were less active than men in the community of Brigstock. The activities of widows in the Brigstock court, however, suggest that their social experiences often more closely matched the male, rather than the female, pattern.

The court networks of wives, as illustrated by the associations formed by Agnes Penifader-Kroyl, were usually small and focused on their husbands. Indeed, wives' networks were even, in a sense, artificially inflated because they usually came to court accompanied by their husbands and dealt predominantly with the associates of their husbands. During her married years, for example, Edith the wife of Gilbert Cocus accumulated a small court network of only 7 contacts with 7 people, and in all but one of these associations she was accompanied by her husband. In widowhood, the court networks of women usually expanded in both breadth of acquaintance and frequency of contact. After her husband died, Edith Cocus independently associated with 12 people in court on 13 occasions, raising a hue, pursuing two pleas, and seeking pledges for her court obligations. Her experiences were typical. Of the 30 women in Brigstock who were active in court as both wives and widows, most interacted as widows not only with more people but also on more occasions; 19 women (63 percent) accumulated larger numbers of associates and contacts than during their married years. The larger court networks of widows were also usually acquired over considerably shorter periods of time—an average of only 9 or 10 years of widowhood as opposed to 16 or 17 years of married life.[55]

Moreover, the pledging associations of widows more closely paralleled those of male householders than those of wives or daughters. Widows, unlike other women, normally turned for pledging assistance not to male relatives, but rather to unrelated friends or neighbors (see Table 6.7). Although daughters were often pledged by their fathers and wives often received such aid from their husbands, widows seldom turned to either brothers or sons for service as legal sureties. Since widows were householders, they had no household head whom they could use for legal assistance, so instead of turning (as was legally permissible) to other male kin, widows usually looked outside of their families for pledging assistance. Once the household basis of reliance on male kin was broken, the importance of such ties apparently weakened quickly. Probably the most striking aspect of Table 6.7, however, is not the divergence of the pledging associations of widows from those of wives and daughters, but their coincidence with the pledging patterns of male householders; 9 percent of widowed litigants used familiar pledges as opposed to 10 percent of male householders involved in the pleas sampled, and 18 percent of both widows and male householders used familial pledges when amerced for petty crimes or offenses. The pledging associations of widows suggest, then, that their social experiences conformed more to the pattern associated with their household position than to the pattern of their gender.

Although the court networks and pledging associations of widows indicate that widowhood was a time of unusual social activity for women, many widows were markedly uninvolved in the public affairs of Brigstock. Fifty-four widows in the community rarely, if ever, used the resources of the court to adjudicate disputes, convey land, or register contracts, and they almost never merited legal notice for criminal actions or commercial sales. Such court activities indirectly reflect social relations since each clerical notation of a land trade, broken contract, ale sale, and the like indicates an informal interaction between villagers. Men and women active in the society of Brigstock almost inevitably had some of their disagreements, crimes, contracts, and sales enrolled in the court record. As a result, the 54 widows who seldom merited court attention for such matters were, compared to other villagers, relatively inactive in the social life of Brigstock. Nothing suggests, it should be reiterated, that these widows were not privately active as householders and landholders, but they were probably not as publicly active in local society as other

TABLE 6.7. Familial Pledging of Widows in Brigstock

| Category | Widows | | Percent for Wives (from samples) | Percent for Daughters (from samples) | Percent for Male Householders (from samples) |
	Number	Percent			
Litigation					
Litigant used some familial pledges	3	9%	32%	33%	10%
Litigant used only nonfamilial pledges	30	81	68	67	90
Total litigants using pledges	33	100	100	100	100
Crime					
Familial pledges	7	18	75	56	18
Nonfamilial pledges	31	82	25	44	82
Total pledges	38	100	100	100	100

Note: Percentages have been rounded to produce integral numbers.

women and men. To be sure, these widows probably spoke with their neighbors and cultivated friendships outside of their families, but such associations, as indicated by the silence of the record, were comparatively limited in both breadth and depth. These women, it seems, took control of their free bench lands and retired to the private management of their households.

Court records, then, offer two contrary pictures of how widows fit into the social community of Brigstock. On the one hand, about half of the widows traced on the manor actively participated in the public life of Brigstock in ways that suggest that they were more independent of familial ties than most women. On the other hand, about half of Brigstock's widows were publicly inactive, rarely bringing any business before the local court. Two factors probably encouraged social inactivity. Some women became widows at an age of social withdrawal, not involvement. As illustrated by the male careers summarized in Table 6.1, men withdrew from public activity as they aged, and it is likely that many widows did the same. Other widows supervised such poor households that neither they nor their husbands were very active in public affairs; over two-thirds of the publicly inactive widows of Brigstock had husbands who never held local office.[56] When such factors, however, did not distract widows from the public realm, the Brigstock evidence suggests that widows often became so active in their communities that their social horizons had more in common with the experience of male householders than with those of daughters or wives.

As a householder, a landholder, and a villager, each widow in Brigstock personally experienced the inconsistencies of her status. She took on most of the responsibilities of householding, but accrued few of its advantages. She held extensive properties, but her control was limited by both tenurial restrictions and familial obligations. And she either participated more actively in public affairs than was common for other women or was exceptionally uninvolved in the social circles of her community. Widows, in short, certainly did not wholly step into the positions vacated by their husbands, but they also seldom meekly retired to the care of a married son. Faced with the expanded legal, economic, and social options of widowhood, most women in Brigstock actively exploited at least some of their new opportunities.

The particular customs and economy of Brigstock in the early fourteenth century probably promoted the autonomy and assertiveness of its widows. To begin with, the manor's diverse economy and active land market assured the very existence of widowhood, since remarriage was very common in areas where land was both precious and scarce; on land-hungry manors like Houghton-cum-Wyton, widows remarried so quickly that few women long experienced the status of widowhood.[57] Brigstock's active land market also probably assured that many widows were not solely dependent on inalienable free bench lands. Because some held properties acquired through inheritance or purchase that were not bound by the restrictions of free bench tenure and others devised methods of circumventing the custodial nature of free bench, the vigorous land market of Brigstock encouraged widows to be active, not passive landholders. And Brigstock's custom of divided inheritance, which gave younger sons their fathers' inherited lands, might also have worked to the advantage of widows by more often placing them in control of minor heirs.

The activities of widows in Iver suggest, however, that the customs and economy of Brigstock caused differences of degree, not kind, in the experiences of widows in the medieval countryside. Iver, like Brigstock, was not a land-hungry agrarian community, but instead relied largely on animal husbandry and boasted a fairly active market in land. Widows in Iver only rarely remarried; of the 34 widows identified in the pre-plague records of the manor, only 5 (15 percent) sought second husbands. Iver, however, differed from Brigstock in its provisions for widows; a widow in Iver only claimed a third of her husband's properties which was, it seems, not formally separated from the tenement of the eldest son and sole heir. Because the widow's portion was intermingled with the heir's property, conveyances or leases of free bench were discouraged if not outrightly forbidden; no widow in Iver ever independently transferred lands explicitly identified as free bench. Yet Iver widows, like their counterparts in Brigstock, seldom retired from active management of their households and properties.[58]

As householders, Iver's widows never pledged for their children in the local court, but they were accorded the other responsibilities that usually fell to heads of households. Widows, as householders, were directly charged for the conduct of their dependents; in 1337 Katrina the widow of William Peys paid an amercement because she had not prevented her son from fishing illegally.[59] Similarly, Iver's widows paid amercements for offenses typically committed by households—the trespass of animals, the illegal felling of trees, and the failure to clean ditches.[60] Widows in Iver also often received full legal custody of their husbands' minor heirs. Women like Alice the widow of John Sprot not only acquired physical custody of these children, but also obtained the right to administer their lands and properties. And Iver's widows took over another common responsibility of householders; they paid the merchets of their daughters.[61] Of the 16 widows active in Iver between 1322 and 1348, 9 were cited for such householder responsibilities, and only 2 evinced any interest in retirement. Neither case provides definitive evidence of any social expectation that widows should retire to the protection of their sons. Although Margery the widow of John Lawrence paid to relax her obligation to attend court in January 1346, she was still sufficiently active to be fined several months later for failing to clean a ditch. And although Alice the widow of John Popelin contracted a maintenance agreement with a couple to whom she was not related in 1345, this retirement came after 13 years of active widowhood.[62] As in Brigstock, the widows of Iver were not content to retire into households headed by their sons; instead they usually took control of the truncated households left by their husbands.

As landholders, widows in Iver were less active than their counterparts in Brigstock, but they nevertheless managed their lands effectively. One-fourth of Iver's widows brought properties to the land market. Some transferred land directly to children, others transferred land through children to third parties, and still others directly conveyed property outside of the family. None, it is worth noting, immediately transferred land after the death of her husband, and none conveyed away all of her property. Widows in Iver could not as freely convey land as did widows in Brigstock, but they used their properties for essentially similar purposes—for maintenance, for profit through sales or leases, for endowing their children.[63]

As villagers, the experiences of widows in Iver were as varied as those of widows in Brigstock. As in Brigstock, half of Iver's traceable widows were inactive in the manor, appearing in court only once or twice to pay obligatory fines. Yet the other widows traced in Iver were quite active in the community, paying amercements for misdemeanors, pursuing disputes through litigation, and trading land with their neighbors. Like their counterparts in Brigstock, these active widows only infrequently relied on male relatives for legal assistance when they brought business before the court. The social experiences of widows in Iver varied enormously, but those who chose to be active in local affairs were often very active indeed.[64]

Widowhood in the medieval countryside has been so little studied by historians that the typicality of the activities of widows in Brigstock cannot be firmly assessed. The comparative experiences of widows in Brigstock and Iver suggest, however, that different customs of tenure and inheritance affected the options of widows, but did not alter their essential responsibilities and opportunities. One manor practiced divided inheritance; the other followed the custom of primogeniture. One offered widows easy access to land trading; the other more closely restricted the conveyances of widows. Yet in both communities, women stepped into new public roles—as householders, as landholders, as villagers—when their husbands died. On many medieval manors, few women lived for long as widows because they quickly found second husbands, but on those manors whose economies discouraged remarriage, widows were often active and powerful members of their communities.

Widowhood was not a time of absolute advantage for women in Brigstock. It probably often brought many personal and emotional problems; bereaved of their husbands with whom they had shared many years and experiences, widows often also coped with the disabilities and frustrations of old age. This time of life also varied so enormously according to individual circumstances that not all widows were either willing or able to emulate Alice Avice's vigorous assumption of public responsibilities and opportunities. But despite much variety and much ambivalence, most widows took some advantage of the new public roles offered by their changed status, and in most instances, their public presence exceeded that of both daughters and wives. Widows were often heads of small, disintegrating households, but they were householders, neither semi-independent daughters nor dependent wives. Despite customs that restricted their control of free bench properties, widows' tenures were both substantial (exceeding those held by most daughters) and independent (as opposed to the submergence of wives' properties into the conjugal estate). Although some widows reacted to bereavement by withdrawing from village society, those widows who remained active in local life built social networks larger and more independent of kin than the associations formed by either daughters or wives. Widows were, in short, the most publicly active of all women in the medieval countryside. Although their public presence fell short of that typical of male householders, it surpassed the female norm.

The interplay of gender and household position in Brigstock before the plague, then, seldom disturbed the continuity of men's lives, but usually created discontinuities in the lives of women. For men, gender and household position were roughly identical; all men—as either future, current, or past householders—were accorded extensive public privileges and responsibilities throughout their lives. Yet for women, the prescriptions of gender sprang from only one household position; the public reticence expected of all women reflected the public reticence of wives alone. As adolescent daughters and widows, women enjoyed legal, economic, and social opportunities that contrasted sharply with their limited activities as wives.

VII

Medieval Countrywomen in Perspective

The conjugal households of Brigstock shaped the social relation of the sexes in contradictory ways. On the one hand, conjugality reinforced gender stereotypes by encouraging the authority of husbands and the dependency of their wives. Maleness was associated with the public activity of householders, and femaleness was defined by the public passivity of household dependents. On the other hand, conjugality inevitably gave rise to situations that blurred distinctions of gender. Neither adolescents nor widows strictly conformed to the expectations of their gender. The conjugal households of Brigstock before the plague created an assumption of public males (householders) and private females (dependents), but regularly moderated this assumption by allowing many household circumstances that fit poorly with male authority and female dependence.

The experiences of women and men in Brigstock offer no support to theories advancing either medieval individualism or medieval sexual equality. The pervasive importance of the household to all peasants, male as well as female, is a feature of rural life that has eluded those who emphasize individualism in medieval villages.[1] Even the most authoritative and independent of medieval peasants, the male householder, was firmly bound to his household by ties of obligation and responsibility. He was not an individualist in any sense of the word. Similarly, the variable influence of the household on the two sexes has escaped others who would resurrect the myth of preindustrial sexual equality.[2] Both women and men could be dependents or householders or some ambivalent status between the two, but women were much more likely than men to spend most of their adult years as dependents in households headed by others. Women, as a group, encountered severely limited public opportunities.

Although women and men were not equally affected by the intersection of gender and household in Brigstock, sex alone did not predetermine an individual's household experiences. Men were not uniformly superordinate, and women were not uniformly subordinate. Instead, householders (including most males) enjoyed access to public privileges and opportunities that were not available to their dependents (including most females). But those men not full householders—adolescent males, bachelors, retired fathers—were less publicly active than male householders, just as those women freed of household dependency—widows, and, in some measure, adolescent daughters—more nearly emulated the public prominence of males. This flexibility meant, for example, that many adolescent sons paid fines for improper gleaning, an offense usually committed by dependent females, and that many widows pledged for their dependent children, a responsibility usually associated with male householders.

The gender system supported by the conjugal households of Brigstock also ensured that the disabilities of femaleness were more situational than inherent. All women faced political, economic, legal, and social disadvantages unknown to men, but practical necessity ensured that these disadvantages waxed and waned over the course of a woman's life. Because daughters married into new and separate households, their parents encouraged them to develop independent resources in the years that preceded their weddings. Because a husband's death left a vacancy that could be filled by neither his sons nor his brothers, widows had to assume the public tasks of householders. Women regularly moved across the boundaries that marked their subordination as a sex, perhaps ensuring by their movement that such boundaries remained flexible and fluid.

Both the independence of daughters and the authority of widows in Brigstock grew directly from the conjugal structures of their households; had they lived in households that were larger and more stable, they would have seldom encountered circumstances requiring public involvement and assertion. In societies both past and present, the subordination of women is greatest when households endure across generations, with sons taking over the households of their fathers and new wives moving into long established households. Probably the best example in Western history of the effect of stable households on women's status comes from Classical Athens where the structures of the *oikos* ensured that citizen women were always under the guardianship of a male. Few family systems in the West have been as pervasive and as perpetual as the *oikos,* and few women have been as confined and secluded as those of Athens in the fourth and fifth centuries b.c.[3] In the Middle Ages, the interplay between household structures and women's lives possibly created broad differences between the experiences of countrywomen in England and those of rural women in another well-documented region, contemporary Tuscany. Much comparative work remains to be done, but it is possible that medievalists will eventually describe two distinct patterns in the history of women in medieval Europe—a northern (or English) pattern where women married late, established new households with their husbands, and enjoyed a companionate marriage in the sense that both spouses were of roughly equivalent age, and a southern (or Mediterranean) pattern where women married young and moved into the established households of their much older husbands.[4] Such a contrast would suggest that women in the English countryside encountered opportunities unknown to their counterparts in southern Europe.

Nevertheless, the lot of women in early fourteenth-century Brigstock was not enviable. All women shared certain public disabilities; excluded from politics, they were treated legally as second-rank constituents of their courts, disadvantaged economically as both landholders and workers, and less active socially than men. All women also experienced discontinuity in their public opportunities. Man's activities changed over the course of the male life-cycle, but these changes ran along a single continuum; adolescent males were "householders-in-training," most males in the prime of life were full householders, and males who reached old age were either retired householders or heads of small, truncated domestic groups. Women's public experiences, however, changed abruptly and discontinuously because the public passivity expected of wives matched poorly the independent actions of many daughters and widows. The public activities of women in Brigstock varied widely, but all women shared both disadvantage and discontinuity.[5]

Women in Brigstock doubtless did not seek public equality with their fathers, husbands, and brothers, and they might well have derived much satisfaction and power from private associations unreported in the extant records. There can be no doubt, however, that the sorts of activities recorded in the courts of manors like Brigstock were respected and valued in the very public society of the medieval countryside. Political authority and legal competency gave men control over the governance of their communities, just as their economic and social privileges enhanced their prestige and power. The public activities reported in court rolls comprise only one part of gender relations, but it was an exceedingly important part; only men enjoyed full access to the major political and social institution in their community. It is certainly possible that medieval countrywomen accrued prestige from their private activities as wives and mothers and also exercised power informally through influencing the public decisions and actions of men. Yet it is equally likely that the public subordination of women was not offset in private. Indeed, public activities (such as the exclusion of women from tithings) often reflected private realities (in this case, the assumption that all women were privately governed by male householders).[6] If women's status is broadly defined as "the differential power, prestige, rights, privileges and importance of women relative to men," the status of women in early fourteenth-century Brigstock was certainly very low.[7]

Women's status was not only low, but also relatively invariable. Although women from poorer households in Brigstock doubtless encountered many hardships and challenges unknown to more privileged women, the public activities of women of modest circumstances differed little from those of women related to wealthy and powerful villagers. The desperation of destitute and wandering women is a matter of speculation alone; such women so rarely merited notice by manorial clerks that their lives will forever elude historical studies. The public lives of more settled women, however, varied little according to the socioeconomic status of their households. Similarly, changes in the economy of Brigstock during the early decades of the fourteenth century slightly altered the public activities of women without generating any fundamental changes in their status. The public experiences of women in Brigstock were dramatically affected by household position—daughter, wife, widow—but little altered by economic circumstance.

Socioeconomic Rank and Women's Status

Because the most straightforward and accurate measure of socioeconomic status in Brigstock is officeholding, the inhabitants of Brigstock have been divided into upper and low ranks based on whether they (or men to whom they were related) ever held local office.[8] These divisions strongly affected the public activities of men, but much less surely altered women's public opportunities. A man of upper-rank status came regularly to court for a variety of purposes—to sell or buy land, to settle disputes with his neighbors, to serve as a juror or other officer, to pledge for his friends. A lower-rank man went to the Brigstock court much less frequently and for many fewer reasons; he never served as an officer, he seldom traded land, he rarely settled disputes through the court, and he only occasionally pledged for others. As illustrated in Table 7.1, an upper-rank man in Brigstock came to court, on the average, about three times as frequently as did a man of lower status. Similar patterns prevailed in both Iver and Houghton-cum-Wyton.

For women, however, social rank had less influence on their public activities. Women attended their manorial courts for reasons different from those of men; never serving as officers and seldom acting as pledges, women came to court most often to conclude specific business, to answer for brewing offenses, or to respond to criminal charges. Social rank only minimally altered the involvement of women in such public matters. In Brigstock, an upper-rank woman usually appeared in court on only three occasions more than a woman of lower rank, and in both Iver and Houghton-cum-Wyton, women of both ranks accumulated roughly equal numbers of court appearances (see Table 7.1). These figures reflect the involvement of women of both ranks in all the facets of female public life that are reported in court records. During the transitional years of adolescence, daughters of both upper-rank and lower-rank parents managed to acquire independent economic resources. Of the 4 Brigstock women whose premarital careers betrayed evidence of economic independence, 2 were daughters of officeholders and 2 had fathers

TABLE 7.1. The Court Appearances of Women and Men of Different Social Ranks in Brigstock, Iver, and Houghton-cum-Wyton

Category	Upper Rank			Lower Rank		
	Males	Females	Female/Male Ratio	Males	Females	Female/Male Ratio
Appearances						
Brigstock	20,292	4,981	25/100	4,006	2,002	50/100
Iver	4,131	430	10/100	2,694	677	25/100
Houghton-cum-Wyton	2,292	269	12/100	583	180	31/100
Average appearances per individual						
Brigstock	29.9	9.4		8.5	6.4	
Iver	14.9	3.3		6.3	3.8	
Houghton-cum-Wyton	8.1	1.9		3.6	1.9	

who never held office. Of the 31 adolescent daughters who acquired land in the transactions sampled, 16 were upper-rank, 12 were lower-rank, and 3 were of unknown status. After marriage, women of both ranks similarly worked to support their households through commercial brewing. Of the 38 ale-wives in Brigstock, 13 were married to officeholders, 22 had husbands who never acquired office, and 3 were of unknown status. When their husbands died, widows of both ranks also accepted the duties and responsibilities of householders. Of the 24 women who acted as pledges in the Brigstock court, 12 were upper rank, 10 were lower rank, and 2 were of unknown status. Social rank clearly shaped the public business of men, but scarcely affected at all the public activities of their daughters, wives, and mothers.

Nevertheless, lower-rank women in Brigstock, Iver, and Houghton-cum-Wyton were consistently better represented in their local courts, relative to the men in their rank, than were women of higher status. In Brigstock, for example, upper-rank women appeared in court on only 25 occasions for every 100 appearances recorded for upper-rank men, but lower-rank women claimed 50 court citations for every 100 appearances by males of their rank. Consider the activities of two Kroyl brothers and their wives—the lower-rank Robert Kroyl and his successful, upper-rank brother Henry junior. The network of court associations formed by Robert's wife Alice fell below that of Robert in terms of both number of people (7 versus 30) and frequency of contacts (7 versus 48). But Alice actually appeared in court more frequently than did Robert; her 65 citations (most associated with her work as a brewer) far exceeded the 41 court references to her husband. Although the court careers of Robert and Alice Kroyl were not equivalent, they were clearly more equitable than the careers of Henry junior and his wife Agnes. Henry junior's court network (322 contacts with 156 people) vastly exceeded that of his wife (31 contacts with 11 people), as did the number of times he appeared before the court (559 appearances versus only 29 for Agnes). Such patterns suggest that, for women of the lower stratum, the limitations imposed by their gender were seemingly mitigated by the limitations imposed by rank. In other words, the status of lower-rank women vis-à-vis lower-rank men was possibly enhanced by the public disabilities faced by men of low socioeconomic status. All women knew political, legal, economic, and social handicaps peculiar to their sex, but less privileged men also encountered barriers to their full participation in the public life of their villages; they held less land, they less frequently acted as pledges or otherwise participated in the sociopolitical networks of their communities, and they rarely served in any official capacities. Although lower-rank men still enjoyed privileges usually unavailable to women (preference in inheritance, membership in tithings, and status as householders), they were much less publicly active than men of higher social standing. Women of all ranks, in short, faced roughly equivalent restrictions on their public behavior, but these restrictions might have been less telling for lower-rank women whose husbands, fathers, and sons were unable to exploit fully the public options available to wealthy male householders.

The internal dynamics of household economy and demography probably also fostered more egalitarian sexual relations among the especially poor. Christopher Middleton has argued that wealthier peasants were able to confine women more exclusively in the home, creating, in effect, a "housewifely" role. Wives of substantial tenants certainly worked hard in the home and croft, but they less often ventured outside the domestic area to work in the fields, to labor for wages, or to perform required services for their lords. Poorer peasants could not afford the luxury of wives or daughters who did not work in the fields or labor for payment.[9] For these poorer women, however, the necessity of extra domestic work might have turned into an asset because their "social" labor was more highly valued than the "domestic" labor of more privileged women.[10] The demographic fragility of poorer households also possibly promoted greater sexual equality within the lower ranks of the peasantry. Marriages were more likely to be delayed or to be casual, temporary affairs; children might have been fewer and might have left home at younger ages; widowhood probably occurred earlier and more frequently. The harsh realities of poverty in the medieval countryside, in short, not only restricted the authority that poor householders could assert over their dependents, but also expanded women's opportunities for greater autonomy as adolescent daughters, spinsters, and widows.

Yet the effect of socioeconomic position on the status of women in Brigstock should not be overdrawn. The comparative advantage of lower-rank women illustrated in Table 7.1 was caused more by changes in male opportunities than by any fundamental differences in female experiences; women of all ranks faced roughly similar public disabilities and used their local courts with roughly similar frequency. Moreover, the slightly expanded opportunities of lower-rank women, founded in the privileges of upper-rank males and the fragility of domestic life among the poor, were born of oppression and deprivation. Because these women were disadvantaged by rank as well as gender, the limitations brought by either variable were seemingly eased. But the combined disadvantages were nonetheless both real and harsh; it is hard to imagine that a virgater's wife ever envied a cottar's widow or a poor spinster. Although the latter might have enjoyed a closer equality with men of her lower rank, she was also unprotected, poor, and powerless. Even if the relative symmetry of public presence demonstrated by males and females of lower rank translated into a domestic equality not paralleled in more privileged households, it was an equality of disadvantage and poverty.

Social rank in Brigstock, then, only minimally affected the gender rules of the community. Wives of virgaters, semi-virgaters, and cottars faced different daily chores and challenges, but they, as women, faced roughly equivalent public responsibilities and opportunities. Insofar as rank did affect their public activities, its influence was ambivalent and unwelcome. These patterns in Brigstock raise the possibility that rank only slightly shaped gender rules among all the strata—aristocratic, urban, and rural—of late medieval England. To be sure, social rank affected the daily lives of all medieval women. Raised in different types of communities, peasant women, townswomen, and feudal women lived in different dwellings, ate different foods, dressed differently, worked at different tasks, and even, in the century after the Conquest, spoke different languages. Yet these women, despite the dramatically distinct material conditions of their lives, shared roughly similar domestic circumstances. Expected to work in support of their marital households, women of all ranks faced fundamentally parallel opportunities and restrictions. As a result, differences of rank created little more than incidental variations in the social relation of the sexes in medieval England.

In terms of politics and law, similar customs governed the lives of medieval Englishwomen of all ranks. Countrywomen never served as reeves, townswomen never acted as mayors, and feudal women never went to parliament to advise their king. Politics—whether rural, urban, or royal—was the business of men and men only.[11] Because the customary law of the countryside and the mercantile law of the towns often emulated the common law of the realm, women of all ranks also shared equivalent legal disabilities. Widows and unmarried women could often plead cases alone—whether at manorial, urban, or royal courts—but wives were usually accompanied by their husbands. And inheritance laws similarly transcended distinctions of rank, usually preferring sons over daughters whether the property was acreage and pasture, townhouses and shops, or manors and fiefs. Proprietal laws at all levels of society also placed the assets of wives under the control of their husbands and designated some portion of conjugal estates to widows.[12]

Moreover, the daily tasks that occupied medieval Englishwomen retained a similarity across rank that contrasts sharply with the different occupations of their fathers and husbands. As bearers of children, women undertook whatever child-care and housekeeping tasks were required by their social status. Women also specialized in two commodities not dictated by their biological capabilities—foodstuffs and textiles. A knight could not plow and a plowman could not fight from horseback, but the wives of both knights and plowmen spun thread with equal ease. And although the business of obtaining and preparing food was very different in cottages, townhouses, and castles, women were invariably more active and more familiar with such duties than were their fathers and husbands. The relegation of food and textiles to women can perhaps be most clearly seen in its commercial uses; the hawking of prepared foods and used clothes were distinctively female specialties in medieval markets and towns.

The sexual division of labor in medieval England also largely transcended rank. Whether in villages, towns, or feudal courts, the major economic enterprise of a household was assigned to males and a myriad of other, supportive tasks to women. In Brigstock, women complemented the field work of men not only by undertaking many ancillary tasks but also by always being available to help in the fields at planting and harvest. Similar patterns characterized the work of urban and feudal women. Urban households centered around the trade or craft of the husband; a townswoman both supported her householder's work (as illustrated by the common exemption of wives and daughters from guild regulations prohibiting the employment of women) and supplemented that work through wage labor (particularly in service) or by-industries (especially in cooking, brewing, and textiles). A townsman's work was skilled and steady; except for the very poor, most men followed a single occupation throughout their lives. A townswoman, however, toiled intermittently at many low-skill tasks; no matter what the social status of her husband, an urban wife fulfilled a variety of subsidiary tasks and remained ever-ready to accommodate her work to that of her husband.[13]

The experiences of women of feudal rank were not much different. The military ethic of the feudal elite assured that the primary occupation of that rank was closed to women. But while men focused on the highly skilled business of war, women were busied by a variety of tasks that, although less skilled and less prestigious, were equally crucial to the welfare of their families. Responsible for the provisioning, staffing, and daily maintenance of their households, gentlewomen managed home farms, monitored estate and domestic servants, stockpiled food and drink, ordered needed repairs, and if wealthy enough to possess several homes, organized the moves that were such a common part of elite life. In addition, they worked hard at the politicking that was so important to elite fortunes; they constantly entertained, they sought audiences with influential lords and bishops, they pleaded cases for their absent husbands. Feudal women had many servants to assist them in their tasks, but they were not idle. They were, like peasant women and townswomen, their husbands' helpmeets.[14]

Medieval women of all ranks, then, spent their married lives busied with a multitude of tasks essential for their households, but secondary to the work of their husbands. They also remained ready to assist or even replace their husbands at any time; peasant women left their work in crofts and dairies to help at harvests, townswomen forsook prior occupations when they married in order to better support their husbands' work, and as illustrated by the defense of Caistor Castle by Margaret Paston, feudal women stood in for their husbands in even the most extreme of circumstances. A medieval wife, in short, was both her husband's assistant and his understudy. Her tasks varied somewhat according to rank, but her objectives remained the same.

These striking similarities in the gender rules that shaped the lives of medieval women of all social ranks do not mean, of course, that peasant, urban, and feudal women either recognized their shared experiences or cultivated notions of a common female culture or experience. Christine de Pisan argued in the fifteenth century that her rules of female conduct could "apply to every woman of whatever class she may be," but both her education and her feminism made her an unlikely representative of her sex.[15] These similarities also do not belie the profound differences that economic privilege created in the daily lives of medieval Englishwomen; a feudal woman could exercise an authority over her serfs—male as well as female—that eluded both townswomen and peasant women. But compared to the distinctions that economic rank created in the lives of men, differences of rank among women seem relatively incidental. For medieval Englishwomen, rules of gender cut across distinctions of rank.

In Brigstock before the plague, the rules that shaped the lives of all women and men were supported by the conjugal household and its ideal dichotomy of public men and private women. Even though that ideal was regularly contradicted by the activities of men who were not householders and women who were not wives, it nevertheless structured the social relation of the sexes in the community. Although much more research is needed on the household structures of the urban and landed elites, the experiences of townswomen and feudal women suggest that their lives were similarly shaped by conjugality. Two extraordinary townswomen—the fictional Wife of Bath and the very real Margery Kempe—illustrate how the lives of townswomen were as inextricably bound to their households as were the lives of countrywomen. The Wife of Bath was a clever and ambitious woman who "bettered those of Ypres and Ghent" in her clothworking skills, but she grew wealthy through marriage, not trade or craft.[16] The fortunes of Margery Kempe were just as closely, although less successfully, tied to the results of marriage. When her husband proved to be a less successful merchant than her father had been, the proud daughter of the one-time mayor of Lynn helplessly lost status in the eyes of her neighbors. Because she would not "be content wyth the goodys that God had sent hire, as hir husband was," she tried to earn money through the low-status trades open to women. When her businesses failed she took a bold and individualistic step. Unable to maintain high status through her husband, she sought it on her own through religion.[17] The Wife of Bath's success provided the occasion for misogynistic ribaldry, while Kempe's dilemma was born of her pride and circumstance, but their experiences nevertheless illustrate how profoundly domesticity shaped the lives of women in medieval towns.

Conjugality similarly limited the experiences of women among the landed elite. The letters exchanged between Margaret and John Paston leave no doubt that Margaret was a vigorous and competent woman. In addition to provisioning the Paston household, managing the Paston servants, and supervising the Paston children, Margaret also collected rents from the tenants of the Paston estate, lobbied for Paston causes before lords and bishops, and even fought off an attack on one of the Paston manors. But she was always first a dependent wife—deferring to her husband, downplaying her own contributions to the family fortunes, and focusing always on the collective interests of the Pastons.[18] Eleanor de Montfort played a similar role in the fortunes of her thirteenth-century family.[19] The activities of such women suggest that feudal women, like women in villages and towns, were expected to be supportive dependents of their husbands.

Distinctions of rank, to be sure, altered the experiences of women in late medieval England, but little changed the social relations of the sexes. Just as socioeconomic variations within the Brigstock community only minimally affected the public activities of women, so distinctions of rank among peasant, urban, and feudal women likely only changed incidentally the subordinate position characteristic of all women. Indeed, the Brigstock evidence suggests that the small differences found in the status of women of different ranks were rooted more in the expanding or contracting options of men than in any substantive changes in female experiences. In medieval England, social rank changed neither the fact nor the foundations of female subordination.

Economic Change and Women's Status

Economic change similarly affected the status of women in minimal and ambivalent ways. The early fourteenth century was a time of enormous crisis in the rural economy of England. As population levels outstripped productive resources, wage rates fell, food prices increased, and the rising demand for land forced the cultivation of marginal, unproductive fields. Successive years of bad weather added to the crisis by yielding poor harvests between 1315 and 1322, when probably 10 percent of the English population died of starvation or disease. Reflecting this general crisis in the English rural economy, the standard of living in Brigstock began to decline dramatically in the early fourteenth century. The public activities of women on the manor responded to these economic changes, but in ways that never substantially altered the social relation of the sexes.

In the six decades that preceded the plague, population in Brigstock stabilized, fell, and then grew slightly. Between 1287 and 1325, the number of men in the community was high, but stable; between 1326 and 1340, male population dropped to less than three-fourths of former levels; and between 1341 and 1348, Brigstock began to recover some of this loss (although it never again reached the high levels characteristic of earlier decades). The economy of Brigstock underwent similar changes. Field crimes associated with poverty and economic hardship increased dramatically in the first decades of the century and then remained at the new, higher level until the plague. Debt cases, reflecting the growing inability of villagers to repay outstanding loans, also increased in the early fourteenth century, stabilized, and then grew again in the decade that preceded the plague. Sales of land similarly grew in the face of economic pressures, doubling in the early fourteenth century, leveling off for a few years, and then growing again. Even court amercements suggest the growing poverty of Brigstock, with average sums paid by brewers falling steadily in the early decades of the century, recovering slightly in the 1330s, and then falling to new levels just before the mid-century mark. The uneven economic decline of Brigstock during these years matched the demographic fortunes of the community. When the economy began to falter seriously in the early fourteenth century, population was high, but stable; a slight economic recovery in the 1320s and 1330s was complemented by a sharp population decline; and renewed population growth accompanied renewed economic decline in the 1340s.[20]

During these decades of unsteady economic deterioration, women began to participate more actively in the public economy of Brigstock. Women's involvement in the local baking industry rose from only one-fifth of the amercements levied in the late thirteenth century to over four-fifths of amercements between 1341 and 1348. As shown in Table 7.2, this movement was fairly steady, with a minor setback during the 1330s that corresponds to the time of improving economic prospects in the community. Women so thoroughly dominated the other major industry in Brigstock during these decades—brewing—that no increase in female involvement was possible, but the growing importance of women in the brewing industries of both Iver and

TABLE 7.2. Women and Men in the Baking Industry
of Brigstock, 1287–1348

Period	Male Citations		Female Citations		All Citations	
	No.	Row Percent	No.	Row Percent	No.	Row Percent
1287–1300	27	79%	7	21%	34	100%
1301–1310	9	69	4	31	13	100
1311–1320	20	45	24	55	44	100
1321–1330	15	34	29	66	44	100
1331–1340	17	38	28	62	45	100
1341–1348	9	17	43	83	52	100

Note: This table excludes the one citation for baking made against a person of unknown sex. Percentages have been rounded to produce integral numbers.

Houghton-cum-Wyton suggests that more and more countrywomen
throughout England were profiting from food trades in the early
fourteenth century.[21] Women also became more active in the local
land market during the course of the early fourteenth century, and as
shown in Table 7.3, greater female involvement in land trading corresponded closely to the growth of the land market during these same
years. Constituting only 14 percent of those trading land in 1301–
1303, women accounted for 23 percent of land traders by 1343–
1345. Although the trends are more gradual than those traced in
baking amercements, female participation in the land market also
seems to have increased most dramatically in the first decades of the
fourteenth century, stabilized briefly thereafter, and resumed growth
in the 1340s.

Changing patterns of reported female criminality in Brigstock suggest that greater social activity matched the growing economic prominence of women in the early fourteenth century. Women accounted
for an increasing proportion of reported criminals, rising from 26
percent of those reported in 1301–1304 to 29 percent in 1318–1322
to 35 percent in 1340–1343. This increase was probably not caused
simply by any growing tendencies to report the crimes of women; if
Brigstock's tithingmen had grown more interested in presenting female offenders, they would have certainly continued to report the one
exclusively female crime, fornication, but after 1299, no woman in
Brigstock was amerced for improper sexual activity. The increase

TABLE 7.3.   Women and Men in the Brigstock Sample of Land
Transactions, 1301–1345

Period	Male Traders		Female Traders		All Traders		Average Number of Land Exchanges per Court
	No.	Row Percent	No.	Row Percent	No.	Row Percent	
1301–1303	73	86%	12	14%	85	100%	1.16
1314–1316	166	79	43	21	209	100	2.64
1331–1333	130	79	34	21	164	100	2.26
1343–1345	248	77	73	23	321	100	3.38

Note: Percentages have been rounded to produce integral numbers.

also was not caused by changes in the types of offenses reported at views of frankpledge; although crimes against specific persons were reported less frequently through these decades, the chronology of this decline does not match the growth in reported female criminals.[22] Instead of being caused by changes in presentments, the growth in reported female criminality probably reflects the increased public activity of women. The slight increase in reported female victims (from 38 percent of victims in 1301–1304 to 44 percent in 1340–1343) supports this conclusion. As women became more prominent in local life, they also became more liable to either criminal action or criminal victimization.

In addition, female criminals in Brigstock became less likely during the early fourteenth century to seek pledging assistance from relatives and instead increasingly received such aid from persons to whom they were presumably not related; whereas 10 of 11 female criminals pledged in 1301–1304 used kin (91 percent), only 37 of 92 female criminals were pledged by kin in 1340–1343 (40 percent). Data on pledging in the samples of land transactions and litigation are more equivocal, but the sample of crimes suggests that fewer and fewer women were relying on kin for assistance in meeting their legal obligations. Curiously, at the same time that female criminals were turning to kin less often, men began using pledges to whom they were related more frequently (familial pledging of male criminals rose from 11 percent in 1301–1304 to 26 percent in 1340–1343).[23]

Women were also more prominent as householders in Brigstock in the 1340s than earlier. They accounted for none of the householder crimes listed in the views for 1301–1304, but by 1318–1322 they constituted 21 percent of those guilty of crimes associated with householding, and in 1340–1343 that proportion had risen to 27 percent. The most telling evidence of the growing presence of women as householders in Brigstock, however, comes from data on female pledging. Before 1340, only 17 instances of female sureties were found in the Brigstock records, but 29 female pledges (mostly widows) were accepted by the court between 1341 and 1348 (see Table 6.3). This sudden increase in female pledging was not caused by changes in court procedure or by increased reporting of the sorts of petty crimes for which female pledges could be accepted. Nor was it precipitated by a growth in the number of households headed by widows during these last two decades. As shown in Table 7.4, the number of widows

TABLE 7.4.   The Chronology of Widowhood in Brigstock

Date of First Citation as Widow	Number of Widows	Percent of All Widows
1287–1299	13	12%
1300–1309	24	23
1310–1319	24	23
1320–1329	14	13
1330–1339	12	11
1340–1348	19	18
Total	106	100

Note: Percentages have been rounded to produce integral numbers.

cited in the courts (using the date of first citation as a widow) waxed and waned over these decades in a pattern unrelated to the sudden burst of female pledging in the 1340s. Instead of responding to new procedures, different patterns of criminality, or growing numbers of widows, the Brigstock court seems simply to have more readily accepted female householders as sureties in the 1340s than earlier.

Only one aspect of female public activity in Brigstock declined during the first half of the fourteenth century. Women appeared before the Brigstock court as litigants more often in the early years of the century than later (see Table 7.5). Moreover, wives, who frequently pursued cases alone in the early decades of the fourteenth century, always acted jointly in litigation with their husbands in the samples from the 1330s and 1340s. A growing business in debt cases

TABLE 7.5.   Women in the Brigstock Sample of Civil Pleas, 1301–1345

Period	Female Suitors		Percentage of Cases Involving Pleas of Debt	Wives as Litigants	
	Number	Percent of All Suitors		Acted Alone	Acted Jointly
1301–1303	36	33%	6%	5	7
1314–1316	16	15	10	4	5
1331–1333	23	20	8	0	10
1343–1345	11	10	44	0	4

Note: Percentages have been rounded to produce integral numbers.

partly contributed to these trends; since women were seldom party to suits of debt, their litigation occupied a smaller proportion of the court's agenda as debt cases played a more prominent role. But the decline in female litigation more closely matched—in an inverse relationship—economic trends in Brigstock than changes in debt litigation. Whatever its causes, the declining involvement of women in litigation provides a puzzling contrast to the increased activity of women as bakers, pledges, land traders, criminals and victims, and householders.

As is so often the case in the history of women, some of these changes in female public activity might have been more illusory than real. It is certainly possible, for example, that a growing male interest in the commercial opportunities of regional markets lay behind the growth in women's brewing and baking at the local level; as men looked toward more profitable trade, women took over the sectors they abandoned. Similarly, women might have become acceptable pledges precisely because pledging was becoming less important to men. In the early decades of the fourteenth century, the power of royal government in rural life grew steadily; local men fought in the king's wars, worked with the king's tax collectors, and served on the king's juries. As the political horizons of men expanded, local political activities (like pledging) might have waned in importance. Widows might, in other words, have become more active as pledges in Brigstock at the very time that such associations were losing importance for men. In short, women might have been moving into areas of activity no longer valued by men, rather than actually acquiring prestigious opportunities.

Moreover, these changes represented only variations in the enduring pattern of female subordination in Brigstock. Women were more active in many aspects of the local economy and society in the 1340s than in earlier decades, but these new activities never conferred upon them the basic public privileges of males. The lines that distinguished male and female public life remained intact. Thus the growing public presence of women during these decades never substantially altered the social relation of the sexes.

Ever since Joan Kelly questioned the idea of a Renaissance for women, feminist historians have critically examined the assumption that "good times" for men were also "good times" for women.[24] In Brigstock, the experiences of women inversely matched the economic circumstances of their community; the numbers of women appearing as bakers, land traders, and widows grew during the economic decline of the early fourteenth century, fell during the economic stabilization of the late 1320s and 1330s, and grew again in the wake of renewed economic crisis just before the plague. This correlation between economic crisis and expanding female action in Brigstock moves counter to the modern commonplace that women (and minorities) fare best in times of economic growth and quickly lose ground when the economy falters. Why should the experiences of medieval countrywomen have been different? The answer lies in the importance of the household in shaping the personal circumstances of working women in communities like Brigstock. A peasant woman was seldom an independent worker, but instead worked within the constraints of her natal or marital household. In good times, householders could afford to remove their daughters and wives from public activity, but bad times brought women into public life—as they sought to bring extra cash into their households and as they took over the public functions of fathers and husbands dead from famine or disease. The public activities of women expanded in bleak economic times because of hard necessity, not happy opportunity. Just as it is likely that few virgaters' wives envied women of lower rank, so it is likely that few women in the late thirteenth century would have envied their publicly more active descendants who lived in the troubled decades before the plague. Accompanied by dearth, hardship, and death, the public activities of women expanded only at great cost.[25]

Because economic changes affected women as members of households, daughters and widows probably benefited more than wives from the new opportunities of the early fourteenth century. Daughters were no longer liable for sexual amercements, widows were increasingly allowed to pledge for their children, and both contributed to the growing numbers of women cited for householder crimes. Indeed, the famine and hardship of these years meant that more women lived outside of the authority of male householders, as the premature deaths of fathers and husbands left women not only bereaved but also more independent. The chronology of widowhood in Brigstock shows how more widows appeared before the court when the economy worsened and fewer appeared in years of economic improvement. More widows appeared during the bleak first decades of the fourteenth century, fewer in the brief period of economic stabilization in the 1320s and 1330s, and more again the decade of decline before the plague (see Table 7.4). In contrast to the expanding numbers and opportunities of independent women, the experiences of wives changed only minimally. A few married women profited from new opportunities in the baking industry, but the experience of ale-wives suggests that women exercised little control over such work and gained little public benefit from it. Wives also clearly lost ground in the one area of declining activity for women—civil litigation. These trends suggest that the expanding public presence of women in the early fourteenth century reflected the new activities of daughters and widows, not wives. The most anomalous and least protected women in Brigstock were participating more actively in the public life of the manor.

In early fourteenth-century Brigstock, then, the expansion in women's public activities was so limited and so ambivalent that it never substantially changed the status of women. The social relation of the sexes remained fundamentally unchanged. With implications that extend far beyond the experiences of women on one English manor before the plague, this pattern calls into question the economic history of medieval Englishwomen in its most crucial transition, the decades after the plague. Assuming that women's status contracted in times of economic hardship and improved in times of economic expansion, English historians have argued that the status of women rose in the decades that followed the first devastation of the Black Death in 1348–1349. Freed by the plague from the constraints of overpopulation, the late fourteenth-century economy was buoyant and expansive—commonly called a "golden age" for both rural and urban workers. In the context of this economic growth (which slowed and then reversed in the fifteenth century), the status of women, it is argued, improved dramatically—as shown in the narrowing of wage gaps, the growth of female emigration to towns, and the passage of legislation that permitted women to practice many crafts while restricting men to only one.[26]

But this evidence can be read in other ways. Only a minority of women, after all, worked for wages, and they were among the least envied members of rural (and urban) society. Women's wages also, although comparatively improved in the late fourteenth century, seldom matched the wages of men. Female emigration to towns was possibly caused as much by lack of opportunity in rural areas ("push") as by attractive urban opportunities ("pull"). And the labor legislation of the late fourteenth century could suggest that males were specializing in trades and crafts while women continued to work in many low-skill, low-status jobs. More important, the experiences of women in pre-plague Brigstock suggest that the model linking economic growth with improved female status inverts the actual experiences of women. Evidence from a single manor before the plague cannot rewrite the economic history of women in late medieval England, but it does indicate a need for continued research and possible revision.

The history of women in the medieval English countryside is a story of ambivalencies and contradictions. The conjugal household both limited women's options (by creating the gender norms of publicly active males and publicly inactive females) and freed women (by creating many circumstances in which those norms could not be sustained). Economic hardship—experienced because of either social rank or general economic crisis—brought into women's lives not only new responsibilities and opportunities but also dearth and death. Insofar as these women had choices about their lives, the choices were always poor ones. Marriage brought private security, but public subordination, and life as a spinster or widow brought public independence, but vulnerability. Times of economic hardship brought grief, but expanded activities, and prosperous times brought an easier, but more restricted life. Tied to either increased personal vulnerability, lower social rank, or times of economic stress, increased public activity for women was always a mixed blessing. Such ambivalence probably helped to assure that most women would be content with very limited public roles.

The experiences of women in Brigstock also demonstrate how enduring the subordination of women to men has been in the history of England. In the centuries that followed the plague, the capitalization and commercialization of the English rural economy might have further devalued women's work, and the growth in the powers of royal government might have further isolated women within the private household.[27] But such changes do not necessarily suggest a prior golden age in the medieval countryside. While the development of a commercial economy and a centralized state in the fifteenth through seventeenth centuries might have adversely affected the status of women, neither capitalism nor state formation was a necessary cause of women's second-rank status in English society. The subordination of women in Brigstock was rooted in neither government nor economy, but rather in the household.

APPENDIX

A Note on Method

The entries found in the records of manorial courts are fairly straight-forward, but their use by social historians has become both complex and controversial. When scholars first turned to these archives for social in-formation, they used manorial courts as the historian's equivalent of the anthropologist's field notes. Searching these records for unusually de-tailed or complicated cases, they recreated medieval rural society through illustration and example.[1] This approach, while profitable and lively, has proven to be too impressionistic and too prone to mistake the atypical for the norm. As a result, it is now usually supplemented by the tech-niques of historical aggregation and reconstruction. In addition to search-ing manorial courts for particularly revealing cases, students of the medieval countryside now also systematically use these records to recon-struct the lives of individuals, their families, and their communities.

No consensus, however, has yet been reached on even the most basic aspects of social reconstruction from manorial records. The primary controversy centers on the stability and reliability of surnames. Early forays into the use of manorial records for social history were justifiably criticized for too freely associating surnames and families, as well as for relying on surnames that were too fluid or too unspecific to warrant precise identification. Dissension also extends to such other issues as the tracing of demographic changes and the delineation of socioeconomic groupings.[2] Reflecting lessons learned from these controversies, the tech-niques used to study the experiences of women in Brigstock also introduce new methods designed specifically to study gender relations. These innovations might themselves provoke further comment and criticism. Such discussions are essential to developing a firm historical methodology for studying rural society from manorial records, but the objective of these disagreements must be final agreement. Although manorial recordkeeping varied widely in ways that reflect seigneurial needs, administrative structures, and local circumstances, the social information found in the manorial archives of England can nevertheless be comparatively analyzed if subjected to generally accepted techniques of historical reconstruction. To date, attempts to generalize about the experiences of the medieval peasantry have been hindered by the particular interests and methods of each investigator; J. Ambrose Raftis, Edwin DeWindt, Edward Britton, Richard Smith, and Zvi Razi have each used different sources in different ways to answer different questions.[3] The idiosyncrasies of manorial records ensure that medievalists will never employ such highly systematized techniques as those used by the Cambridge Group for the History of Population and Social Structure to analyze the parish registers of early modern England, but agreement on basic issues of method and analysis is within reach.[4]

Reconstructing the Families of Brigstock, Iver, and Houghton-cum-Wyton

The initial stages of historical reconstruction from manorial records are the least controversial parts of the process. Once the extant archives of Brigstock, Iver, and Houghton-cum-Wyton were chosen for analysis, all named citations from their records were noted on cards that include full recapitulations of the original entries (identification of source, type of action and its resolution, names of other participants).[5] Each named citation was recorded on a separate slip of paper to facilitate later reshuffling and reevaluations of the person(s) actually identified by that name. Although this process consumed such enormous time and produced such immense files that computer-assisted analysis seemed attractive, these initial stages were done by hand because early analyses were too complex and idiosyncratic to be amenable to standardized programming. Since the separating of individuals from names and families from surnames often presented unique problems and required unique solutions, neither step was well-suited to computerized analysis.[6]

Once the cards were sorted alphabetically, the preliminary identification of individuals began. Two problems complicated the linkage of names to individuals. First, certain persons were identified at different times by different surnames; the recorded court actions of John Kroyl and John Wolf in Brigstock, for example, were the activities of only one person. Fortunately, clerks sometimes merged multiple surnames, as in the reference in the Brigstock court of May 1338 to property acquired by John Wolf Kroyl. Manorial records also provide such detailed information that many cases of multiple surnames became clear from individual patterns of activity; between 1332 and 1348, one of the aletasters for Brigstock proper was identified variously as John Kroyl, John Wolf and occasionally, Wolf Kroyl.[7] The second problem is an inversion of the first problem, arising from the possible identification of several individuals by the same name. Because the pool of forenames used by medieval villagers was exceedingly small, certain persons inevitably shared common forenames and surnames. But this problem was often solved directly by manorial clerks who used additional modifiers to differentiate persons carrying the same name contemporaneously. Fathers and their namesake sons were usually clearly separated (Henry Kroyl senior versus Henry Kroyl junior), and other persons were distinguished by geographical locators (William Norgent de Thorney or William Norgent de Sutton) or by occupational titles (Richard Aylward le Miller or Richard Aylward le Reeve).

Despite the fluidity of naming practices in the early fourteenth century, the challenges of linking names to individuals are not insurmountable because all administrative bodies—the monarchy, the manor, and the village—needed to ensure that their records firmly identified and differentiated all persons. The compilers of records like the lay subsidy rolls would have been wasting their time had the individuals they were assessing been able to evade later payment by claiming misattribution. The entire system of manorial recordkeeping was similarly predicated on the precise identification of tenants; how were lands to be administered and rents to be collected if several villagers shared an indistinguishable name? One might imagine that peasants cultivated confusion in order to limit royal and seigneurial interference in their lives, but villagers themselves also had a vested interest in assuring the reliability of name citations. Since persons involved in disputes or controversies often requested that the rolls of prior courts be searched to verify their claims, the validity of land transactions, concords, maintenance contracts, and all other contractual agreements between villagers would have been seriously undermined if one person was identified by several names or if one name applied to several persons. It was this concern that motivated the men of the town of Godmanchester to include in their custumal of 1324 the requirement: "That every one pleading in pleas shall answer and be called by that name and surname by which he is most commonly called without taking exception."[8]

Because it is impossible to identify precisely all cases in which one person used several names or several persons used one name, no reassuring statistics can be cited about the frequency with which these two problems of name linkage occurred in the preliminary analyses of Brigstock, Iver, and Houghton-cum-Wyton. But the breadth and depth of the information provided in manorial court rolls greatly aided the identification of individuals. Name changes and name differentiations are particularly problematic for scholars working with censuses or parish registers. The abbreviated entries of such records, coupled with the passage of many years between references to a given name, make precise linkages between individuals and names particularly risky. In contrast, manorial rolls can provide literally hundreds of citations to a single villager who regularly attended the court of his or her manor every three weeks for decades. With such abundant and consecutive data, peculiarities that complicate name identification are easily traced by considering not only names themselves, but also activity patterns. In the final analysis, however, we must admit our dependence on the written records. If the Brigstock records had never betrayed the identity of John Wolf with John Kroyl, these two names would have been treated as two separate individuals. Even the linkage of all citations mentioning John Kroyl to one individual, however, provides some picture of his life. Without the linkage with John Wolf, the picture would have been incomplete, but nevertheless both accurate and worthwhile.

The next analytical stage—the linkage of individuals into family groups—has generated the most controversy among medievalists using manorial court rolls to study rural society. Early researchers optimistically assumed that persons identified by the same surname were ipso facto related to one another. They also employed surnames that were clearly imprecise in designation—especially those based on occupations (John le Miller), offices (Henry le Reeve), geographic locations (Richard atte Well), and personal names (John son of Hawisa). It is certainly true, as some have argued, that surnames do not automatically constitute families, but it is also true that surnames are generally reliable guides to familial groupings. Only rarely did two closely related individuals (two siblings, a parent and child, a husband and wife) not use a common surname. The only regular exceptions were married women who, because they usually adopted their husbands' surnames, were identified by surnames different from those used by their parents and siblings. This is, of course, a familiar practice. But, although related persons did usually share a common surname, shared surnames could be used by nonrelated individuals. Consider a case found in the fourteenth-century records of Iver. When Thomas Coupere died in the 1349 plague, his properties in Iver were inherited by Robert Coupere who was, according to the entry of that year, related to the deceased (*consanguineous*). Over a decade later, however, a panel of jurors in Iver declared that Robert Coupere held these lands unjustly because he was not, in fact, related to Thomas Coupere (*non est de sanguine suo*).[9] Robert Coupere's experiences exemplify the researcher's problem; a shared surname did not guarantee a familial relationship, but even contemporaries were inclined to assume that a common surname did, in fact, indicate a familial tie.

Relying solely on explicit statements of kinship was determined to be a poor solution to the problems posed by surname unreliability for three reasons. First, it immediately skewed all analyses toward the wealthiest and most privileged sectors of Brigstock, Iver, and Houghton-cum-Wyton. Because genealogical statements were usually incidental to court business, each surviving reference to an individual increased the chances that the manorial clerk might have specified his or her familial relationship to another villager. As a result, the better representation of wealthy villagers in court rolls significantly enhanced efforts to reconstitute their families.[10] Second, relationships beyond the nuclear family unit were exceedingly difficult to trace—even for the most completely reconstructed families. Almost all statements of kinship in manorial rolls were phrased in terms of close family ties (spouses, children, siblings); more distant relationships can only be reconstructed when sufficient parental, sibling, and marital linkages were specified in the courts. Often only the wife and children of one male in each generation were traced through specified links, and cousins and affines were extraordinarily difficult to trace.[11] Third, reconstruction of families from explicit statements was seldom thoroughly successful. Most families included a few daughters whose marriages could not be traced, a few wives whose families or origin were unknown, and a few individuals identified by the common surname of the family who nevertheless lacked explicit genealogical information.

In short, neither wholesale identification of surnames with families nor total reliance on specified kinship satisfactorily solved the problem of linking individuals into familial groups. To resolve this dilemma, the individuals identified in Brigstock, Iver, and Houghton-cum-Wyton were separated into three analytical groups. In the first group (*isolated appearances*) fell those whose familial ties could not be estimated. Some persons were identified by incomplete or damaged citations. Others used surnames attributed only to them. Still others were identified by imprecise surnames; if no stated relationships survived linking the holders of such unstable surnames to one another, they were treated as isolated individuals.[12] As a rule, the proportion of isolated appearances found in the records of these manors related inversely to the size of the extant collection; the fewer the records, the more unlinked individuals. But even quite small archives, such as that extant for Houghton-cum-Wyton, yielded less than one-fifth of all citations in this category (see Table A.1).

TABLE A.1. Isolated Appearances in Brigstock, Iver,
and Houghton-cum-Wyton

Category	Brigstock	Iver	Houghton-cum-Wyton
Isolated appearances	2,227	1,465	738
Appearances linked to surnames	31,281	7,932	3,324
Total appearances	33,508	9,397	4,062

The second category (*surname groups*) includes surnames that were too unstable to be treated as familial groups, but were nevertheless sufficiently stable for inclusion in aggregative analyses. Some surnames in this group were imprecisely based on common occupations and the like, yet they included persons for whom the manorial clerks had specifically noted relationships with one another. For example, the ad Fontem surname in Brigstock seemed unreliable because of its topographic basis, its Latin form, and its use of a preposition. But the Brigstock clerks specified relationships between several persons using this surname—Henry ad Fontem, his wife Alice, daughter Emma, and son John; the two sons of Gilbert ad Fontem, Walter and Richard; Roger ad Fontem and his unnamed widow. Links between these kin groups, however, could not be traced, and one individual (Cristina ad Fontem) was never explicitly linked to any of the others. Other surnames included in the category of *surname groups* had opposite characteristics from those typified by the ad Fontem case; they were linguistically stable, but lacked any specified linkages between individuals. The Brigstock surname Hardy, for example, betrayed no evidence of imprecision, but no relationship was ever noted by the clerks between the two men who used this surname, Robert and Galfridus. Both types of surnames—unstable with some specified linkages, and stable without specified linkages—were judged to provide fair but not excellent indications of familial relationship.

All surnames that betrayed a strong familial basis were included in the third group (*presumptive families*). A few unstable surnames were placed in this category because all relationships between persons using this surname were known from explicit statements made by manorial clerks. The Brigstock surname of de Felde did not meet the criteria for surname precision, but only two persons, Hugh de Felde and his wife Isabella, used the surname in the late thirteenth and early fourteenth centuries. Most of the surnames designated *presumptive families*, however, were linguistically precise and included at least some individuals whose kin relationships were stated in the court records. The Kroyl surname

TABLE A.2. The Distribution of Surnames in Brigstock, Iver,
and Houghton-cum-Wyton

Category	Brigstock	Iver	Houghton-cum-Wyton
Surname groups	101	113	78
Presumptive families	176	80	50
All reliable surnames	277	193	128

in Brigstock for which all linkages are known, save for the relationship of a Matthew Kroyl active between 1287 and 1292, is a good example. As shown in Table A.2, proportions of *surname groups* and *presumptive families* varied according to the size of extant collections (with larger archives yielding more *presumptive families*).

This careful evaluation of the surnames used in Brigstock, Iver, and Houghton-cum-Wyton before the plague represents a compromise between the overestimation of kinship caused by equating it with surnames and the undervaluing of kinship caused by relying solely on specified linkages. The use of reliable surnames—classified as either *surname groups* or *presumptive families*—offers, in a sense, a middle position between two extreme alternatives. On the one hand, with each surname carefully evaluated and every linkage carefully analyzed, these surnames provide fairly reliable guides to familial relationships. Some unrelated persons doubtless used the same apparently reliable surname, and others who were related doubtless used different surnames, but most of the persons who shared reliable surnames were certainly related to one another. On the other hand, this method is as inclusive as possible because it excludes neither underrepresented socioeconomic groups nor extended, but usually unspecified, kinship ties. But no system of reconstructing families from manorial records can be foolproof. Little interested in kinship and genealogies, manorial administrators supplied such incomplete and tentative familial information that no historical methodology can produce both definitive and thorough family trees from their records. As a result, the quantified results reported in this study have been simply stated, with percentages rounded whenever possible and no statistical tests applied. It seemed deceptive to apply a veneer of precision to figures that are necessarily more suggestive than definitive. By taking account of the strengths and weaknesses of manorial sources, however, the methods outlined above allow a reasonable estimation of kinship patterns in the medieval English countryside.[13]

Brigstock Before the Plague

Population and Economy

Court rolls contain a wealth of social information, but they are frustratingly silent about the basic perimeters of human life. Many of the problems of linking names to individuals, for example, redound less upon the reconstruction of personal histories than upon demographic calculations; treating John Kroyl and John Wolf as two separate people would have artificially inflated the count of adult males in early fourteenth-century Brigstock. The demographic value of manorial court rolls is also limited by their failure to provide full information on births, marriages, and deaths. Births were never noted in manorial rolls. Marriages were often recorded because unfree women were obliged to pay fines for marriage licenses. But many women were not subject to such fines, and the specification of the bride's intended husband, which was usually irrelevant to the payment, was left to the clerk's discretion. As a result, only some marriages were noted, and most lack the names of both spouses. The situation is not much better for tracing deaths. Clerks usually noted the deaths of tenants in the course of supervising the inheritance of their lands, but deaths of nontenants—wives, children, subleasees, laborers—did not merit legal notice. As a result, basic demographic trends on manors like Brigstock are notoriously difficult to trace.

Despite the severe demographic limitations of manorial court rolls, tabulating the number of adult males cited in the courts of Brigstock provides a rough estimate of population levels. Since men attended court more regularly than women and children, they were the most reliably represented segment of the rural population. As a result, changes in the total population of Brigstock can be broadly reconstructed by tracing shifts in the numbers of adult males who appeared before the court in different periods. Raw counts of males, however, must be adjusted to account for different numbers of extant courts surviving for each period. This adjustment was obtained by using the period most amply documented (1336–1340 with 78 courts) as the base period. Since 4.5 new individuals were recorded for each court session in 1336–1340, the adjusted figures for each period in Table 1.1 represent the addition of 4.5 persons for each court in that period not surviving up to the base of 78 courts.[14] Estimates of population trends from manorial rolls are necessarily tentative and general, but they suggest that Brigstock's population before the plague stabilized (c. 1287–1325), declined sharply (c. 1326–1340), and finally grew slightly (c. 1341–1348).

Reconstructing economic trends from manorial court rolls is almost as difficult as tracing demographic patterns, but several measures suggest that the local economy of Brigstock reacted strongly to the changing population levels of the community before the plague. Field crimes associated with poverty took up a growing proportion of the court agenda in Brigstock in the early decades of the fourteenth century. In the views held in 1301–1304, field crimes accounted for only 9 percent of the offenses noted, but less than two decades later (1318–1322), 20 percent of all cited offenders were guilty of gleaning badly, taking sheaves improperly, or pilfering hay. In the last views sampled (1340–1343), the proportional importance of field crimes remained fairly steady at 19 percent of all reported offenses. These figures imply that the economy of Brigstock might have worsened dramatically in the first decades of the fourteenth century, forcing more and more inhabitants of the manor to resort to petty agrarian offenses in order to survive.

The Brigstock land market also reflected the economic pressures of the early fourteenth century, growing, declining, and growing again in the decades before the plague. In the sample for 1301–1303, an average of only 1.2 land conveyances were recorded in each meeting of the court, but by 1314–1316 the frequency of such transfers had more than doubled to an average of 2.6 transactions per court. Land conveyances fell slightly in 1331–1333 with an average of 2.3 transfers in each court, and finally peaked in the last sample before the plague (1343–1345) at an average of 3.4 transfers in every session. Laconic records of land transfers betray no information about the motivations of buyers and sellers, but it is reasonable to suppose that most peasant landholders preferred to retain, not sell, their properties. If this was the case in early fourteenth-century Brigstock, the burgeoning land market in 1314–1316 and 1343–1345 implies that worsening economic circumstances were forcing many landholders to relinquish their properties.[15]

The varying incidence of debt in Brigstock complements the evidence of field crimes and land transactions. In the sample of civil pleas, debt cases accounted for only 6 percent of pleas in 1301–1303 and then rose to 10 percent of cases sampled in 1314–1316, suggesting that these latter years were a time of economic difficulty in Brigstock. The proportion of debt cases then fell slightly to 8 percent in 1331–1333, but finally jumped dramatically to 44 percent of the sampled cases in 1343–1345. Correlating strongly with the growing land market in the community, this sharp jump in debt litigation suggests that the years just before the plague were especially difficult for many households in Brigstock.

Changes in the incidence of field crimes, land transfers, and debt cases, then, suggest that the economy of Brigstock seriously faltered in the early decades of the fourteenth century, brightened slightly in the 1330s, and worsened again in the 1340s. These trends might be more precisely dated

TABLE A.3.   Brewing Amercements in Brigstock, 1287–1348

Period	Number of Amercements	Average Amercement (pence)	Standard Amercement (pence)	Number of Standard Amercements Paid
1287–1290	10	6.0	6	10
1291–1295	14	3.9	6	6
1296–1300	34	6.7	6	18
1301–1305	42	4.5	3	17
1306–1310	56	4.4	3	31
1311–1315	373	3.5	3	243
1316–1320	351	2.6	2	167
1321–1325	188	2.1	2	165
1326–1330	246	2.2	2	223
1331–1335	350	2.6	3	181
1336–1340	556	2.8	3	286
1341–1345	710	2.5	2	388
1346–1348	80	1.3	1	60

by a fourth measure—the level of amercements levied for infractions against brewing regulations. Although ale amercements varied slightly in most years, they were fairly standardized; between 1326 and 1330, for example, 223 of 246 ale amercements were assessed at 2 pence. But, as shown in Table A.3, the most commonly assessed amount (or standard amercement) varied considerably in the decades before the plague, falling from 6 pence in the late thirteenth century to only 2 pence in the 1320s, rising to 3 pence in the 1330s, and falling to only 1 pence in the late 1340s.

Two factors could explain these changing levels of ale amercements. On the one hand, lower amercements might reflect growing numbers of offenders. As suggested by the legal historian John Beckerman, manorial administrators might have lowered amercements in order to obtain as many convictions as possible for petty offenses.[16] The trends shown in Table A.3 do not support this theory. In 1321–1325, for example, officers collected only about one-half of the amercements they had collected in 1316–1320, but the standard amercement remained steady at 2 pence and the average amercement payment actually fell. Indeed, the number of amercements assessed in 1311–1315 far exceeded those levied in any of the four subsequent quinquennial periods, but levels of amercements fell rather than rose after 1311–1315. On the other hand, court assessors might have determined amercement amounts according to the ability of offenders to meet their legal obligations.[17] If this was the case in early fourteenth-century Brigstock, changing amercement levels would reflect changing economic circumstances, with worsening conditions until the late 1320s, slight improvement for two decades, and renewed decline at the end of the 1340s.

Estimates of both population and economy in Brigstock before the plague are necessarily tentative, but they do suggest that Brigstock, like many other contemporary communities, was haunted by the classic Malthusian imbalance between population and resources. The stabilized population of the late thirteenth century probably represented the maximum number of inhabitants that Brigstock's economy could accommodate. In the first decades of the fourteenth century, the growing strain between people and resources led to a declining standard of living, as reflected not only in increased numbers of field crimes, debt cases, and land sales but also in falling levels of ale assessments. Once population reacted to the bleak economic situation by beginning to fall in the mid-1320s, the local economy quickly revived. But this revival was short-lived, as renewed population growth in the decade just prior to the plague was accompanied by new economic difficulties. It seems likely that external pressures only aggravated this indigenous imbalance in Brigstock between people and resources. Brigstock's economy was probably already in trouble before 1315, but the famines and diseases that swept through the English countryside between 1315 and 1322 only added to the difficulties of the community.[18] Aside from payments in the lay subsidies, little is directly known about how the growing demands of the Crown for men, money, and provisions affected the inhabitants of pre-plague Brigstock, but certainly such new impositions only compounded the economic problems of these years.[19]

Geographical Mobility

Movement in and out of medieval manors was as difficult for lords to regulate as it is for historians to reconstruct. Some lords levied fines (chevage) for the privilege of living away from their manors, but these fines were difficult to collect and many peasants absconded without any seigneurial notice. In Brigstock, no such fines were ever assessed. Nevertheless, some measure of the mobility of Brigstock's inhabitants has been obtained by tracing patterns in the disappearance and appearance of the 277 reliable surnames identified in the manorial rolls. Surname instability, of course, arose from a variety of factors. Surnames disappeared through not only emigration but also extinction of a family line or inheritance by daughters only. The occurrence of a new surname probably indicated immigration into the community or the creation of a new surname to account for multiple branches of a large resident family. Although surnames per se cannot reveal demographic trends, their general patterns of stability can be used in two ways to outline broadly the social composition of Brigstock.

First, each of the 277 surnames in the community was assigned to a duration group based on the dates of the surname's first and last appearances in the records of the court. This categorization revealed enormous mobility in Brigstock, with less than one-third of the surnames enduring throughout the six decades prior to the plague. The categories and their distribution are as follows:

Duration Group I (*89 surnames: 32 percent*).   These surnames appeared from the 1290s through the 1340s.

Duration Group II (*57 surnames: 21 percent*).   These surnames appeared in the 1290s, but disappeared before the 1340s.

Duration Group III (*90 surnames: 32 percent*).   These surnames appeared after the 1290s and continued to appear through the 1340s.

Duration Group IV (*41 surnames: 15 percent*).   These surnames appeared after the 1290s, but disappeared before the 1340s.

Second, trends in mobility over the period were estimated by tabulating the appearance and disappearance of surnames in quinquennial blocks. To obtain accurate estimates of appearances and disappearances, periods prior to 1300 and after 1340 were excluded; new arrivals could not be measured for the first years of extant courts (1287–1300), just as exits could not be estimated for the last years. For comparative purposes, Table A.4 includes the adjusted count of resident males.

These two estimates suggest that geographical mobility was a constant, but gradual feature of Brigstock life. Although only a third of Brigstock's surnames were cited throughout the late thirteenth and early fourteenth centuries, surname instability was spread evenly through these decades. At least four out of every five surnames remained stable during every quinquennial period between 1301 and 1340. The best period for surname stability, 1321–1325, witnessed Brigstock's population peak before the slight fall of the late 1320s and 1330s. Although new surnames had outnumbered lost surnames prior to the 1320s, the balance shifted thereafter. Nevertheless, the proportion of stable surnames in the community remained fairly constant throughout the first half of the fourteenth century, with only gradual introduction and loss of surnames. Because the fluidity of Brigstock's composition developed slowly over the decades, the community was able to absorb in small stages the social impact of its continuous immigration and emigration.

TABLE A.4. Surname Stability in Brigstock, 1301–1340

Period	Stable Surnames		Appearing Surnames		Disappearing Surnames		Adult Male Residents (adjusted count)
	No.	Row Percent	No.	Row Percent	No.	Row Percent	
1287–1300	135	—	—	—	11	—	—
1301–1305	132	84%	21	13%	4	3%	430
1306–1310	147	89	13	8	5	3	489
1311–1315	155	84	20	11	10	5	495
1316–1320	161	84	20	10	12	6	467
1321–1325	168	92	5	3	10	5	490
1326–1330	162	89	10	5	11	6	459
1331–1335	164	88	12	7	10	5	412
1336–1340	151	81	10	5	25	14	355
1341–1348	160	—	20	—	—	—	—

Note: Percentages have been rounded to produce integral numbers.

211

Commercial Brewing

As in the courts of many medieval manors, ale presentments were a regular feature of the sessions of the Brigstock court which took place every three weeks. Providing an extraordinarily rich source for studying industry and commerce, 3,844 ale citations survive from pre-plague Brigstock. A rough approximation of the dispersion of brewing activity was obtained by categorizing reliable surnames according to the number of ale amercements received. Over half of Brigstock's 277 surnames were never cited for brewing, while the remainder fell into two equal groups— those mildly involved and those intensely involved in the business. The categories and their distribution are as follows:

Assize Group X (67 surnames: 24 percent). Ten or more brewing citations were received by persons identified by these surnames.

Assize Group Y (67 surnames: 24 percent). Less than ten brewing citations were received by persons identified by these surnames.

Assize Group Z (143 surnames: 52 percent). No brewing citations were received by persons identified by these surnames.

Individual participation in commercial brewing was widely dispersed in Brigstock, but three features distinguish the personnel involved in this industry. First, almost all brewers were female. Only 20 men received a total of 47 ale citations (accounting for only 1.2 percent of all ale presentments). Second, brewing was a common female occupation. Of the 843 women identified in the reliable surnames of the community, 309 were cited for brewing (37 percent), and the 3,797 brewing presentments against women account for 51 percent of all female appearances before the court (7,449 total female citations). Third, Table A.5 shows that female brewing was roughly divided between a few dozen major brewers and several hundred women who only intermittently dabbled in the ale market.

Social Stratification

Although all students of medieval rural society agree that the peasantry was divided by sharp socioeconomic distinctions, they have disagreed about how best to reconstruct these divisions. Both Keith Wrightson and Zvi Razi criticized the early studies of J. Ambrose Raftis, Edward Britton, and Edwin DeWindt for their pioneering, but flawed attempts to differentiate families based on whether persons identified by familial sur-

TABLE A.5. The Distribution of Ale Amercements in Brigstock

Category	Number of Persons	Number of Citations
Major female brewers	38	2,265
Minor female brewers in surname groups	273	1,412
Minor female brewers: isolated individuals	—	120
Male brewers	20	47
All identified brewers	331	3,844

Note: Two major female brewers were isolated individuals.

names held many offices (Group A), some offices (Group B), or no offices (Group C). Wrightson and Razi argued that these methods not only placed too much socioeconomic importance on official duties but also ignored variations over time and within families.[20] The first criticism is overdrawn, for official activity clearly constitutes an easily retrievable and relatively accurate index of socioeconomic status. For example, Anne DeWindt's careful study of a wide variety of factors contributing to socioeconomic status (a study that merited praise by Razi) has proven that officeholding was closely correlated to success in other areas (as judged by landholdings, numbers of animals, pledging activities, and the like).[21] The second criticism is more serious and has been resolved in the analyses of Brigstock by using two levels of categorization. The first level assigned a social rank to each reliable surname; the second assigned a specific rank to individuals based on either that person's official activities or (in the case of females) the activities of fathers and husbands. Because both approaches provide only rough approximations of socioeconomic status, only two categories were used—upper and lower rank. The 277 reliable surnames of Brigstock were assigned rankings as follows:

Upper Rank (98 surnames: 35 percent). These surnames were used to identify officeholders.

Lower Rank (179 surnames: 65 percent). These surnames were never associated with officeholding.

Every index developed to study social structures in Brigstock confirmed the correlation between officeholding and socioeconomic privilege. The 1319 rental of semi-virgaters and quarter-virgaters contained a gross disproportion of officeholding surnames (88 percent of those cited). Similarly, Table A.6 shows that officeholding surnames were not only especially active in the profitable brewing industry but also par-

TABLE A.6. Brigstock: Distribution of Surnames by Ranks

Category	Upper Rank			Lower Rank			Both Ranks		
	No.	Column Percent	Row Percent	No.	Column Percent	Row Percent	No.	Column Percent	Row Percent
Assize Group X	47	48%	70%	20	11%	30%	67	24%	100%
Assize Group Y	23	23	34	44	25	66	67	24	100
Assize Group Z	28	29	20	115	64	80	143	52	100
All assize groups	98	100	35	179	100	65	277	100	100
Duration Group I	58	59	65	31	17	35	89	32	100
Duration Group II	16	16	28	41	23	72	57	21	100
Duration Group III	19	19	21	71	40	79	90	32	100
Duration Group IV	5	5	12	36	20	88	41	15	100
All duration groups	98	99	35	179	100	65	277	100	100

Note: Percentages have been rounded to produce integral numbers.

TABLE A.7. Brigstock: Court Appearances by Ranks

Category	Upper Rank		Lower Rank		Both Ranks	
	No.	Percent	No.	Percent	No.	Percent
Individuals	1,209	61%	783	39%	1,992	100%
Appearances	25,273	81	6,008	19	31,281	100
Average individuals per surname	12.3		4.4		7.2	
Average appearances per individual	20.9		7.7		15.7	

Note: Percentages have been rounded to produce integral numbers.

ticularly successful at maintaining long residence in the area. And the social power of officeholders and their families was reflected in their better representation in the manor court. As demonstrated in Table A.7, the average upper-rank surname boasted almost three times as many identified individuals as did lower-rank surnames, and each person from an officeholding surname averaged almost 21 appearances against less than 8 average appearances for those identified by nonofficeholding surnames.

Analyzing the Social Relation of the Sexes in Brigstock

The Sample of Crimes

To study how criminal activity reflected the experiences of women and men in medieval Brigstock, a sample of criminal cases was extracted and analyzed. This sample was taken from three clusters of views of frankpledge chosen to represent the early, middle, and later stages of the six decades covered by the pre-plague records of the manor. Each cluster contains three adjacent views that have survived in excellent condition. Although all criminal cases were extracted from these courts, noncriminal citations (defaults, commercial amercements, tithing entries) were not included in the sample. In addition, some crimes could not be recovered or were recovered imperfectly because of damaged court rolls. Representing a separate clerical entry and a single criminal, each case was coded for sex and marital status of criminal, sex and marital status of victim(s), type of crime, and relationship of criminal to victim(s) and pledge(s). Because six criminals were of unknown sex, the gender analysis of the sample involved only 554 criminals (176 females and

TABLE A.8. The Brigstock Sample of Crimes

Category	Sources	Number of Cases
Early cluster	View 21/9/1301	99
	View 6/10/1302	
	View 17/9/1304	
Middle cluster	View 30/9/1318	172
	View 21/9/1319	
	View 27/9/1322	
Late cluster	View 21/9/1340	289
	View 24/9/1341	
	View 25/9/1343	
Total sample		560

378 males). It should be noted that the count of criminals does not correspond to individuals, but rather correlates to cases. Excluding 10 persons of unknown sex, the count of 290 victims included 171 males and 119 females. Table A.8 summarizes the basic configurations of the crime sample.

The Sample of Land Transactions

The participation of women in the land market of Brigstock has been studied through a sample of land transactions. The sample consists of four clusters of court sessions chosen to represent different portions of the pre-plague period.[22] The clusters include all available courts for the years noted. Each land transaction was treated as a separate case and was coded for biographical information on grantors and receivers (sex, marital status, relationship to joint actors), size of land and entry fine, special encumbrances on grant, and relationship of grantor(s) and pledge(s) to receiver(s).[23] The sample yielded 396 grantors and 383 receivers of known sex; as in the analysis of crimes, these figures represent actors in land transactions, not individuals. As actors, men outnumbered women by a ratio of four to one (617 males to 162 females). The land transaction sample is summarized in Table A.9.

The Sample of Civil Litigation

The legal competence of women was studied through a sample of civil pleas based on the same four clusters used for the sample of land trans-

TABLE A.9. The Brigstock Sample of Land Transactions

Category	Sources	Number of Cases
Early cluster	1301–1303 (36 courts)	42
Early middle cluster	1314–1316 (42 courts)	102
Late middle cluster	1331–1333 (34 courts)	77
Late cluster	1343–1345 (42 courts)	142
Total sample		363

actions. Picking up cases consecutively, the sample drew 50 pleas from each cluster and traced each plea through the extant courts. Slightly under two-thirds of the pleas were traced to their final resolution (124 out of 200 cases). The conclusions to the remainder were either never recorded in the court or were recorded in courts whose records have not survived. These 200 cases include the normal civil actions found in the Brigstock courts (pleas of trespass, contract, and debt, as well as simple quarrels or *loquelae*), but exclude the occasional dispute about land ownership. Two-thirds of all cases were pleas of trespass and most known resolutions ended with concords (74 percent) rather than court judgments (26 percent). Each case was coded for plea information (type, resolution, fines), biographical data (sex, marital status, relationship to joint actors) on defendant(s) and plaintiff(s), and data on assistors (number and relationship to person assisted). As in the sample of land transfers, men outnumbered women by a 4:1 ratio (348 males versus 86 females).

The Kroyl-Penifader Analysis

The aggregative trends revealed in the samples of crimes, land transactions, and civil pleas were supplemented, whenever feasible, by more detailed studies of the experiences of women and men in Brigstock before the plague. The information obtained from the sample of land transactions on the landholding experiences of daughters and sons was, for example, confirmed by examining the economic activities of all women and men known to have been unmarried prior to a certain date. Such in-depth studies not only compensated for the error inherent in the samples, but also highlighted factors often obscured in general trends. The most important detailed analysis was that of the Kroyl and Penifader families joined together by the marriage of Henry Kroyl junior and Agnes Penifader in 1319. The Kroyls and Penifaders, as members of the upper strata of a heterogeneous rural population, were not strictly representative of all the medieval peasantry, but detailed analysis of their experiences allowed unusual insights into the social importance of family and kinship in medieval villages.

The narrow focus of the Kroyl-Penifader microcosm, moreover, provided an ideal setting for network analysis. This system of charting and analyzing individual contacts must necessarily be applied only to small groups because personal networks can quickly grow to unwieldy proportions.[24] In everyday speech, the word *network* is used loosely to describe the bonds that link an individual to others, but the anthropological use of social networks is more precise and analytical.[25] Evolving in response to the inadequate coverage of informal social activities found in most structuralist-functionalist studies, network analysis examines how connections between individuals both reflect and affect social behavior. Although there is no formal theory of social networks, network analysis has, in the last few decades, produced an elaborate set of analytical techniques and devices. The basic methodology is simple and straightforward; the researcher charts and analyzes the contacts that an individual develops with members of his or her community. The actual application of network analysis is becoming increasingly sophisticated; the qualitative content and directional flow of contacts must be considered, as well as the extent of independent interactions between two members of a third person's network. In short, network analysis provides a set of measurements for assessing the importance of personal associations within a given environment.

Figure A.1 sets forth the reconstructed genealogies of the Kroyls and Penifaders. The fathers of both families belonged to the privileged elite of Brigstock. Robert Penifader was a substantial landholder in Stanion who served in several community offices.[26] He and his wife Alice produced eight known children (three sons and five daughters). The careers of all three sons were traced in the Brigstock records. The life histories of two daughters who appeared only sporadically in the courts could not be fully reconstructed.[27] Of the other three daughters, Cecilia Penifader never married, Cristina Penifader married an outsider and emigrated (although she later made appearances in the Brigstock court to either claim or transfer land), and Agnes Penifader, just one year after her father's death, married Henry Kroyl junior in 1319.[28] The father of Henry Kroyl junior, like Robert Penifader, held substantial lands and offices in the community, but his main holdings were located in Brigstock rather than Stanion.[29] Together with his wife Agnes, Henry Kroyl senior had four sons and no known daughters. William Kroyl ceased to appear in the courts in the early 1320s, but his three brothers pursued important careers in the community through the 1340s. Table A.10

FIGURE A.1. The Penifader and Kroyl Genealogies

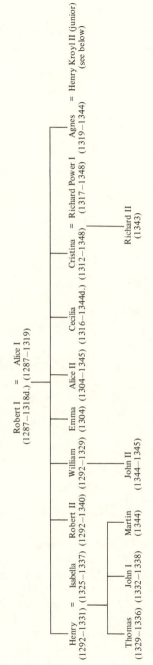

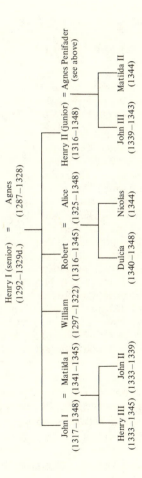

Note: All of the relationships shown were explicitly stated in court entries. Dates indicate period covered by court appearances (not life span). Known deaths are indicated by a "d." after the date.

TABLE A.10. The Court Appearances of the Kroyls and Penifaders

Person	Number of Appearances
Henry Kroyl I (senior)	210
Agnes wife of Henry Kroyl I	13
John I son of Henry Kroyl I	439
Matilda wife of John Kroyl I	2
Henry III son of John Kroyl I	2
John II son of John Kroyl I	4
William son of Henry Kroyl I	9
Robert son of Henry Kroyl I	41
Alice wife of Robert Kroyl	65
Dulcia daughter of Robert Kroyl	5
Nicholas son of Robert Kroyl	1
Henry II (junior) son of Henry Kroyl I	586
Matilda II daughter of Henry Kroyl II	1
John III son of Henry Kroyl II	2
Robert Penifader	226
Alice I wife of Robert Penifader I	16
Henry son of Robert Penifader I	72
Isabella wife of Henry Penifader	13
Thomas son of Henry Penifader	3
John I son of Henry Penifader	3
Martin son of Henry Penifader	4
William son of Robert Penifader I	78
John II son of William Penifader	4
Robert II son of Robert Penifader I	60
Emma daughter of Robert Penifader I	1
Alice II daughter of Robert Penifader I	2
Cecilia daughter of Robert Penifader I	30
Cristina daughter of Robert Penifader I	22
Richard Power I (Cristina's husband)	21
Richard II son of Richard Power I	1
Agnes daughter of Robert Penifader I	29

breaks down the 1,965 appearances made by the Kroyls and Penifaders in the extant Brigstock courts held between 1287 and 1348.

Personal networks were constructed for each of these individuals by listing the person with whom the subject interacted and counting the number of contacts. The content of these transactions was divided into six categories based on whether the subject interacted with another person by (1) receiving assistance, (2) giving assistance, (3) acting jointly, (4) receiving land, (5) giving land, or (6) pursuing a dispute. The granting or receipt of assistance was usually in the form of personal pledging. Joint activity included all instances in which two or more persons acted together; two men who together pledged for a third man were counted as acting jointly. Land transactions included both leases and outright transfers. The dispute category included all controversies that arose between villages (slanders, attacks, unpaid debts, thefts, trespasses). Court citations were not automatically translated into interactions. A dispute that lasted several months and generated numerous court entries has been counted as a single interaction (regardless of the actual number of citations). Because personal pledges, however, could and did change over time, each pledging relationship has been registered as a new interaction. Debt contracts, which rarely appeared in the Brigstock courts, did not merit a separate category; the one debt contract recorded for a member of the Penifaders and Kroyls (when John Hirdman loaned Henry Kroyl junior and his wife Agnes 10 shillings in 1339) was counted in the "assistance received" column. The main configurations of the networks of the Kroyls and Penifaders are described in Table A.11.

The persons and contacts acquired by each member of the Kroyl and Penifader families were divided into three main groups. Cognates included all members of the subject's natal family (parents and siblings) as well as all members of the subject's personal marital family (spouse and children). In addition, descendants (grandchildren, nieces, etc.) and ascendants (grandparents, uncles, etc.) of these families were included. Affines comprised all persons to whom the subject was indirectly related through marriage (wife's brother, sister's husband, etc.). Associations with affines and cognates were occasionally combined into a single category of familial associations. Nonrelatives denoted all persons with whom the subject possessed no known familial ties. In actual fact, however, such individuals are only presumed to be nonrelatives because of the very real possibility that ties existed that remain untraced (especially through incompletely reconstructed marriages). Relationships formed with cognates, affines, and nonrelatives were studied by using a series of rather complex quantitative and qualitative measurements illustrated for the postmarital network of Henry Kroyl junior in Tables 5.6 and 5.7. Multiplexity measured associations that were not only multiple (involving more than one contact between the subject and the person), but also complex (involving more than one *type* of contact). Henry Kroyl junior's premarital relationship with his father, for example, was multiplex because he received assistance from his father on eight occasions and gave assistance once. Multiplex relationships are generally more stable and more important than single-stranded relationships because the variety of contacts fosters stronger bonds. A multiplex relationship

TABLE A.11.   The Court Networks of the Kroyls and Penifaders

Person	Number of Persons in Network	Number of Contacts in Network
Henry Kroyl I	103	182
Agnes Kroyl	4	5
John Kroyl I	116	300
Matilda Kroyl I	4	5
Henry Kroyl III	3	3
John Kroyl II	5	5
William Kroyl	9	9
Robert Kroyl	30	48
Alice Kroyl	7	7
Dulcia Kroyl	7	7
Nicholas Kroyl	2	2
Henry Kroyl II	176	352
Matilda Kroyl II	5	5
John Kroyl III	2	2
Robert Penifader I	97	211
Alice Penifader I	11	16
Henry Penifader	44	69
Isabella Penifader	11	16
Thomas Penifader	2	5
John Penifader I	1	1
Martin Penifader	6	10
William Penifader	42	118
John Penifader II	9	9
Robert Penifader II	36	64
Emma Penifader	2	2
Alice Penifader II	3	3
Cecilia Penifader	22	45
Cristina Penifader	18	34
Richard Power I	15	29
Richard Power II	1	1
Agnes Penifader	11	31

should not be confused with a multiple relationship (involving more than one contact of the same type).[30]

Iver Before the Plague

Lying just below the Chiltern Hills in Buckinghamshire, Iver offered its inhabitants a somewhat different set of living circumstances from those found in Brigstock in the early fourteenth century. The most important difference was economic. With Colne Brook running along its eastern boundary and Alderbourne Stream marking its northern limits, Iver's location promoted intensive animal husbandry and fishing. As early as the Domesday survey, the meadows and fisheries of Iver were firmly established components of its rural economy. Assessed at £22 in 1086, the manor had four fisheries and meadows sufficient for thirty plow teams.[31] Of the 5,531 acres in the modern parish, almost one-half are permanent grass, and only about one-third are arable. Consisting of loam with a subsoil of gravel, the land today is fairly barren, with the northern portion of the parish covered by Iver Heath.[32]

The manorial records extant for Iver before the plague repeatedly emphasize the pastoral focus of the community's economy. Numerous amercements for animal trespasses were noted in every court. The governing hierarchy of the manor included a special official (variously called a *cadaverator* or *coronator*) who presented and explained the deaths of all manorial beasts.[33] While demesne arable was rented by tenants on other manors, demesne beasts were leased in Iver.[34] The community's dependence on the fisheries in the Colne and Alderbourne are similarly reflected in court records. Some holdings included fishing rights, some villagers rented fisheries, and others paid amercements for illegal fishing or illegal sales of fish.[35] The manor included common waters in which all persons could fish, and the manor's fishing rights were jealously guarded against the encroachment of outsiders.[36]

The second important distinction between Iver and Brigstock was manorial. Unlike Brigstock, Iver was not part of the ancient demesne, but rather was held by a Robert Doyley in 1086. By the thirteenth century, the manor was controlled by the Claverings. Upon the death of a Clavering widow in 1345, its ownership passed to Ralph de Neville. Seven years later, he transferred Iver to Edward III who immediately incorporated the manor into the endowment of his new collegiate foundation at St. George's Chapel, Windsor Castle.[37]

In addition, the inhabitants of Iver, unlike those of Brigstock, adhered to the rule of primogeniture in inheritance. Eldest sons inherited their fathers' holdings in Iver. Although this policy was frequently interrupted by inheritance by minor sons, daughters, or other relatives, primogeniture was the governing principle of property devolution in Iver.

Deposited at St. George's Chapel and at the Buckinghamshire Archaeological Society in Aylesbury, the manorial records for Iver from 1287 to 1349 include 71 sessions of the seigneurial court and 9 views of frankpledge. As in Brigstock, the manorial court of Iver met regularly every three weeks. Unfortunately, these records are not spread evenly through the six decades before the plague, but instead include

TABLE A.12. Estimated Adult Male Residents in Iver, 1287–1349

Period	Number of Courts	Number of Males	Adjusted Number of Males
1287–1288	10	155	315
1332–1335	18	335	367
1336–1338	15	374	454
1341–1345	17	355	403
1346–1349	20	312	312

a gap of more than four decades between the 10 courts of 1287–1288 and the substantial collection that begins in 1332. This hiatus, however, is partially covered by extracts from courts now lost that were copied in the fifteenth century into the White Book of Arundel. These selected extracts include merchet payments and land transfers accomplished during the long period for which no full court records have survived.

Iver's limited archive prohibited more than general estimates of its population and economy, but these estimates do suggest that Iver's circumstances were more favorable than those in Brigstock. Table A.12 summarizes the count of males cited in the Iver courts between 1287 and 1349. Although the late thirteenth-century data are too isolated for comparison with later counts, both the raw and adjusted figures in Table A.12 suggest that Iver's population grew significantly during the 1330s, then fell rapidly in the decade prior to the plague. These trends directly contrast with Brigstock where population probably fell during the 1330s and increased slightly in the 1340s.

Moreover, the pastoral basis of Iver's economy apparently protected its residents from the squeeze between people and resources suggested by trends in Brigstock. Between 1332 and 1349, 38 villagers were cited by the court of Iver for the wastage or abandonment of their holdings, a problem that would not have occurred in a community whose resources were stretched by demographic pressures.[38] Since wastage citations continued to appear in the courts of Iver when population was probably falling in the 1340s, the downward trend of this decade might not have been caused by economic hardship.

Iver's distinctive economy and demography, however, did not lead to distinct social structures. The basic features of social organization in Iver varied little from those found in Brigstock. Using the same criteria described above for Brigstock, the 193 reliable surnames of Iver were divided into ranks, assize groups, and duration groups as follows:

Upper Rank:	48 surnames	(25 percent)
Lower Rank:	145 surnames	(75 percent)

Assize Group X:	47 surnames	(24 percent)
Assize Group Y:	76 surnames	(39 percent)
Assize Group Z:	70 surnames	(36 percent)
Duration Group I	66 surnames	(34 percent)
Duration Group II	8 surnames	(4 percent)
Duration Group III	102 surnames	(53 percent)
Duration Group IV	17 surnames	(9 percent)

Several points should be noted. First, as in Brigstock, roughly one-third of the surnames in Iver remained in use throughout the six decades before the plague (Duration Group I), suggesting that on both manors longevity of residence during this half-century was possible for only about one of every three families. Second, roughly one-fourth of the surnames on both manors were associated with intensive brewing (10 or more citations), although proportionally more surnames in Iver were associated with moderate brewing (1 to 9 citations). Third, upper-rank status in Iver was more restricted than in Brigstock where more than a third of all surnames were associated with officeholding. But Tables A.13 and A.14 show that persons identified by Iver's officeholding surnames were, like those in Brigstock, especially well represented in other sectors, appearing in court more frequently, brewing for profit more regularly, and remaining resident on the manor for longer periods of time.

Houghton-cum-Wyton Before the Plague

Resting on the rich soil of the east Midlands, Houghton-cum-Wyton lies in between the villages of Brigstock (to the northwest) and Iver (to the southwest). The history and development of the two separate, but contiguous, villages of Houghton and Wyton had been intertwined since their joint acquisition by Ramsey Abbey in the tenth century, and throughout the medieval period the two communities were administered under the single Ramsey manor of Houghton-cum-Wyton. As in Iver, the inhabitants of Houghton-cum-Wyton followed the rule of primogeniture in passing property between generations. But the economy of this manor provides a contrast to both Brigstock and Iver. Suitable for intensive farming, the clay and loam soil of the manor supported the mixed farming typical of the region. The annual work cycle centered around planting, cultivating, and harvesting corn in the open fields that lay to the north of the manor, but the meadows and pastures to the south also allowed animal husbandry to complement arable farming by

TABLE A.13. Iver: Distribution of Surnames by Ranks

Category	Upper Rank			Lower Rank			Both Ranks		
	No.	Column Percent	Row Percent	No.	Column Percent	Row Percent	No.	Column Percent	Row Percent
Assize Group X	22	46%	47%	25	17%	53%	47	24%	100%
Assize Group Y	22	46	29	54	37	71	76	39	100
Assize Group Z	4	8	6	66	46	94	70	36	100
All assize groups	48	100	25	145	100	75	193	99	100
Duration Group I	27	56	41	39	27	59	66	34	100
Duration Group II	1	2	12.5	7	5	87.5	8	4	100
Duration Group III	19	40	19	83	57	81	102	53	100
Duration Group IV	1	2	6	16	11	94	17	9	100
All duration groups	48	100	25	145	100	75	193	100	100

Note: Percentages have been rounded to produce integral numbers.

TABLE A.14. Iver: Court Appearances by Ranks

Category	Upper Rank		Lower Rank		Both ranks	
	No.	Percent	No.	Percent	No.	Percent
Individuals	406	40%	604	60%	1,010	100%
Appearances	4,561	58	3,371	42	7,932	100
Average individuals per surname	8.5		4.2		5.2	
Average appearances per individual	11.2		5.6		7.9	

Note: Percentages have been rounded to produce integral numbers.

providing brute power for field work and manure for fertilizing the arable.

At the time of the Domesday survey, Houghton and Wyton together possessed fourteen hides of land, two mills, and substantial woodlands and meadows. Their combined value was £15.[39] In the mid-thirteenth century, a Ramsey survey found that each village still included seven hides, but that both the number of virgates in a hide and the number of acres in a virgate were larger in Houghton, reflecting the greater extent of its territory.[40] Today, Houghton contains 1,549 acres of which about two-thirds are arable; 1,470 acres lie in Wyton, which adjoins the western boundary of Houghton.[41]

The ownership of Houghton-cum-Wyton by Ramsey Abbey also differentiated the experiences of its inhabitants from those in Brigstock and Iver, subjecting them to much closer seigneurial control. In both Brigstock and Iver, peasants regularly bought or sold parcels of land, but Ramsey Abbey, intent on keeping holdings intact in the interest of administrative efficiency, effectively prohibited sales of real property in Houghton-cum-Wyton.[42] The officers of Ramsey Abbey also carefully monitored the labor services due from tenants, amercing all those guilty of work defaults (such amercements were infrequent in both Brigstock and Iver). And although the records of Brigstock and Iver never noted whether persons had left or entered these manors, Ramsey Abbey attempted to regulate rural mobility by fining all those who wished to leave Houghton-cum-Wyton.[43] Seigneurial authority was, in short, very much a reality in Houghton-cum-Wyton before the plague.

The officials of Ramsey Abbey usually toured their manors twice yearly, presiding over one court in the summer and one view of frankpledge in the autumn. As a result, the semiannual Houghton-cum-Wyton courts met much less frequently than the triweekly courts of Brigstock and Iver. Deposited at the Public Record Office, the extant courts for Houghton-cum-Wyton are supplemented, for some years, by the annual Michaelmas accounts. The entire collection from 1288 to 1349 includes 32 courts or views and 14 accounts.

Population movements in Houghton-cum-Wyton are exceedingly difficult to trace, but it does seem likely that the manor's population was falling by the second decade of the fourteenth century. Efforts to trace population through counts of adult males cited in the manor's records were obfuscated by the use of many ancillary sources and the sporadic quality of court survival. As a result, it was impossible to evaluate how different sources extant for different periods might have affected the raw count of males. Nevertheless, the general pattern of demographic change is shown in Table A.15 which, combining information on surname stability with data on the unadjusted number of males on the manor, suggests that the population of Houghton-cum-Wyton was falling by the second decade of the fourteenth century.

Houghton-cum-Wyton shared with Brigstock and Iver some basic aspects of social organization. Using the criteria developed for Brigstock, the 128 reliable surnames of the manor were divided into ranks, assize groups, and duration groups as follows:

Upper Rank:	63 surnames	(49 percent)
Lower Rank:	65 surnames	(51 percent)
Assize Group X:	5 surnames	(4 percent)
Assize Group Y:	42 surnames	(33 percent)
Assize Group Z:	81 surnames	(63 percent)
Duration Group I	47 surnames	(37 percent)
Duration Group II	42 surnames	(33 percent)
Duration Group III	25 surnames	(19 percent)
Duration Group IV	14 surnames	(11 percent)

The social structure of Houghton-cum-Wyton was certainly distinct in some respects. A much larger proportion of the manor's surnames were associated with officeholding than in either Brigstock or Iver, suggesting that variations of socioeconomic status were less marked in the Huntingdonshire community. And commercial brewing was more restricted than on the other two manors. But important social features were shared by all three communities. As in both Brigstock and Iver, roughly one-third of the surnames traced in Houghton-cum-Wyton remained stable throughout the late thirteenth and early fourteenth centuries. Surnames associated with officeholding in Houghton-cum-Wyton

TABLE A.15. Demographic Change in Houghton-cum-Wyton, 1288–1349

Period	Stable Surnames		Appearing Surnames		Disappearing Surnames		Adult Male Residents	Number of Extant Courts
	No.	Row Percent	No.	Row Percent	No.	Row Percent		
1288–1300	84	—	—	—	5	—	196	7
1301–1310	76	76%	16	16%	8	8%	205	10
1311–1320	80	79	9	9	12	12	185	5
1321–1330	74	77	5	5	17	18	171	5
1331–1340	66	78	5	6	14	16	139	3
1341–1349	68	—	4	—	—	—	96	2

Note: Percentages have been rounded to produce integral numbers.

TABLE A.16. Houghton-cum-Wyton: Distribution of Surnames by Ranks

Category	Upper Rank			Lower Rank			Both Ranks		
	No.	Column Percent	Row Percent	No.	Column Percent	Row Percent	No.	Column Percent	Row Percent
Assize Group X	5	8%	100%	0	0%	0%	5	4%	100%
Assize Group Y	19	30	45	23	35	55	42	33	100
Assize Group Z	39	62	48	42	65	52	81	63	100
All assize groups	63	100	49	65	100	51	128	100	100
Duration Group I	36	57	77	11	17	23	47	37	100
Duration Group II	16	25	38	26	40	62	42	33	100
Duration Group III	9	14	36	16	25	64	25	19	100
Duration Group IV	2	3	14	12	18	86	14	11	100
All duration groups	63	99	49	65	100	51	128	100	100

Note: Percentages have been rounded to produce integral numbers.

TABLE A.17. Houghton-cum-Wyton: Court Appearances by Ranks

Category	Upper Rank		Lower Rank		Both Ranks	
	No.	Percent	No.	Percent	No.	Percent
Individuals	423	62%	261	38%	684	100%
Appearances	2,561	77	763	23	3,324	100
Average individuals per surname	6.7		4.0		5.3	
Average appearances per individual	6.1		2.9		4.9	

Note: Percentages have been rounded to produce integral numbers.

also, as in both Brigstock and Iver, stood out from other surnames in many respects. As shown in Tables A.16 and A.17, individuals identified by upper-rank surnames were especially likely to bring business to the court, to participate in commercial brewing, and to remain on the manor.

Glossary

Every effort has been made to define terms unfamiliar to general readers the first time they are used in the text. The list below provides definitions of some of the most unusual or frequently used of these words. Although the meanings of many medieval terms are obscure, variable, or controversial, the definitions given here avoid such conundrums in favor of providing general information.

account Official report of the receipts and expenses of a manorial estate.

affeeror Officer responsible for assessing manorial amercements and fines.

aletaster Officer responsible for enforcing the assize of ale.

amercement Sum paid to the lord by a person "in mercy" for an offense.

ancient demesne Manors, held by the king at the time of the Domesday survey, whose tenants enjoyed special legal rights.

assart Land cleared for use in arable farming.

Assize of Bread and Ale Thirteenth-century statute imposing standards of measurement, quality, and pricing upon commercial bakers and brewers; local authorities used the assize as a licensing system by amercing all sellers of bread and ale for supposed infractions of its regulations.

attorney Person accepted by a manorial court to stand in the place of another.

bailiff Chief representative of a lord on a manor (usually an outsider appointed by the lord).

butt Small part of a plowed field, often the portion remaining after plowing.

close Enclosed field or area.

conveyance Transfer of property.

cottar Smallholder (usually holding no more than a cottage and five acres of land).

croft Enclosed land, usually adjacent to the house.

curtilage Yard adjacent to the house.

custumal Written collection of manorial customs.

demesne Lands exploited directly by the manorial lord (as distinct from lands rented to tenants).

domus House or building.

dower Lands designated (often at the time of marriage) for a wife's maintenance in the event of widowhood.

essoin Excuse for failure to appear at court.

essoiner Person presenting another's excuse for failure to attend court.

fine Sum paid to a lord in return for the granting of a favor (such as permission to marry or permission to enter a holding).

free bench Dower lands assigned for a widow's maintenance.

hamsoken Housebreaking.

heriot Payment due to a manorial lord upon a tenant's death.

hue and cry Outcry alerting others to pursue a criminal.

mainpast To assume responsibility for another; to be under the guardianship of another.

merchet Payment due to a manorial lord upon marriage.

messor Officer responsible for supervising the fields.

messuage Site of a home with its outbuildings.

multiplex Term used in network analysis to denote a relationship involving several different kinds of interactions.

pannage Pasturage of pigs in woods; payment for that pasturage.

placia Plot of land.

pledge Legal guaranty; a person who guaranteed that another would meet a legal obligation.

pondbreche Illegal rescue of impounded animals.

presentment Statement made by a sworn jury.

purpresture Illegal enclosure or encroachment.

reeve Officer responsible for the general management of a manor (usually selected from among the manor's tenants).

relief Payment due to a manorial lord upon inheritance.

rental List of rents due from manorial tenants.

rod Variable measurement, usually between 15 and 16.5 feet.

selion Narrow strip of arable land in an open field.

suitor Person obliged to attend court.

survey Official list of the holdings of a manor.

tithing Peace-keeping group of variable size (most men over 12 years of age were enrolled in a tithing).

tithingman Head of a tithing.

toft Site of a house.

view of frankpledge Annual (or biannual) meeting at which tithing-men named all those guilty of infractions against the local peace.

virgate Standard tenant's holding on many manors, but of a size that varied from manor to manor (usually from 20 to 30 acres).

Notes

Chapter I. Introduction

1. Most studies of working women in the Middle Ages have focused on women in English towns. For studies from the early part of the twentieth century, see A. Abram, "Women Traders in Medieval London," *Economic Journal* 26 (1916), pp. 276–285; Mary Bateson, *Borough Customs, Vol. II*, Selden Society 21 (London, 1906), pp. c–cxv; Marian K. Dale, "The London Silkwomen of the Fifteenth Century," *Economic History Review* (1933), pp. 324–335; Eileen Power, "The Working Woman in Town and Country," in *Medieval Women*, ed. M. M. Postan (Cambridge, 1975), pp. 53–75. For more recent studies of women in medieval English towns, see Rodney H. Hilton, "Women Traders in Medieval England," in *Women's Studies* 11 (1984), pp. 139–155, and Maryanne Kowaleski, "Women's Work in a Market Town: Exeter in the Late Fourteenth Century," in *Women and Work in Preindustrial Europe*, ed. Barbara A. Hanawalt (Bloomington, Ind., 1986). Forthcoming books by Martha Howell (University of Chicago Press) and Merry Weisner (Rutgers University Press) will examine the late medieval experiences of women in continental towns.

2. For the few available studies of peasant women in medieval England, see Power, "The Working Woman"; R. H. Hilton, "Women in the Village," in *The English Peasantry in the Later Middle Ages* (Oxford, 1975), pp. 95–110; Barbara A. Hanawalt, "Childrearing among the

Lower Classes of Late Medieval England," *Journal of Interdisciplinary History* 8 (1977), pp. 1–22, and Hanawalt's "Women's Contribution to the Home Economy in Late Medieval England," in *Women and Work in Preindustrial Europe;* and Judith M. Bennett, "The Village Ale-Wife: Women and Brewing in Fourteenth-Century England," also in *Women and Work in Preindustrial Europe.*

3. Olwen Hufton, "Women in History: Early Modern Europe," *Past and Present* 101 (1983), p. 126.

4. Ivan Illich, *Gender* (New York, 1982). See also the critique by Nancy Scheper-Hughes, "Vernacular Sexism: An Anthropological Response to Ivan Illich," *Feminist Issues* 3 (1983), pp. 28–37.

5. Hilton, "Women in the Village," pp. 105–106. Although Hilton concedes that "there may be something special about this part of the world," the thrust of his argument is that women participated in local politics. For other studies emphasizing the relatively high status of medieval women, see Power, "The Working Woman"; Doris Mary Stenton, *The English Woman in History* (London, 1957), pp. 75–99; and Edward Britton, *The Community of the Vill: A Study in the History of the Family and Village Life in Fourteenth-Century England* (Toronto, 1977), esp. pp. 16–37.

6. As quoted in Power, "The Working Woman," p. 75. For a modern translation, see Christine de Pisan, *The Treasure of the City of Ladies,* trans. Sarah Lawson (Harmondsworth, 1985), p. 176. For examples of historians who explicitly judge the status of peasant women to be higher than that of women of other ranks, see Power, "The Working Woman," esp. p. 53; Stenton, *English Woman;* Britton, *Community,* esp. pp. 16–37; Shulamith Shahar, *The Fourth Estate: A History of Women in the Middle Ages,* trans. Chaya Galai (London, 1983), p. 249.

7. Shahar, *Fourth Estate,* p. 89.

8. For the advice of preachers, see G. R. Owst, *Literature and Pulpit in Medieval England,* 2nd edition (New York, 1961), pp. 385–401. The goodwife's caution is from "How the Good Wife Taught Her Daughter," printed in *The Babees Book,* ed. and trans. Edith Rickert (London, 1923), p. 35.

9. Geoffrey Chaucer, "The Knights Tale," line 313. See F. N. Robinson, *The Complete Works of Geoffrey Chaucer* (Boston, 1933), p. 32.

10. The use of "social relation of the sexes" reflects the influence of Joan Kelly-Gadol in her article, "The Social Relation of the Sexes: Methodological Implications of Women's History," *Signs* 1 (1976), pp. 809–823. For medieval definitions of wife and husband, see the appropriate entries in the *Oxford English Dictionary.*

11. Northamptonshire Record Office, Montagu Collection (hereafter

cited as N.R.O.), 20/3/1315. The jurors stated *"vendicio illa nulla est de uxore aliter in absentia mariti sui."*

12. See, for example, the transfer of the custody and lands of the minor John Hayroun by his brother William Hayroun in the court of Brigstock: N.R.O., 3/9/1339.

13. The most important studies of seigneurial estates are: F. G. Davenport, *The Economic History of a Norfolk Manor 1086–1565* (1906; rpt. New York, 1967); Christopher Dyer, *Lords and Peasants in a Changing Society: The Estates of the Bishopric of Worcester, 680–1540* (Cambridge, 1980); John Hatcher, *Rural Economy and Society in the Duchy of Cornwall 1300–1500* (Cambridge, 1970); Barbara Harvey, *Westminster Abbey and Its Estates in the Middle Ages* (Oxford, 1977); P. D. A. Harvey, *A Medieval Oxfordshire Village: Cuxham 1240–1400* (Oxford, 1965); Rodney H. Hilton, *The Economic Development of Some Leicestershire Estates in the 14th and 15th Centuries* (London, 1947); Edward Miller, *The Abbey and Bishopric of Ely* (Cambridge, 1951); Frances M. Page, *The Estates of Crowland Abbey* (Cambridge, 1934); J. Ambrose Raftis, *The Estates of Ramsey Abbey: A Study in Economic Growth and Organization* (Toronto, 1957); Eleanor Searle, *Lordship and Community: Battle and Its Banlieu 1066–1538* (Toronto, 1974).

14. Historians who work with manorial records disagree about many aspects of theory and method, but concurrence on the vitality of village communities before the plague runs throughout their studies. For examples, see Britton ("the village community occupied a place of primacy," *Community,* p. 178) and Zvi Razi ("the medieval village community was far more important than any local organization in later periods" in "Family, Land and the Village Community in Later Medieval England," *Past and Present* 93 [1981], p. 15). For case studies of rural villages, see Britton, *Community;* Edwin Brezette DeWindt, *Land and People in Holywell-cum-Needingworth: Structures of Tenure and Patterns of Social Organization in an East Midlands Village, 1252–1457* (Toronto, 1972); J. Ambrose Raftis, *Warboys: Two Hundred Years in the Life of an English Mediaeval Village* (Toronto, 1974); Zvi Razi, *Life, Marriage and Death in a Medieval Parish: Economy, Society and Demography in Halesowen, 1270–1400* (Cambridge, 1980); Richard M. Smith, "English Peasant Life-Cycles and Socio-Economic Networks: A Quantitative Geographical Case Study," Diss., University of Cambridge, 1974.

15. Lewis Henry Morgan, *Ancient Society,* ed. Leslie A. White (1877; rpt. Cambridge, Mass., 1964). Karen Sacks, *Sisters and Wives: The Past and Future of Sexual Equality* (1979; rpt. Urbana, Ill., 1982).

16. Abraham Farley, ed., *Domesday-Book seu Liber Censualis Wil-*

lelmi Primi, vol. I (London, 1783), p. 219b. A translation of the Domesday entry for Brigstock can be found in W. Ryland D. Adkins and R. M. Serjeantson, eds., *Victoria History of the County of Northampton,* vol. I (London, 1902), pp. 305–306. The tenurial history of Stanion is somewhat complicated, but the parish seems to have been divided into three main manors—Netherhall (held of Brigstock), Overhall (held in the sixteenth century by Thomas Brudenell of Deene), and a manor held of the Honour of Gloucester Fee. I am indebted to Mr. P. I. King, the Chief Archivist of Northamptonshire, for his assistance in tracing the tenurial history of Stanion. See also John Bridges, *The History and Antiquities of Northhamptonshire,* vol. II, ed. Peter Whalley (London, 1791), pp. 284–287 (Brigstock) and pp. 337–338 (Stanion). Stanion shared with Brigstock the peculiar inheritance customs described below, and the two villages were also sufficiently associated in 1334 to be jointly assessed in the lay subsidy; see Robin E. Glasscock, *The Lay Subsidy of 1334* (London, 1975), p. 215.

17. For a discussion of the enormous diversity of economic opportunity provided by the forest, see Jean R. Birrell, "The Forest Economy of the Honour of Tutbury in the Fourteenth and Fifteenth Centuries," *University of Birmingham Historical Journal* 8 (1962), pp. 114–134. For the prevalence of open-field settlements in Rockingham Forest, see Philip A. J. Pettit, *The Royal Forests of Northamptonshire, A Study in Their Economy, 1558–1714* (Gateshead, 1968), pp. 15–16. See also Royal Commission on Historical Monuments, *An Inventory of the Historical Monuments in the County of Northampton, Vol. I: Archaeological Sites in Northeast Northamptonshire* (London, 1975), p. 23, for traces of plowing in Brigstock proper. For a good selection of the sorts of field misdemeanors regularly committed by the inhabitants of Brigstock, see the presentments in N.R.O., 27/9/1322.

18. Assarting in Brigstock had already substantially increased the tillage in the community in the thirteenth century; see J. A. Raftis, *Assart Data and Land Values: Two Studies in the East Midlands, 1200–1350* (Toronto, 1974), pp. 104, 114. Assarts were occasionally mentioned in the manorial rolls of Brigstock before the plague (for examples, see N.R.O. 24/3/1317, 26/5/1317, and 16/6/1317). The custumal of 1391 (N.R.O., Box X371) stated that the heir to any *novus positus* had to pay double the rent as his entry fee. The estimate of Brigstock's arable comes from Pettit, *Royal Forests,* p. 164.

19. Pettit discusses the importance of nonarable lands in the economy of Rockingham Forest in the sixteenth and seventeenth centuries in *Royal Forests,* pp. 141–163. For examples of activities related to animal husbandry in Brigstock, see N.R.O., 12/7/1319 (pondbreche), 3/1/1343 (trespasses by pigs), 30/5/1314 (the obligation of tenants to supply

herders), and Box X371 (regulations in custumal of 1391 about pannage).

20. The custumal of 1391 (N.R.O., Box X371) included provisions about the gathering of wood in the forest. The Brigstock court sometimes granted permission to gather peat; see, for example, N.R.O., 15/12/1301. For the making of charcoal, see *Calendar of Inquisitions Miscellaneous Preserved in the Public Record Office,* vol. I (London, 1916), pp. 355–356 (item 1205). For sales of wood, see the activities of John Pote, N.R.O., 9/12/1300 and 24/3/1301, and the plea of Henry Faber against Henry Dove in N.R.O., 16/1/1315. An authorization for wood to be sold from Brigstock forest can also be found in the *Calendar of the Patent Rolls Preserved in the Public Record Office, 1292–1301* (London, 1895), p. 592. For poaching, see G. J. Turner, ed., *Select Pleas of the Forest,* Selden Society 13 (London, 1901), pp. 29, 30–31, 83–84. See also, Jean Birrell, "Who Poached the King's Deer? A Study of Thirteenth-Century Crime," *Midland History* 7 (1982), pp. 9–25. For plowing in the parks surrounding Brigstock, see Royal Commission on Historical Monuments, *An Inventory, vol. I,* p. 21. For fishing, see the 1391 custumal (N.R.O., Box X371) and provisions in N.R.O., 14/2/1343. For clothworking, see the case of Robert Moke against Galfridus Lambin in N.R.O., 31/5/1303.

21. M. M. Postan first argued that the English countryside was severely overpopulated prior to the plague in "Some Evidence of Declining Population in the Later Middle Ages," *Economic History Review,* 2nd series, 2 (1950), pp. 221–246. See also his article with J. Titow, "Heriots and Prices on Winchester Manors," *Economic History Review,* 2nd series, 11 (1959), pp. 392–411. Postan's viewpoint has not been universally accepted. For contrary arguments, see Barbara F. Harvey, "The Population Trend in England Between 1300 and 1348," *Transactions of the Royal Historical Society,* 5th series, 16 (1966), pp. 23–42, and Josiah C. Russell, "The Preplague Population of England," *Journal of British Studies,* 5, no. 2 (1966), pp. 1–21. Most opposition has, however, waned in recent years, with the exception of the idiosyncratic arguments found in H. E. Hallam, *Rural England 1066–1348* (Glasgow, 1981). The most recent and thorough statement of the demographic crisis of the early fourteenth century can be found in Edward Miller and John Hatcher, *Medieval England: Rural Society and Economic Change 1086–1348* (London, 1978).

22. Ian Kershaw, "The Great Famine and Agrarian Crisis in England, 1315–1322," *Past and Present* 59 (1973), pp. 3–50.

23. See the Appendix for a full discussion of the methods used to trace the demographic and economic history of Brigstock in the early fourteenth century.

24. N.R.O. Box X371. The custumal mentions only younger (*junior*) and elder (*senior*) sons, leaving unclear the disposition of property in cases where a tenant was survived by three or more sons. The latin text reads: *In primis tenens dimidiam virgate terre et prati cum messuagio iunior filius suus post eius obitum erit suus heres si aliquid sibi dimiserit non venditum. Quia dictus tenens si necesse habuerit in vita sua potest vendere omnia quae sibi accidunt hereditarie. Et residuum filius suus iunior heres post obitum suum et recuperet. Et similiter si aliquid perquisierit ultra filius suus senior erit heres si non ea dimiserit alicui. Quia potest vendere omnia quae habet dum vixit. Et hoc senior suus heres post obitum suum residium recuperit.*

25. See, for example, the inheritance inquisition of Richard son of Gilbert, N.R.O., 14/2/1292.

26. Pettit, *Royal Forests,* p. 167.

27. See, for example, the inheritance inquisition concerning the daughters of Robert le Northerne, N.R.O., 30/1/1326.

28. Paul Vinogradoff, *Villainage in England: Essays in English Mediaeval History* (1892; rpt. Oxford, 1968), p. 92; Frederick Pollock and Frederic William Maitland, *The History of English Law Before the Time of Edward I,* vol. I, 2nd edition (1898; rpt. Cambridge, 1968), pp. 383–406; Marjorie Keniston McIntosh, "The Privileged Villeins of the English Ancient Demesne," *Viator* 7 (1976), pp. 295–328.

29. R. Allen Brown et al., *The History of the King's Works: Volume II, The Middle Ages* (London, 1963), p. 902.

30. *Calendar of Fine Rolls Preserved in the Public Record Office, 1307–1319* (London, 1912), p. 372. Pettit also discusses the farming of the manor to the tenants, *Royal Forest,* p. 167.

31. For a discussion of the extensive rights that forest officers exercised over those who resided within forest territories, see Charles Young, *The Royal Forests of Medieval England* (Philadelphia, 1979). J. R. Maddicott describes how all villages, particularly those in the East Midlands, suffered under the growing demands of royal government during this period in *The English Peasantry and the Demands of the Crown 1294–1341* (Oxford, 1975).

32. For a recent discussion of this rural heterogeneity, see Miller and Hatcher, *Medieval England,* pp. 184–188.

33. See the Appendix for fuller descriptions of the histories of Iver and Houghton-cum-Wyton.

Chapter II. Studying Women in the Medieval Countryside

1. For the English rural economy before the plague, see Kershaw, "The Great Famine"; Maddicott, *Demands of the Crown;* Miller and

Hatcher, *Medieval England,* pp. 240–251; Edward Miller, "England in the Twelfth and Thirteenth Centuries: An Economic Contrast?" *Economic History Review,* 2nd series, 24 (1971), pp. 1–14; R. H. Britnell, "The Proliferation of Markets in England, 1200–1349," *Economic History Review,* 2nd series, 34 (1981), pp. 209–221. Medievalists do not concur about the specifics of the changes occasioned by the plague, but they do agree that rural society in the late fourteenth and fifteenth centuries was substantially altered from conditions in the early fourteenth century. For a summary of the debate (and one perspective on late medieval change), see Razi, "Family, Land."

2. For a full introduction to English manorial archives, see J. Z. Titow, *English Rural Society 1200–1350* (London, 1969). For the legal procedures followed in manorial courts, see F. W. Maitland, ed., *Select Pleas in Manorial and Other Seignorial Courts,* Selden Society 2 (London, 1889) and Frederic William Maitland and William Paley Baildon, eds., *The Court Baron,* Selden Society 4 (London, 1891). The most comprehensive introduction to the use of manorial courts for social history is still J. Ambrose Raftis, *Tenure and Mobility: Studies in the Social History of the Mediaeval English Village* (Toronto, 1964).

3. It should be noted that not all medievalists share this confidence. Eleanor Searle, for example, has asserted that manorial court rolls "are only in the most distant sense the record of village life" in her contribution to "Debate: Seigneurial Control of Women's Marriage," *Past and Present* 99 (1983), p. 156. See R. M. Smith's criticisms of Searle's use of court rolls in "Some Thoughts on 'Hereditary' and 'Proprietary' Rights in Land under Customary Law in Thirteenth and Early Fourteenth Century England," *Law and History Review* 1 (1983), pp. 112–114. While no one would deny that court rolls record only results, not processes, and that these tribunals were convened by lords for their fiscal and administrative benefit, most historians are more optimistic than Searle about the capacity of such records to reflect social experiences. Manorial courts, although convened by lords, were controlled in practice by the peasants through their jury panels, their officers, and their local customs. Even the legal historian John Beckerman recognized the social content of court rolls, stating that the manor court "was an organ of administration, not only of justice, but also of an economic routine centered on the manor and of a social order centered on the village." See "Customary Law in English Manorial Courts in the Thirteenth and Fourteenth Centuries," Diss. University of London, 1972, p. 273. Perhaps the different ways in which scholars use court rolls influence their optimistic or pessimistic evaluations of any social content. Searle has recently used rolls from many manors to study one phenomenon—the payment of merchet (a fine due at the marriage of a tenant's daughter). Such a method underem-

phasizes the social institutions of medieval communities and emphasizes legal practice. In contrast, scholars like Edward Britton, Edwin DeWindt, Richard Smith, Ambrose Raftis, and Zvi Razi, who have used the rolls of a single manor to study many aspects of life in one setting, are much more enthusiastic about the reflection of rural society in court records.

4. Although female infanticide, poorer care of female infants, female emigration to towns offering good prospects for employment, and female mortality in childbirth could have led to quite high ratios of males to females, these are matters of speculation, not proof. In light of these uncertainties, Zvi Razi, in the most recent demographic examination of the medieval peasantry, thought it safest to assume that the sexes were roughly balanced (*Life, Marriage,* p. 86). This assumption was one point not criticized in a thorough assessment of Razi's work in L. R. Poos and R. M. Smith, " 'Legal Windows Onto Historical Populations?' Recent Research on Demography and the Manor Court in Medieval England," *Law and History Review* 2 (1984), 128–152.

5. See Table A.10 for the Penifaders and Kroyls. Tim Lomas found roughly similar proportions of individual women identified in the manorial courts of post-plague Durham (22 percent on the manors of the Bishop of Durham and 36 percent on manors held by Durham priory). See his "South-East Durham: Late Fourteenth and Fifteenth Centuries," in *The Peasant Land Market in Medieval England,* ed. P. D. A. Harvey (Oxford, 1984), p. 257.

6. The control of local offices by the wealthy and privileged sector of the peasantry has been noted in many studies. The most thorough examination of the coincidence of economic and governmental power is Anne DeWindt, "Peasant Power Structures in Fourteenth-Century King's Ripton," *Mediaeval Studies* 38 (1976), pp. 236–267. For the social control wielded by officeholders, see Barbara A. Hanawalt, "Community Conflict and Social Control: Crime and Justice in the Ramsey Abbey Villages," *Mediaeval Studies* 39 (1977), pp. 402–423. For an example of the taking of private benefit from public office, see George Caspar Homans, *English Villagers of the Thirteenth Century* (1941; rpt. New York, 1970), pp. 301–302. For an example of an officer fined for dereliction of duty, see N.R.O. 20/1/1317. For attacks against officers, see N.R.O., 21/9/1301 and 6/10/1302. For William Stagnum's fine to avoid serving as reeve, see N.R.O., 3/1/1314. For an exceptional case of women holding local office, see Hilton, "Women in the Village," p. 105. For other isolated examples of women holding office, see Hilton, "Women Traders in Medieval England," note 3.

7. William Alfred Morris, *The Frankpledge System* (New York, 1910). Maitland suggested that women were not included in tithings

because "every woman is the mainpast of some man" (see Pollock and Maitland, *English Law,* vol. I, p. 482).

8. Sometimes officers acted as pledges and sometimes pledges were probably paid for their service, but usually pledging was performed as an unremunerated favor. See Martin Pimsler, "Solidarity in the Medieval Village? The Evidence of Personal Pledging at Elton, Huntingdonshire," *Journal of British Studies* 17, no. 1 (1977), pp. 1–11. Pimsler also noted both "the frequency with which men in positions of responsibility acted as sureties" and that pledges "tended to come from the wealthier segment of the village" (pp. 6–8). See also R. M. Smith, "Kin and Neighbors in a Thirteenth–Century Suffolk Community," *Journal of Family History* 4 (1979), esp. pp. 223–224.

9. See Table 6.3 in which the pledging of women in Brigstock is described in greater detail. No female pledges were recorded in the pre-plague rolls of Iver, but three women were accepted as personal pledges by the court of Houghton-cum-Wyton in 1349. All three women acted as pledges in minor circumstances, guaranteeing the amercements of brewers. The coincidence of these three instances of female pledging with Houghton-cum-Wyton's struggle with the plague suggests that the officers of the court were too harassed by other matters to quibble over the sex of brewing sureties. Pimsler reports one instance of female pledging at Elton, but suggests that it might have been a scribal error ("Solidarity," note 18). On the Yorkshire manor of Wakefield, no woman ever successfully served as pledge, but a cryptic entry in 1298 suggests that widows could do so (Amabel del Botham, when sued for money she had pledged, responded that "she could not pledge for anyone while her husband was alive"). See William Paley Baildon, ed., *Court Rolls of the Manor of Wakefield, Vol. II (1297–1309)* (Leeds, 1906), p. 36.

10. Pollock and Maitland, *English Law,* I, p. 485.

11. N.R.O., 6/10/1302.

12. Several studies have examined the informal power exercised by women in rural communities, see Susan Carol Rogers, "Female Forms of Power and the Myth of Male Dominance: A Model of Female/Male Interaction in Peasant Society," *American Ethnologist* 2 (1975), pp. 727–756; Joyce F. Riegelhaupt, "Saloio Women: An Analysis of Informal and Formal Political and Economic Roles of Portuguese Peasant Women," *Anthropological Quarterly* 40 (1967), pp. 109–126; Rayna R. Reiter, "Men and Women in the South of France: Public and Private Domains," in *Toward an Anthropology of Women,* ed. Rayna R. Reiter (New York, 1975), pp. 252–282; Martine Segalen, *Love and Power in the Peasant Family: Rural France in the Nineteenth Century,* trans. Sarah Matthews (Chicago, 1983). See also Martin King Whyte, *The*

Status of Women in Preindustrial Societies (Princeton, 1978), esp. pp. 167–184.

13. The fundamental limitations on the informal power exercised by women in rural communities are explored in Reiter, "Men and Women."

14. See the Appendix for an explanation of the method used to sample civil litigation in Brigstock. The discussion here is only preliminary; specific aspects of women's participation in pleas will be discussed more fully in subsequent chapters.

15. Pollock and Maitland, *English Law,* II, pp. 399–436.

16. As discussed in the Appendix, women of unknown status were probably either unmarried spinsters or widows. Brigstock was not unusual in the low involvement of women in pleas of debt; Elaine Clark found that only 7 percent of debt litigants in Writtle between 1382 and 1490 were women. See "Debt Litigation in a Late Medieval English Vill," in *Pathways to Medieval Peasants,* ed. J. A. Raftis (Toronto, 1981), p. 252. For the Hayroun-Sutor case, see N.R.O., 8/3/1331, 12/4/1331, and 3/5/1331.

17. Of the 333 litigants who used assistors, 51 (15 percent) turned to family members on some occasions. Women, however, were almost twice as likely as men to use relatives for assistance (24 percent versus 13 percent). Women were not legally obliged to use specified male kin as pledges. On the northern manor of Wakefield, a woman once tried to wage her law with other women, but the procedure was successfully challenged (and she lost the case). See Baildon, ed., *Court Rolls of the Manor of Wakefield, Vol. I (1274–1297)* (Leeds, 1901), pp. 194, 212.

18. See N.R.O., 2/8/1303 for the Morice-Cocus case. In the Brigstock sample of pleas, 6 of the 12 persons who clearly lost cases on the basis of legal errors were women. In addition, at least two women in Brigstock claimed that they were incapable of answering the charges brought against them. In 1301, Alice ad Solarium responded to a plea brought against her by stating *"non teneri respondere quia sectam non habuit vivam"* (N.R.O., 29/9/1301). In 1315, Alice Cocus denied an accusation and stated *"non habuit clientem nec nescuit in forma iuris respondere"* (N.R.O., 16/1/1315). Both cases were terminated quickly by court adjudication.

19. Case type did not significantly affect the mode of resolution; most suits of trespass, contract, and debt were resolved with concords. Women, of course, might have preferred court judgment to concords. Barbara Hanawalt found that juries and judges were considerably less willing to convict women of felonies than men, and Maryanne Kowaleski has similarly discovered that juries in Exeter were particularly lenient on female defendants. See Barbara A. Hanawalt, "The Female Felon in Fourteenth-Century England," in *Women in Medieval Society,* ed. Susan Mosher

Stuard (Philadelphia, 1976), pp. 125–140, and Kowaleski, "Women's Work." A similar bias in the Brigstock court might have encouraged women to pursue their cases to final judgment. Indeed, although judgments were heavily biased in favor of plaintiffs (who won about 85 percent of their cases), women, who appeared more frequently as defendants than as plaintiffs, were nevertheless roughly as successful in their final resolutions as men. For a recent discussion of the use of concords to resolve litigation, see Michael Clanchy, "Law and Love in the Middle Ages," *Disputes and Settlements: Law and Human Relations in the West,* ed. John Bossy (Cambridge, 1983), pp. 47–68.

20. N.R.O., 12/3/1310, 2/4/1310, 23/4/1310, 14/5/1310, 4/6/ 1310, and 25/6/1310. Because the courts for 1310 stop with Emma's third essoin in the last court for June, it is not known whether Simon persisted in his claim despite the long delays of his opponents.

21. The term "social adulthood" is used here to describe the status of those who enjoyed full access to the public organizations—political, legal, economic, and social—of their communities. Because it is an artificial, not a natural, status, it is distinct from chronological adulthood.

22. All of these matters are discussed more fully in subsequent chapters. For women's paid and unpaid work, see Chapter V. For the holding of land by daughters, wives, and widows, see Chapters IV, V, and VI respectively.

23. See the Appendix for an explanation of the methods used to sample land transactions in Brigstock. See N.R.O., file 31, for the rental of 1319. The proportion of land controlled by women might have been somewhat high in Brigstock. For lower estimates of landholding by women, see Britton, *Community,* pp. 79–86; DeWindt, *Land and People,* pp. 117–121, 148–150; Hilton, "Women in the Village," pp. 98–101; Titow, *English Rural Society,* p. 87; Bruce M. S. Campbell, "Population Pressure, Inheritance and the Land Market in a Fourteenth-Century Peasant Community," in *Land, Kinship and Life-Cycle,* ed. Richard M. Smith (Cambridge, 1984), p. 96. Rates similar to those of Brigstock, however, were found in Redgrave, Suffolk where 20 percent of the holdings were possessed by women in 1289 (I am grateful to Richard Smith for this information). Even higher rates were found in the Essex communities of Great Waltham and High Easter, where women held 23 percent of the land in 1328. See L. R. Poos, "Population and Resources in Two Fourteenth-Century Essex Communities: Great Waltham and High Easter, 1327–1389," Diss. University of Cambridge, 1983, p. 214.

24. Ernestine Friedl, "The Position of Women: Appearance and Reality," *Anthropological Quarterly* 40 (1967), pp. 97–108, and Friedl's *Vasilika: A Village in Modern Greece* (New York, 1962).

25. N.R.O., 17/9/1304.

26. Rickert, ed. and trans., *Babees Book,* pp. 35–36.

27. Although women came to court less often than men and under restricted circumstances, the persons with whom they interacted on such occasions nevertheless reliably reflect relationships formed outside of court. Most men attended court so frequently and so regularly that influential social ties found their diluted reflection in court records; when a man needed a personal pledge to back up a legal obligation, he turned to a friend, not a stranger. His land sales, debt contracts, property disputes, complaints about neighbors, and tales of physical assaults or thefts similarly betray his networks of friendship and enmity. To be sure, every social interaction did not merit a court notation, but male villagers were so publicly active that the transactions they recorded in their triweekly community court are fair indicators of their most important social relationships. Tracing the social activities of females through court records, however, is more difficult because women, lacking basic political and legal options, had many fewer opportunities for court action. But contacts formed by women in court, although less frequent and more restricted than those of men, were not legal artifacts. Records of women proffering pledges, buying land, assaulting neighbors, or complaining about trespasses might be less common than those for men, but they do reflect, as with men's legal actions, women's social relations outside of court. It is worth repeating that the same political and legal restrictions that so complicate the historian's task of reconstructing the social experiences of women also restricted the social opportunities of women.

28. The problem of unreported crime plagues all studies of public misbehavior reported in legal records, and the possibility that the crimes of women and men were reported to the Brigstock court with different alacrity cannot be ignored. Nevertheless, reported crime provides a particularly good measure of female social activity because it is relatively unaffected by the legal and political handicaps of women. For example, since women seldom served as pledges, loaned money, or traded land, their friendships are less clearly reflected in such legal activities, but women were reported so frequently for trespasses, assaults, thefts, and other offenses that criminal reports provide an especially good base for comparing the everyday activities of women and men. See the Appendix for an explanation of the method used to sample criminal presentments. This discussion of reported crime in Brigstock is a preliminary introduction to the more detailed discussions to be found in later chapters.

29. For Henry Cocus' citations, see N.R.O., 21/9/1295, 21/9/1300, 6/10/1302, 17/9/1304, 10/2/1317, 27/9/1322, 21/9/1340. All four men were reported for insolence to their tithingmen (N.R.O., 21/9/1319 and 21/9/1340); the one woman refused to allow entry to officers (*clausit hostium contra visores*), N.R.O., 6/10/1302.

30. Barbara Hanawalt also found that men were more often reported for violent crimes, see "Female Felon," pp. 128–129.

31. See N.R.O., 25/9/1343. Barbara Hanawalt reached a similar conclusion about female motivations in "Female Felon," p. 133.

32. Women were especially active in appealing cases to the Huntingdonshire eyre in the late thirteenth century, despite the restricted rights of women to appeal. Since most cases came before the eyre by presentments of juries, it seems possible that appeals by women were admitted because their grievances were especially likely to be ignored by juries. See Anne Rieber DeWindt and Edwin Brezette DeWindt, *Royal Justice in the Medieval English Countryside* (Toronto, 1981), I, pp. 45–50.

33. Mary Ritter Beard, *Woman as a Force in History* (1946; rpt. New York, 1962).

34. Peggy R. Sanday, "Toward a Theory of the Status of Women," *American Anthropologist* 75 (1973), pp. 1682–1700 (quotation from p. 1682).

35. Heidi Hartmann, "Capitalism, Patriarchy, and Job Segregation by Sex," in *Woman and the Workplace,* ed. Martha Blaxall and Barbara Reagan (Chicago, 1976), p. 142. See also the essay by Berenice A. Carroll, "Mary Ritter Beard's *Woman as a Force in History:* A Critique," in *Liberating Women's History,* ed. Berenice A. Carroll (Urbana, Ill., 1976), pp. 26–41.

36. Jack Goody, *Production and Reproduction: A Comparative Study of the Domestic Domain* (Cambridge, 1976).

37. Whyte, *Status of Women.*

38. More likely than not, the culture and attitudes of the peasantry were deeply influenced by the traditions of the elite. R. H. Hilton has said that "in so far as one has evidence at all, the ruling ideas of medieval peasants seem to have been the ideas of the rulers of society as transmitted to them in innumerable sermons." See *English Peasantry,* p. 16. For two excellent general introductions to elite attitudes toward women, see Power, "Medieval Ideas about Women," in *Medieval Women,* pp. 9–34, and Carolly Erickson, *The Medieval Vision* (New York, 1976), pp. 181–212.

39. See especially Carol Gilligan, *In a Different Voice: Psychological Theory and Women's Development* (Cambridge, Mass., 1982).

Chapter III. Rural Households Before the Plague

1. See especially the depiction of the medieval family and household in Lawrence Stone, *The Family, Sex and Marriage in England 1500–1800* (New York, 1977). For a summary of how historians have fit the medieval family into their arguments about the transition from medieval

to modern society, see R. M. Smith, "Some Reflections on the Evidence for the Origins of the 'European Marriage Pattern' in England," in *The Sociology of the Family: New Directions for Britain,* ed. Chris Harris (Keele, Eng., 1979), esp. pp. 85–91.

2. Although household (denoting those sharing residence and work as well as kinship) is used in this book in distinction to family (those sharing a relationship through birth or marriage), neither is necessarily a natural organization. For discussions of the defining characteristics of households, see Peter Laslett, "Introduction," in *Household and Family in Past Time,* ed. Peter Laslett with Richard Wall (Cambridge, 1972), pp. 1–89; Olivia Harris, "Households as Natural Units," in *Of Marriage and the Market,* 2nd edition, ed. Kate Young et al. (London, 1984), pp. 136–155; Richard Wall, "Introduction," in *Family Forms in Historic Europe,* ed. Richard Wall with Jean Robin and Peter Laslett (Cambridge, 1983), pp. 1–63. For discussions of the family as a social unit, see Rayna Rapp, Ellen Ross, and Renate Bridenthal, "Examining Family History," *Feminist Studies* 5 (1979), pp. 174–200.

3. See the Appendix for an introduction to the methods used to study the social relationships of Henry Kroyl junior and other members of the Kroyl and Penifader families in Brigstock. See also my article, "The Tie That Binds: Peasant Marriages and Families in Late Medieval England," *Journal of Interdisciplinary History* 15 (1984), pp. 111–129.

4. This point has been discussed extensively by historians. For major studies, see Helen Cam, "Pedigrees of Villeins and Freemen in the Thirteenth Century," in *Liberties and Communities in Medieval England: Collected Studies in Local Administration and Topography* (London, 1963), pp. 124–136; M. M. Postan, "Legal Status and Economic Condition in Medieval Villages," in *Essays on Medieval Agriculture and General Problems of the Medieval Economy* (Cambridge, 1973), pp. 278–289; R. H. Hilton, "The Social Structure of the Village," in *English Peasantry,* pp. 20–36.

5. E. A. Kosminsky, *Studies in the Agrarian History of England in the Thirteenth Century,* ed. R. H. Hilton (Oxford, 1956).

6. For examples, see J. A. Raftis, "Social Structures in Five East Midland Villages: A Study of Possibilities in the Use of Court Roll Data," *Economic History Review,* 2nd series, 18 (1965), pp. 83–100; DeWindt, "Peasant Power Structures"; Hilton, "Social Structure"; DeWindt, *Land and People,* p. 35; M. M. Postan, *The Medieval Economy and Society* (1971; rpt. Harmondsworth, 1975), pp. 142–147.

7. For the high incidence of intragroup contact, see DeWindt, *Land and People,* pp. 242–275; Britton, *Community,* pp. 103–114; Smith, "Kin and Neighbors." For discussions of how socioeconomic status affected

family size and kinship, see Razi, *Life, Marriage,* pp. 83–88; Smith, "Kin and Neighbors"; Edward Britton, "The Peasant Family in Fourteenth-Century England," *Peasant Studies* 5, no. 2 (1976), pp. 2–7. For explorations of how the privileges of wealthy peasants were nevertheless too limited and too temporary to make them a distinct class, see Postan, "Legal Status," and the work of R. H. Hilton, especially *A Medieval Society: The West Midlands at the End of the Thirteenth Century* (London, 1966), pp. 149–166, and Hilton's "Conflict and Collaboration," in *English Peasantry,* pp. 54–75. For intergroup tensions, see Britton, *Community,* pp. 115–123; Hanawalt, "Community Conflict."

8. See the Appendix for evidence on the social structures of Brigstock, Iver, and Houghton-cum-Wyton.

9. J. A. Raftis' study of the Ramsey estates suggests that manorial officials were particularly unconcerned about regulating the emigration of their tenants in the years that preceded the plague. He found that "there was no great pressure to retain villeins on their 'home' manor" in the early fourteenth century, but that after 1400 Ramsey officials became increasingly concerned about rural mobility and recorded in great detail the whereabouts and activities of those who had left their manors. See *Tenure and Mobility,* pp. 129–182, quote from p. 141.

10. See especially, Raftis, *Tenure and Mobility,* pp. 129–182; Peter McClure, "Patterns of Migration in the Late Middle Ages: The Evidence of English Place-Name Surnames," *Economic History Review,* 2nd series, 32 (1979), pp. 167–182.

11. See the Appendix. See also the article by L. R. Poos, "Population Turnover in Medieval Essex: The Evidence of Some Early Fourteenth-Century Tithing Lists," in *The World We Have Gained: Essays in Honour of Peter Laslett,* ed. Lloyd Bonfield, Richard Smith, and Keith Wrightson (Oxford, 1986). Poos suggests that rates of pre-plague rural mobility might closely parallel the high turnovers found in the late seventeenth-century villages of Clayworth and Cogenhoe.

12. In the Brigstock court, for example, tenants were regularly amerced for harboring itinerants for long periods (*hospitare*). See also Raftis, *Tenure and Mobility,* pp. 130–138.

13. Britnell, "Markets, 1200–1349." The growing importance of rural markets by the late thirteenth century is also illustrated by an increase in both the minting and dissemination of small coinage. See R. H. Hilton, "Lords, Burgesses and Hucksters," *Past and Present* 97 (1982), pp. 5–6.

14. Unlike Henry junior and John, who both served repeatedly in local offices, Robert Kroyl never acquired official responsibility. When their father died in 1329, his property was divided between Henry junior and John with no known provision for Robert. See N.R.O., 8/9/1329.

15. See Chapter V for a discussion of how Cristina Penifader's marriage to Richard Power of Cranford affected her public relationships with her siblings.

16. For a discussion of how kinship reckoned bilaterally lacks "clear structural persistence over time," see Keith Wrightson, "Household and Kinship in Sixteenth-Century England," *History Workshop* 12 (1981), pp. 151–158, quote from p. 155.

17. Cam, "Pedigrees."

18. See, for example, discussions in Barbara A. Hanawalt, "The Peasant Family and Crime in Fourteenth-Century England," *Journal of British Studies* 13, no. 2 (1974), p. 2; Smith, "Kin and Neighbors," pp. 252–254; Jack Goody, *The Development of the Family and Marriage in Europe* (Cambridge, 1983), pp. 262–278.

19. See Chapter V for a full discussion of Henry Kroyl junior's network of court interactions. For discussions of the limited importance of kinship in medieval villages, see Smith, "Kin and Neighbors," and Bennett, "The Tie That Binds." For similar conclusions about the relative importance of kin and neighbors in an early modern village, see Keith Wrightson and David Levine, *Poverty and Piety in an English Village: Terling, 1525–1700* (New York, 1979), pp. 73–109. A debate on this subject has recently clarified many issues. See Miranda Chaytor, "Household and Kinship: Ryton in the Late 16th and Early 17th Centuries," *History Workshop* 10 (1980), pp. 25–60; Richard Wall, "Household and Kinship," *History Workshop* 12 (1981), p. 199; Olivia Harris, "Households and Their Boundaries," *History Workshop* 13 (1982), pp. 143–152; Wrightson, "Household and Kinship"; Rab Houston and Richard Smith, "A New Approach to Family History?" *History Workshop* 14 (1982), pp. 120–131; Christopher Hill, "Note: Household and Kinship," *Past and Present* 88 (1980), p. 142.

20. Charles Donahue, Jr., "The Policy of Alexander the Third's Consent Theory of Marriage," in *Proceedings of the Fourth International Congress of Medieval Canon Law*, ed. Stephen Kuttner (Vatican City, 1976), pp. 251–281; John T. Noonan, Jr., "Power to Choose," *Viator* 4 (1973), pp. 419–434.

21. Michael M. Sheehan, "The Formation and Stability of Marriage in Fourteenth-Century England: Evidence of an Ely Register," *Mediaeval Studies* 33 (1971), pp. 228–263; Sheehan's "Choice of Marriage Partner in the Middle Ages: Development and Mode of Application of a Theory of Marriage," *Studies in Medieval and Renaissance History*, new series, 1 (1978), pp. 3–33; R. H. Helmholz, *Marriage Litigation in Medieval England* (London, 1974).

22. Maddicott, *Demands of the Crown.*

23. One historical sociologist has recently placed especially heavy

focus upon how seigneurial policies shaped the rural household. See Christopher Middleton, "The Sexual Division of Labor in Feudal England," *New Left Review* 113–114 (1979), pp. 147–168, and Middleton's "Peasants, Patriarchy and the Feudal Mode of Production in England: A Marxist Appraisal" (in two parts) *Sociological Review,* 29 (1981), pp. 105–154. It is worth noting that Middleton still maintains that most households in the medieval countryside were extended to include more than a single nuclear family.

24. M. M. Postan, *The Famulus: The Estate Labourer in the XIIth and XIIIth Centuries,* Economic History Review Supplements 2 (Cambridge, 1954).

25. For examples, see N.R.O., 13/12/1314 (presentment against John Babel) and 6/2/1315 (Robert Pidenton versus William Sanin).

26. Razi, "Family, Land," p. 31. It is possible that the populous era before the plague—when workers were many and wages low—especially encouraged the hiring of servants. Razi found that only 20 percent of households in Halesowen after the plague employed servants ("Family, Land," p. 31). Richard Smith similarly established that 20 percent of households in Rutland in 1377 included a live-in servant; see his "Hypothèses sur la nuptialité en Angleterre aux XII–XIV siècles," *Annales, économies, sociétés, civilisations* 38 (1983), pp. 107–136. But Smith has used the findings of Ann Kussmaul to suggest that the period after the plague witnessed a growth, rather than a decline, in the incidence of service (because the use of servants is especially high when wages are high, living costs low, and pastoralism important); see Smith "Some Issues Concerning Families and Their Property in Rural England 1250–1800," in Smith's *Land, Kinship and Life-Cycle* (Cambridge, 1984), esp. pp. 22–38. See also Ann Kussmaul, *Servants in Husbandry in Early Modern England* (Cambridge, 1981); Britton, *Community,* pp. 135–137; DeWindt, *Land and People,* pp. 91–95; Raftis, *Warboys,* pp. 203–207.

27. George Homan's notion that only one child in each generation had access to land and that this heir had to wait to marry until parental death brought inheritance (*English Villagers*) has been successfully challenged by Edward Britton who demonstrated that many families established several sons on holdings in early fourteenth-century Broughton (see his "Peasant Family"). See also Richard M. Smith, "Families and Their Land in an Area of Partible Inheritance: Redgrave, Suffolk 1260–1320," in *Land, Kinship and Life-Cycle,* esp. pp. 149–185, and Jack Goody, Joan Thirsk, and E. P. Thompson, eds., *Family and Inheritance: Rural Society in Western Europe 1200–1800* (Cambridge, 1976).

28. For major discussions of the peasant land market, see M. M. Postan, "The Charters of the Villeins," in *Carte Nativorum,* ed. C. N. L.

Brooke and M. M. Postan (Oxford, 1960) pp. xxviii–lx; Harvey, *Peasant Land Market;* Smith, *Land, Kinship and Life-Cycle;* Raftis, *Tenure and Mobility;* Rosamund Jane Faith, "Peasant Families and Inheritance Customs in Medieval England," *Agricultural History Review* 14 (1966), pp. 77–95; Edward King, *Peterborough Abbey 1086–1310: A Study in the Land Market* (Cambridge, 1973); Paul R. Hyams, "The Origins of a Peasant Land Market in England," *Economic History Review,* 2nd series, 23 (1970), pp. 18–31.

The issue of whether the peasant land market extended to all properties or instead left certain family holdings intact is complex and controversial. On the one hand, Alan Macfarlane lays great emphasis on the legal ability of medieval peasants to disinherit future generations by alienating all properties. Macfarlane ignores the fact that the peasantry rarely used this legal option; see his *The Origins of English Individualism: The Family, Property, and Social Transition* (Oxford, 1978), esp. pp. 102–130. On the other hand, Cecily Howell claims that early fourteenth-century holdings were inalienable and passed along intact from generation to generation. But Howell's methodology is poorly explained, and her findings have not been corroborated in other studies. See Howell's *Land, Family and Inheritance in Transition* (Cambridge, 1983). Actual practice probably ranged somewhere between these two extremes, with most households trying to maintain a core property supplemented with other acreage as necessary. See Faith, "Peasant Families," p. 86; Harvey, *Westminster Abbey,* pp. 294–330; King, *Peterborough Abbey.*

29. For the Penifader grants, see N.R.O., 22/1/1312, 20/6/1314, 8/8/1314, ?/10/1316. Parental gifts of land to unmarried children are discussed more fully in Chapter IV.

30. J. Z. Titow (*English Rural Society,* pp. 64–96) has argued that a household of 4.5 persons would need at least 10 acres to survive on its agricultural produce. Since the estimates of scholars like E. A. Kosminsky have shown that from one-third to one-half of households in most villages farmed less than 10 acres, economic opportunities in nonagricultural sectors were clearly vital to many households.

31. Jean Birrell, "Peasant Craftsmen in the Medieval Forest," *Agricultural History Review* 17 (1969), pp. 91–107; Britton, *Community,* pp. 87–92; DeWindt, *Land and People,* pp. 235–240; Raftis, *Warboys,* pp. 193–210; Bennett, "The Village Ale-Wife."

32. Britnell, "Markets, 1200–1349."

33. N.R.O., 15/12/1301 (collecting peat), 16/1/1315 (timbering), 31/5/1303 and 2/5/1315 (clothworking), 14/2/1343 (fishing), 30/5/ 1314 (selling meat).

34. Of eight women whose premarital activities in Brigstock could be traced, four clearly enjoyed economic autonomy before marriage. Of

four men, two displayed considerable premarital independence. The evidence about the activities of these twelve young people is discussed in Chapter IV, which also explores other information that suggests the semi-independence of adolescents in Brigstock before the plague. For a discussion of premarital economic independence in the early fifteenth century, see Judith M. Bennett, "Medieval Peasant Marriage: An Examination of Marriage License Fines in the *Liber Gersumarum*," in Raftis, *Pathways*, pp. 193–246.

35. For a theoretical discussion of marriage settlements in rural societies, see Lutz K. Berkner, "Rural Family Organization in Europe: A Problem in Comparative History," *Peasant Studies Newsletter* 1 (1972), pp. 145–156. For the Kroyl-Penifader settlement, see N.R.O., 31/5/1319.

36. The social changes occasioned by marriage are fully discussed in Chapter V.

37. For a discussion of how household size and structure change as the head ages, see Lutz K. Berkner, "The Stem Family and the Developmental Cycle of the Peasant Household: An Eighteenth-Century Austrian Example," *American Historical Review* 77 (1972), pp. 398–418.

38. Razi, *Life, Marriage*, pp. 83–88; Smith, "Kin and Neighbors" and "Some Issues," pp. 22–38; Britton, "Peasant Family."

39. E. A. Wrigley, "Fertility Strategy for the Individual and the Group," in *Historical Studies of Changing Fertility*, ed. Charles Tilly (Princeton, 1978), pp. 135–154. See also Smith, "Some Issues," pp. 38–62, and Jack Goody, "Strategies of Heirship," *Comparative Studies in Society and History* 15 (1973), pp. 3–20.

40. Ian Kershaw estimated that perhaps as much as 10 percent of the English population perished during these years ("The Great Famine"). L. R. Poos suggests that mortality was nearer to 15 percent in "The Rural Population of Essex in the Later Middle Ages," *Economic History Review*, 2nd series, 38 (1985), pp. 515–530.

41. Razi, *Life, Marriage*, pp. 43–45. See criticisms of Razi's calculations in Poos and Smith, "Legal Windows?" and Razi's response, "The Use of Manorial Court Rolls in Demographic Analysis: A Reconsideration," *Law and History* 3 (1985), pp. 191–200.

42. H. E. Hallam, "Some Thirteenth-Century Censuses," *Economic History Review*, 2nd series, 10 (1958), pp. 340–361, and "Further Observations on the Spalding Serf Lists," *Economic History Review*, 2nd series, 16 (1963), pp. 338–350. J. C. Russell took issue with Hallam's findings in "Demographic Limitations of the Spalding Serf Lists," *Economic History Review*, 2nd series, 15 (1962), pp. 138–144. R. M. Smith has recently argued that these listings recorded families (including deceased members) not households, and therefore are genealogies, not censuses (see "Hypothèses sur la nuptialité," esp. pp. 120–124).

43. George Homans argued that the custom of partible inheritance promoted large joint-family households with married siblings forming a single household, *English Villagers,* esp. pp. 110–120. If, as Berkner has suggested ("Rural Family Organization"), partible inheritance promotes both joint-family households and nuclear-family households, the presence of nuclear households in the Lincolnshire lists is less surprising than the virtual absence of joint-family households.

44. See Hallam's "Thirteenth-Century Censuses" and "Further Observations"; J. Krause, "The Medieval Household: Large or Small?" *Economic History Review,* 2nd series, 9 (1957), pp. 420–432; Josiah Cox Russell, *British Medieval Population* (Albuquerque, 1948), esp. pp. 22–31 and Russell's "Preplague Population"; Titow, *English Rural Society,* esp. pp. 83–90; Razi, *Life, Marriage,* esp. pp. 83–88, 92–93; Howell, *Land, Family,* pp. 199–236; Lomas, "South-east Durham," pp. 257–258.

45. Maurice Beresford and John G. Hurst, *Deserted Medieval Villages* (London, 1971), esp. pp. 76–181; R. K. Field, "Worcestershire Peasant Buildings, Household Goods and Farming Equipment in the Later Middle Ages," *Medieval Archaeology* 9 (1965), pp. 105–145; Hilton, *Medieval Society,* pp. 90–103.

46. R. M. Smith has suggested, however, that retiring parents usually preferred to live separately from the younger generation (in a building separate from the main dwelling); see "Rooms, Relatives and Residential Arrangements: Some Evidence in Manor Court Rolls 1250–1500," *Annual Report of the Medieval Village Research Group* 30 (1982), pp. 34–35. The apparent contradiction between some written evidence of additional dwellings for retirees and little archaeological evidence of such structures might indicate that retirements were fairly uncommon, but did result in separate dwellings when they occurred.

47. Studying only retirements that involved fathers and sons, Razi found that 20 percent of the fathers who handed their holdings over to their sons in Halesowen before the plague also contracted formal maintenance agreements. On the basis of these figures, he suggests that maintenance agreements were only used when a villager "had reason to believe that he would be mistreated by his heir"; see "Family, Land," p. 7–8. But Razi brings forth neither evidence from the text of maintenance agreements nor data on the other court activities of these fathers and sons to support his notion of distrust. It is hard to imagine, moreover, why fathers who distrusted their sons would have decided either to retire or to use their sons as maintainers. The subject certainly merits further inquiry, for it seems just as likely that most landholders who lived long enough to retire contracted maintenance agreements, but that

only some were enrolled in the manor court. See also Smith, "Rooms, Relatives."

48. Elaine Clark, "Some Aspects of Social Security in Medieval England," *Journal of Family History* 7 (1982), pp. 307–320.

49. See note 26. The activities of servants in medieval villages are explored more fully in Chapter IV.

50. N.R.O., 11/6/1339 and 9/4/1344. Barbara Hanawalt also discusses the endowment of servants in "Women's Contribution."

51. Peter Laslett, "Parental Deprivation in the Past," in *Family Life and Illicit Love in Earlier Generations* (Cambridge, 1977), pp. 160–173. See also Chaytor, "Household and Kinship."

Chapter IV. Daughters and Sons

1. For Cristina Penifader's landholdings, see N.R.O., 22/1/1312, 8/8/1314 (this land was granted *ad opus*), and ?/10/1316. See the Appendix for information about the analysis of the court networks of the Penifaders and Kroyls. Cristina Penifader's premarital court network included 15 contacts with 7 people. Her only multiplex relationship was with her father (with whom she interacted on 7 occasions). Her father had independent multiplex relationships with the only 2 other people with whom Cristina Penifader interacted more than once (2 contacts each), and he also associated independently with 2 of the remaining 4 persons in his daughter's network. She required legal assistance on 11 occasions before her marriage; her father provided the needed aid in 4 instances. For her obligation to attend court, see essoins offered in such courts as N.R.O., 24/8/1316 and 26/5/1317.

2. For Henry Kroyl junior's premarital acquisitions of land, see N.R.O., 18/11/1316, 14/4/1317, 5/5/1317, 26/5/1317, 4/1/1319, and 31/5/1319. For a full discussion of his premarital court network, see my article "The Tie That Binds." For examples of his assisting others in court, see N.R.O., 18/8/1317 (pledge), 7/7/1317 (essoiner), and 19/4/1319 (attorney).

3. Adolescence is used in this study in the standard sense, as defined in the *Oxford English Dictionary,* of "the period which extends from childhood to manhood or womanhood." Historians, like Philippe Ariès, have usually downplayed the importance of this transitional period; see Ariès' *Centuries of Childhood: A Social History of Family Life,* trans. Robert Baldick (New York, 1962). But it has received more notice in recent years, most notably in the study by John R. Gillis, *Youth and History: Tradition and Change in European Age Relations 1770–Present* (New York, 1974). Because adolescents in Brigstock accepted many but

not all of the responsibilities of older villagers, they are considered in this study as "adults" rather than children, but not as "full adults."

4. N.R.O., 3/9/1339. George Homans cites another example of the arrangement of a minor heir's marriage; see *English Villagers*, p. 162. Arranged marriages were subject to the final approval of the principals when they reached the age of consent.

5. Buckinghamshire Archaeological Society, 128/53 (hereafter cited as B.A.S.), m. 17, 7/5/1337.

6. N.R.O., 27/9/1303.

7. The status of children was roughly similar under the common law; their properties were protected, but they were usually "covered" by guardians. See Pollock and Maitland, *English Law*, II, pp. 436–445.

8. J. B. Post, "Ages at Menarche and Menopause: Some Medieval Authorities," *Population Studies* 25 (1971), pp. 83–87; Darrel W. Amundsen and Carol Jean Diers, "The Age of Menarche in Medieval Europe," *Human Biology* 45 (1973), pp. 363–369.

9. Helmholz, *Marriage Litigation*, p. 98.

10. According to Morris, *Frankpledge System*, pp. 70–71, young men entered tithings at 12 years of age. At King's Ripton in the late thirteenth century, an inquest reported that women reached legal maturity at 13½ years of age and that men reached maturity at 14½ years. See Maitland, *Select Pleas in Manorial Courts*, p. 121. In Iver, however, heirs could not claim their inheritances until at least 16 years of age; when John Forde died in 1349, the court put his minor heir in custody because *"filius et heredes predicti Johannis infra etate est scilicet xvi annorum"* B.A.S., m. 47, 6/6/1349. And in Halesowen, the minimum age for holding land was 20 years (Razi, *Life, Marriage*, p. 43). The age of legal maturity in Brigstock was never stated in the extant manorial records.

11. Pollock and Maitland, *English Law*, II, 438–439. The relatively low ages of maturity among the peasantry probably reflects first, the greater need of rural parents for the labor of their children and, second, the comparatively low levels of training required to prepare peasant children for adulthood.

12. Shahar, *Fourth Estate*, p. 238; Homans, *English Villagers*, pp. 191–193. Of the 17 minor heirs placed in custody between 1332 and 1376 in Iver, custody in 7 cases (41 percent) was awarded to the minor's mother.

13. Hanawalt, "Childrearing among the Lower Classes."

14. E. A. Wrigley, "Mortality in Pre-Industrial England: The Example of Colyton, Devon, Over Three Centuries," *Daedalus* 97 (1968), pp. 546–580 (especially Tables 9 and 15). See also Roger Schofield and E. A. Wrigley, "Infant and Child Mortality in England in the Late

Tudor and Early Stuart Period," in *Health, Medicine and Mortality in the Sixteenth Century*, ed. Charles Webster (Cambridge, 1979), pp. 61–95, and Schofield and Wrigley's "English Population History from Family Reconstitution: Summary Results 1600–1799," *Population Studies* 37 (1983), esp. pp. 160–161. In the French village of Challain in the seventeenth century, 35 percent of all children died in the first year and 53 percent died before their twentieth birthdays (see Charles Tilly, "Population and Pedagogy in France," *History of Education Quarterly* 13 [1973], p. 119).

15. Two articles have recently cited compelling evidence of parental love for children during the Middle Ages, see Hanawalt, "Childrearing among the Lower Classes," and Lorraine C. Attreed, "From *Pearl* Maiden to Tower Princes: Towards a New History of Medieval Childhood," *Journal of Medieval History* 9 (1983), pp. 43–58. For similar evidence from the early modern period, see Linda A. Pollock, *Forgotten Children: Parent-Child Relations from 1500 to 1900* (Cambridge, 1983).

16. Edwin DeWindt's survey of personal names in Holywell-cum-Needingworth found that over three-fourths of all males were identified by a half-dozen names (John, Robert, William, Nicholas, Richard, Thomas), and that only two-thirds of females were named from such a small pool of names (Johanna, Margaret, Matilda, Alice, Agnes, Elena). Although his survey included three times the number of males (664 males versus 211 females), only 10 additional names were used by males (33 forenames versus 23 forenames). DeWindt commented on the fact that male names were "sometimes numbingly repeated from generation to generation within the same family." See *Land and People*, pp. 184–185. Similar patterns were found in Iver between 1332 and 1376, where 45 male forenames and 38 female forenames were used (despite the fact that roughly three times as many males were identified in the records). See also Daniel Scott Smith, "Child-Naming Practices as Cultural and Familial Indicators," *Local Population Studies* 32 (1984), pp. 17–27.

17. See, for example, Emily Coleman, "Infanticide in the Early Middle Ages," in *Women in Medieval Society*, ed. Stuard, pp. 47–70; Richard C. Trexler, "Infanticide in Florence: New Sources and First Results," *History of Childhood Quarterly* 1 (1973), pp. 98–116; Glynis Reynolds, "Infant Mortality and Sex Ratios at Baptism as Shown by Reconstruction of Willingham, a Parish at the edge of the Fens in Cambridgeshire," *Local Population Studies* 22 (1979), pp. 31–37; Richard Wall, "Inferring Differential Neglect of Females from Mortality Data," *Annales de démographie historique* (1981), pp. 119–140; Barbara D. Miller, *The Endangered Sex: Neglect of Female Children in Rural North India* (Ithaca, N.Y., 1981).

18. R. H. Helmholz, "Infanticide in the Province of Canterbury during the Fifteenth Century," *History of Childhood Quarterly* 2 (1975), pp. 379–390, esp. p. 385. See also Barbara A. Kellum, "Infanticide in England in the Later Middle Ages," *History of Childhood Quarterly* 1 (1973–1974), pp. 367–388.

19. Hanawalt, "Childrearing among the Lower Classes," pp. 10–14.

20. For discussions of the unnderenumeration of females, see Russell, *British Medieval Population,* esp. pp. 166–168; Hallam, "Thirteenth-Century Censuses"; Smith, "Some Reflections." For a discussion of the many factors that can produce skewed sex ratios, see Wall, "Inferring Differential Neglect of Females."

21. Hanawalt, "Childrearing among the Lower Classes."

22. Ivy Pinchbeck and Margaret Hewitt, *Children in English Society, Volume I: From Tudor Times to the Eighteenth Century* (London, 1969), pp. 22–23.

23. Hanawalt, "Childrearing among the Lower Classes."

24. Florentine adolescence is discussed extensively in Richard C. Trexler, *Public Life in Renaissance Florence* (New York, 1980). See also Thomas Kuehn, *Emancipation in Late Medieval Florence* (New Brunswick, 1982), and David Herlihy, "Vieillir à Florence au Quattrocento," *Annales économies, sociétés, civilisations* 24 (1969), pp. 1338–1352. The extensive political, legal, economic, and social changes occasioned by marriage in Brigstock are discussed in Chapter V.

25. J. Hajnal, "European Marriage Patterns in Perspective," in *Population in History: Essays in Historical Demography,* ed. D. V. Glass and D. E. C. Eversley (Chicago, 1965), pp. 101–143, and Hajnal's "Two Kinds of Pre-Industrial Household Formation System," in *Family Forms in Historic Europe,* ed. Richard Wall (Cambridge, 1983), pp. 65–104. For a detailed discussion of attempts to trace the medieval origins of the European marriage pattern, see Smith, "Some Reflections."

26. Razi, *Life, Marriage,* pp. 60–64. See criticisms of Razi's calculations by Poos and Smith in "Legal Windows?" pp. 144–148, and Razi's response, "Use of Manorial Rolls," pp. 198–199. Much higher estimates of marital age were reached by Cicely Howell in her study of Kibworth Harcourt after the plague, see *Land, Family,* pp. 221–225.

27. Of the six young people in Brigstock for whom premarital activities could be traced, two appeared in the courts only in the year of their marriages, three appeared three years before they married, and one was active in the courts for five years before marriage. Because only certain types of activities merited court attention, the interval between first citation and marriage provides a minimum figure for the duration of adolescence. It is worth noting that Razi does cite two individual cases in which marital age was clearly stated—two heiresses who married at 19 years

and 21 years. The marriages of heiresses, however, have might occurred unusually early.

28. Hallam, "Thirteenth-Century Censuses"; Smith, "Hypothèses sur la nuptialité."

29. Homans, *English Villagers,* pp. 136–137. Because of their unmarried status, the few servants encountered in the Brigstock samples have been analyzed as adolescents.

30. The uncertainty of this issue is probably best illustrated by the work of Richard Smith who has tried to deduce indirect evidence of the European marriage pattern in medieval England (both before and after the 1348 plague), but has stopped short of proclaiming its existence in the English countryside of the early fourteenth century. See "Hypothèses sur la nuptialité" and "Some Reflections."

31. N.R.O., ?/12/1344.

32. Table 6.1 shows how the political activities of men in Brigstock grew slowly during adolescence, peaked during the prime of life, and declined with old age.

33. Much has been made of the special rowdiness of medieval adolescents. See, for example, Britton, *Community,* pp. 38–43 and Barbara Hanawalt, *Crime and Conflict in English Communities, 1300–1348* (Cambridge, Mass., 1979), pp. 125–127. But such assertions have been based more on anecdotal evidence than comparative data. Table 4.4 suggests that adolescents were no more violent and disruptive than were full adults. In some cases, the numbers of sons and daughters in the sample are so small that apparent divergences from the patterns of their genders must be discounted (i.e., the slightly lower incidence of concords for adolescents of both sexes; the lower rate of success for daughters; the total absence of daughters from suits of debt or contract).

34. In order to trace precisely the premarital activities of a villager, one must, of course, know the date of first marriage; all activities prior to that date can then be confidently analyzed as part of the premarital adolescent stage of life. The activities of eight women and four young men in Brigstock could be reconstructed in this fashion. It should be noted that this method necessarily excludes spinsters and bachelors (who were never explicitly identified as such by the clerks) because no date of marriage confirms a prior unmarried state. The persons for whom no premarital economic activities were traced were: (a) unnamed daughter of Alan Hale, married 14/2/1292; (b) Beatrice daughter of Walter Helkok, married 1/1/1304 (see court for 29/7/1306); (c) Agnes daughter of Robert Penifader, married 31/5/1319; (d) Isabella daughter of William Pidenton, possibly married 11/7/1348; (e) Robert son of Egidius Smith, possibly married 11/7/1348; (f) Adam Gothirde, married 20/6/1298. For traced premarital experiences, see notes 1 and 2 above

(Cristina Penifader and Henry Kroyl junior) and the following courts in the N.R.O.: Isabella Brother, 20/1/1317; Alice Orgoner, 4/6/1310 and 25/6/1310; Isabella Huet, 29/9/1295, 21/9/1295, and 20/6/1298; Henry Cocus, 24/2/1301 (Cocus received only future rights to land). The fathers of Agnes Penifader, Alice Orgoner, Henry Kroyl junior, Henry Cocus, Cristina Penifader, Isabella Pidenton, and the unnamed daughter of Alan Hale held offices; the fathers of Isabella Brother, Isabella Huet, Beatrice Helkok, Robert Smith, and Adam Gothirde were never cited for official activity. See the Appendix for a full discussion of socioeconomic distinctions within Brigstock. It is worth noting that several persons who married widowers (but were not themselves known to be widowed) also acted independently before marriage. See Adam Werketon, 17/6/1295, 9/12/1300, 31/5/1303, and 21/6/1303; William Kykhok, 28/9/1297, 13/3/1304, and 17/12/1305; Elicia Sephirde, 9/5/1314 and 31/5/1319.

35. Although adolescents of both social ranks were equally active in the Brigstock land market, young people of upper rank were disproportionately represented. The best comparative evidence comes from rank assignments based on surnames, not the official activities of fathers; a ranking of all of Brigstock's villagers, based on the official activities of their fathers, would have been a lengthy and artificial task (since paternal office-holding is most relevant for determining the social ranks of adolescents). Although 60 percent of the individuals identified in Brigstock were upper rank (based on surnames), 70 percent of adolescents active in land trades were upper rank (based on surnames). Edward Britton found that social rank strongly affected the ability of parents to settle noninheriting children in Broughton before the plague; see "Peasant Family."

36. Of the 35 future grants in the sample, 20 were to sons and 5 to daughters. Of the 27 encumbered grants or leases, 8 were to sons and 3 to daughters. For the Kroyl transfer, see N.R.O., 31/5/1319.

37. Of the daughters who received land, 55 percent obtained property from their parents, as opposed to only 25 percent of sons who received land. For future grants, see note 36.

38. See discussion of commercial brewing in Chapter V.

39. Smith, "Some Issues," esp. pp. 22–38. In early modern England, servants accounted for probably one-third to one-half of all hired labor (Kussmaul, *Servants in Husbandry,* p. 4).

40. William Beveridge, "Wages in the Winchester Manors," *Economic History Review* 7 (1936–1937), pp. 22–43; James E. Thorold Rogers, *A History of Agriculture and Prices in England, Vol. I: 1259–1400* (Oxford, 1866), pp. 252–325. Women's wages are discussed more fully in Chapter V.

41. N.R.O., 21/9/1336, 11/6/1339, 9/4/1344. For other examples, see Hanawalt, "Women's Contribution."

42. For major studies of service in medieval and early modern England, see Postan, *Famulus;* Smith, "Some Issues"; Kussmaul, *Servants in Husbandry;* Marjorie K. McIntosh, "Servants and the Household Unit in an Elizabethan English Community," *Journal of Family History* 9 (1984), pp. 3–23.

43. As noted by many scholars, the disproportionate numbers of women found in late medieval towns might have resulted from rural daughters moving to urban areas offering female employment in textile crafts, service, food trades, and the like. Rodney Hilton found that about three-quarters of the immigrants to the borough of Halesowen in the late thirteenth century were women ("Women Traders," p. 149). See also the essay by P. J. P. Goldberg, "Female Labor, Service and Marriage in the Late Medieval Urban North" forthcoming in *Northern History.* Clearly, the question merits further inquiry, but the records of Brigstock unfortunately provide no information on migration out of the manor.

44. See notes 1 and 2 in this chapter.

45. The 38 pledges were: fathers, 23; mothers, 4; masters, 3; brothers, 4; persons of unknown relationship (but shared surname), 4.

46. Daughters accounted for 19 percent of reported female crimes (34 of 176 crimes), and sons constituted 16 percent of presentments against males (62 of 378 crimes).

47. It is worth noting that one reported offense not covered by the Brigstock sample of crimes was particularly biased toward daughters; no men were ever cited (or even mentioned as accessories) in any of the eight amercements for fornication (leyrwytes) levied in the manor courts. These citations were: Matilda Bate (28/11/1298); Alice Durant (29/8/1287); Emma the daughter of John Prepositus (28/11/1298 and 13/2/1299); Alice ad Solarium (25/6/1287); Alice the daughter of Mablia Tulk (11/8/1298); Alice the daughter of Peter Medicus (18/1/1292); and Margery the daughter of Hugh Swon (27/3/1299). The courts for 28/11/1298, 13/1/1299, and 27/3/1299 are in the Public Record Office, SC-2, 194/65. All others are in the appropriate rolls of the N.R.O. collection. No leyrwytes were levied in Brigstock after 1299.

48. N.R.O., 30/5/1343.

49. The 29 adolescents included 20 females (of whom 9 held properties and 1 was active in timbering) and 9 males (of whom 1 worked as a brewer before marriage). Four of the landholding women had definitely received their properties from their fathers. Of the 49 merchets recorded in the Iver courts, 13 were paid by daughters and 7 by bridegrooms. Although no published studies provide strictly comparable data,

both Britton and Razi found that sons were often settled on land before the deaths of their fathers. See Britton, *Community,* pp. 38–56; Razi, *Life, Marriage,* pp. 50–60.

50. Of the 14 merchets found in the Houghton-cum-Wyton courts, 10 were paid by daughters and 2 by bridegrooms. Of the 15 women whose premarital careers were traced, only 1 was economically active. Of the 4 men traced, only 1 probably held land. For the Prepositus dispute, see Public Record Office (hereafter cited as P.R.O.), SC-2, 179/15: 8/11/1308. For a printed transcription of the Latin text of the dispute, see Homans, *English Villagers,* p. 437 (chapter XII, note 4). The dispute ended with Stephen Prepositus producing pledges to guarantee that he would maintain his son and his son's wife according to the original agreement.

51. Smith, "Some Issues," pp. 68–85; Richard Wall, "Real Property, Marriage and Children: The Evidence from Four Pre-industrial Communities," in *Land, Kinship and Life-cycle,* ed. Smith, pp. 443–479.

52. For a discussion of the importance of birth order, see Richard Wall, "The Age at Leaving Home," *Journal of Family History* 3 (1978), pp. 181–202. For examples of how a single marriage could often result in changes for unmarried siblings, see my article "Medieval Peasant Marriage," esp. pp. 235–239. Agnes Penifader's marriage settlement was recorded in May 1319; her father had died by 31 August 1318.

53. Seigneurial interest in marriage has recently received much attention by historians. See Jean Scammell's "Freedom and Marriage in Medieval England" and "Wife-Rents and Merchet," in *Economic History Review,* 2nd series, 27 (1974), pp. 523–537 and 29 (1976), pp. 487–490; Eleanor Searle, "Freedom and Marriage in Medieval England: An Alternative Hypothesis," *Economic History Review,* 2nd series, 29 (1976), pp. 482–485, and "Seigneurial Control of Women's Marriage: The Antecedents and Function of Merchet in England," *Past and Present* 82 (1979), pp. 3–43; and contributions by Searle, Paul A. Brand and Paul R. Hyams, and Rosamund Faith to "Debate: Seigneurial Control of Women's Marriage," *Past and Present* 99 (1983), 123–160.

54. Donahue, "Alexander the Third's Consent Theory of Marriage," and Noonan, "Power to Choose."

55. Helmholz, *Marriage Litigation,* pp. 25–111; Sheehan, "Stability of Marriage" and "Choice of Marriage Partner."

56. William Langland, *The Book Concerning Piers the Plowman,* trans. and ed. Donald and Rachel Attwater (1907; rpt. London, 1959), p. 73. I am grateful to Tess Tavormina of Michigan State University for her willingness to discuss Langland's treatment of marriage with me. Since apostrophes were not used in the original texts of *Piers Plowman,*

I have altered the Attwaters' editorial placement of the apostophe in the phrase "by the fathers' will."

57. N.R.O., 29/7/1306 and 24/2/1301. For additional information on dowries, see Maitland, *Select Pleas in Manorial Courts,* pp. 32, 46–47, and Searle, "Seigneurial Control," pp. 19–20. Dowries were usually a form of premortem inheritance that excluded daughters from further claims upon their parents' properties. In Iver, for example, a daughter was excluded from an inheritance in 1352 because it was the custom of the manor that if any women *per bona et catalla antecessorum extra tenementum fuerit maritata nichil iuris in predictos tenementos post mortem antecessorum suorum clamare potest nec debet.* B.A.S., m. 55r., 5/3/1352.

58. Church courts readily overturned marriages in which consent was coerced. See Helmholz, *Marriage Litigation,* esp. pp. 199–201, 220–228. Contemporary literature also emphasized the importance of consent (as in the description from *Piers Plowman*). See also the passages in Robert Mannyng's *Handlyng Synne,* quoted by Homans, *English Villagers,* p. 163. The right of consent was most threatened in the cases of minor heirs placed in other households in anticipation of marriage at a future date, but even such attempts to arrange the marriages of minors often recognized that children might choose to terminate the agreement when they reached maturity. In 1339, for example, William Hayroun came to the Brigstock court and transferred the custody of his minor brother John to Thomas Dandelin, providing that, if John later married Thomas' daughter Emma, Thomas would endow his daughter with chattels that matched John's movable goods. William Hayroun and Thomas Dandelin certainly hoped that the children would marry as planned, but their contract nevertheless included the crucial conditional clause, *"si nubat Emmam filiam dicti Thome."* N.R.O., 3/9/1339.

59. Professor Homan's description of wedding customs is still very useful, *English Villagers,* pp. 160–176. See also the later practices described by John Brand in *Observations on the Popular Antiquities of Great Britain,* vol. 3 (1848–1849; rpt. New York, 1970), pp. 87–177. Whether private marriage threatened claims to property is yet unclear. Homans argued that, as under the common law, a Church wedding was necessary to ensure both the widow's dower and the children's inheritance. Eleanor Searle, however, has stated that "In the manorial world bastardy seems rarely to have mattered" ("Seigneurial Control," p. 36). Richard Smith has disagreed with her, concurring with Homans on the importance of publicly recognized marriage in ensuring the rights of children, but leaving open the question of what constituted a legally sufficient marriage ("Hereditary and Proprietary Rights in Land," pp.

112–114). Although proprietal disputes centered around bastardy do appear in manorial courts, they do not explicitly arise from clandestine marriages. Clearly, the subject merits further research.

60. See the case cited by Homans, *English Villagers,* p. 173, of a man amerced for failing to provide a wedding feast, and cases cited by Rosamond Faith in her contribution to "Debate: Seigneurial Control of Women's Marriage," pp. 137–140.

61. N.R.O., 29/7/1306.

62. Attempts to use such amercements to estimate rates of illegitimacy have failed. Richard Smith originally calculated high rates of illegitimacy (about 10 percent) in late thirteenth-century Redgrave and Rickinghall, and Razi found even higher rates in Halesowen during the same years. See Smith, "Life-Cycles," pp. 456–457, and Razi, *Life, Marriage,* pp. 64–71. But Smith has now retracted his estimates (see Poos and Smith, "Legal Windows?" note 72), and Razi has failed to defend his (see "Use of Manorial Rolls," pp. 198–199).

63. This issue is discussed more fully in my article, "The Tie That Binds."

64. Of the 23 marriages examined in Brigstock, 14 (61 percent) united persons from equivalent backgrounds. Of the 21 marriages traced in Iver, 13 (62 percent) were intragroup. Intergroup marriages did not follow specific patterns; both men and women married into higher social strata.

65. Rates of geographic exogamy are difficult to trace because exogamous marriages were more likely to be recorded than endogamous unions. In the *Liber Gersumarum,* 32 percent of the known marriages were exogamous, see Bennett, "Medieval Peasant Marriage" esp. pp. 219–221. An analysis of fourteenth-century marriage cases also indicated that roughly one-third of all marriages might have united persons from different villages; see Michael M. Sheehan, "Stability of Marriage," p. 251.

66. For the Iver case, see B.A.S., m.19., 1/12/1337. For the Brigstock case, see N.R.O., 9/5/1314 and 31/5/1319. See also Searle, "Seigneurial Control," pp. 19–20; Hanawalt, "Women's Contribution."

Chapter V. Wives and Husbands

1. Sheehan, "Stability of Marriage," and Helmholz, *Marriage Litigation.*

2. Estimates of marital duration were obtained by tracing the recorded activities of fifty widows who appeared in the Brigstock court while still married. The median time elapsed between first citation as a wife and first mention of bereavement was 15 years; the average was 17.1 years.

See fuller discussion in Chapter VI, note 3. Estimates of life expectancy rely on Razi who calculated that men in Halesowen before the plague could expect, at the age of twenty years, to live another 25 to 28 years (*Life, Marriage,* pp. 43–45). For a debate about the validity of these estimates, see Poos and Smith, "Legal Windows?," pp. 141–142, and Razi, "Use of Manorial Court Rolls," pp. 196–197. Demographic calculations for medieval villagers are necessarily tentative and general, but our best current estimates suggest that most men and women married at about the age of 20 years (see discussion in Chapter IV) and died no more than three decades thereafter. The incidence of remarriage is discussed in Chapter VI.

3. See especially, Stone, *Family, Sex and Marriage.* In addition, others have claimed that sexual pleasure was also rare in the preindustrial world. See Edward Shorter, "Illegitimacy, Sexual Revolution, and Social Change in Modern Europe," *Journal of Interdisciplinary History* 2 (1971), pp. 237–272, and "Female Emancipation, Birth Control, and Fertility in European History," *American Historical Review* 78 (1973), pp. 605–640.

4. For cases brought before Church courts, see Sheehan, "Stability of Marriage," and Helmholz, *Marriage Litigation.* For the Pole-Note affair, see P.R.O., SC-2, 179/13, courts for 15/7/1308 and 9/7/1310. This affair was probably particularly objectionable because Stephen Note was a very peripheral member of the Houghton community whereas Agnes Pole's husband was a person of considerable local consequence. For a concise description of Church teaching on marital companionship, see Shahar, *Fourth Estate,* pp. 67–68.

5. For the Hirdman estate, see cases in N.R.O., 2/11/1342, 6/2/1344, and 30/4/1344. Keith Wrightson has noted that, for the early modern era, "no clearer tribute to the practical experience and economic competence of women and to the trust placed in them by their husbands exists than the . . . naming of a wife as executor," *English Society 1580–1680* (London, 1982), p. 94. See also Hanawalt, "Women's Contribution."

6. See N.R.O., 25/9/1337 (Peter Aylward—elsewhere identified as the son of Richard and Elicia Aylward—amerced for drawing the blood of his brother Treuelove) and 29/9/1335 and 21/9/1336 (William Treuelove cited for petty crimes and pledged by Elicia the widow of Richard Aylward).

7. Natalie Zemon Davis, " 'Women's History' in Transition: The European Case," *Feminist Studies* 3 (1976), p. 89; see also Shahar, *Fourth Estate,* p. 71 (and note 23). Because of the presumed connection between conception and sexual pleasure, a rape victim who became pregnant could not press charges under the English common law, see Shahar, *Fourth Estate,* p. 17.

8. Pierre J. Payer, *Sex and the Penitentials: The Development of a Sexual Code, 550–1150* (Toronto, 1984), esp. pp. 19–36. Payer's careful analysis of the sexual content of penitentials has led him to conclude that "it is reasonable to assume that their contents reflect what was in fact being done" (p. 12).

9. See note 62 in Chapter IV for information on illegitimacy in medieval villages.

10. Emmanuel Le Roy Ladurie, *Montaillou: The Promised Land of Error*, trans. Barbara Bray (New York, 1978), esp. pp. 139–203.

11. Power, "Medieval Ideas about Women," in *Medieval Women*, pp. 16–19; Hanawalt, "The Peasant Family and Crime," p. 5; Le Roy Ladurie, *Montaillou*, pp. 192–203; James Buchanan Given, *Society and Homicide in Thirteenth-Century England* (Stanford, 1977), p. 195.

12. Rogers, "Female Forms of Power"; Reigelhaupt "Saloio Women"; Reiter, "Men and Women"; Segalen, *Love and Power*.

13. Both Barbara A. Hanawalt, "Violent Death in Fourteenth- and Early Fifteenth-Century England," *Comparative Studies in Society and History* 18 (1976), esp. pp. 309–310, and Given (*Society and Homicide*, esp. pp. 41–65) found that domestic homicides accounted for a relatively small proportion of homicides in medieval England. These observations have been compared with early modern data in J. A. Sharpe, "Domestic Homicide in Early Modern England," *Historical Journal* 24 (1981), 29–48.

14. Henry Kroyl junior first served as an officer in N.R.O., 14/9/1319. Of the other three men in Brigstock whose premarital careers could be traced, none served in offices as bachelors and all assumed official responsibilities during their married years. Although men identified explicitly as sons by the court clerks frequently acted as essoiners or pledges in Brigstock, they were rarely cited as officers (and such citations, as discussed in Chapter IV, probably indicate more the need for further identification than the unmarried status of the officer). Table 6.1 also illustrates how the political activities of males in Brigstock peaked during the middle years of adult life. DeWindt closely studied qualifications of jurors in Holywell-cum-Needingworth and concluded that most jurors were tenants of at least 30 years of age (*Land and People*, pp. 216–220). Although Britton showed that many sons in Broughton became jurors while their fathers were still alive, he did not consider whether such sons were married (*Community*, pp. 47–49).

15. N.R.O., 9/12/1300 (Brum); 28/7/1331 (Cissor); 18/8/1317 (Kut); 28/11/1325 (Golle).

16. The only exception was in contracts; husbands in Brigstock seem, like husbands in towns, to have been responsible for the business arrangements of their wives. In 1331, for example, John Hayroun sued both

Strangia Sutor and her husband John, alleging that Strangia had reneged on a sales contract (N.R.O., 8/3/1331 through 3/5/1331). See also Robert Pidenton's plea against both Alice Tulke and her husband William for Alice's alleged failure to deliver some grain she had sold him (N.R.O., 10/5/1319). The responsibility of husbands for the contracts of their wives (*femmes couvertes*) was a common feature of commerce in towns (see Bateson, *Borough Customs, Vol. II*, pp. cxi–cxv).

17. For Cristina Penifader, see N.R.O., 16/6/1317 (her last essoin), 28/7/1317 (her marriage), 4/1/1319 (fine by her husband to avoid court suit). For examples of Cecilia Penifader's essoins, see N.R.O., 14/2/1343, 5/12/1343, and subsequent courts. For the Northern inheritance, see N.R.O., 30/1/1326. For practices under the common law, see Pollock and Maitland, *English Law*, II, pp. 399–414.

18. Pollock and Maitland, *English Law*, II, p. 406 (note 3).

19. N.R.O., 2/8/1303 and 13/9/1303.

20. N.R.O., 22/8/1314 (Hayroun vs. Helkok); 5/12/1314 through 26/12/1314 (ad Crucem vs. Westwode); 9/5/1343 through 26/12/1343 (Molendinarius vs. Aukyn); 8/2/1331 (Faber vs. Suig).

21. Pollock and Maitland, *English Law*, II, p. 405.

22. Pollock and Maitland, *English Law*, II, pp. 399–436.

23. Despite their disputed testamentary rights, both serfs and wives often left wills. See Michael M. Sheehan, *The Will in Medieval England* (Toronto, 1963), esp. pp. 70–71 and 253–254.

24. For the dispute over the Helkok marriage settlement, see N.R.O., 29/7/1306. For another case that excluded the wife, see Maitland, *Select Pleas in Manorial Courts*, pp. 46–47. Of the eight women in the Brigstock sample of pleas sued for debt or broken contract, two were women of unknown status, three were widows, and three were wives acting jointly with their husbands. For the custumal of 1391, see N.R.O., Box X371.

25. Middleton, "Peasants, Patriarchy," 1, pp. 120–121.

26. Joint ownership of the main holding might have often been part of the marriage settlement. In 1319, for example, the marriage of Henry Kroyl junior and Agnes Penifader included the future grant to them of a semi-virgate from his parents (N.R.O., 31/5/1319). The wife's joint ownership of the household's main holding was also noted by Raftis for many of the Ramsey manors, *Tenure and Mobility*, pp. 36–42.

27. Ada Elizabeth Levett, *Studies in Manorial History* (1938; rpt. London, 1962), p. 335. For instances of wives examined separately to ensure their acquiescence to a land transfer, see Beckerman, "Customary Law," pp. 170–171, and Smith, "Hereditary and Proprietary Rights," p. 111. For instances of sales accomplished without the wife's consent, see Beckerman, "Customary Law," pp. 105–106. Others have also assessed wives as subordinate co-tenants of their husbands. See Middleton,

"Peasants, Patriarchy," 1, p. 121, and Raftis, *Tenure and Mobility,* p. 36 (note here that the wife, as co-tenant, did not hold the land until after her husband died).

28. No cases in Brigstock indicate that wives retained any rights over the lands held independently by their husbands, but in some villages wives could claim their dower from such properties. See Maitland, *Select Pleas in Manorial Courts,* pp. 41–42.

29. For the three wives who granted lands independently, see N.R.O., 28/3/1314 (Strangia Pikard), 18/11/1316 (Nella ad Solarium), and ?/12/1344 (Edith Tulke). For the ad Crucem case, see N.R.O., 20/3/1315. The jurors stated *"vendicio illa nulla est de uxore aliter in absentia mariti sui."* Richard Smith also found that most joint conveyances involved spouses, see "Hereditary and Proprietary Rights in Land," note 72.

30. Searle has suggested that seigneurial restrictions worked to the advantage of women, see "Seigneurial Control," p. 18. For Maitland's observation, see Pollock and Maitland, *English Law,* II, p. 402. It should be noted that Edward Britton (*Community,* pp. 19–37) would not agree with this interpretation of the rough equivalency in the treatment of wives under common and customary law. His discussion of the public activities of wives in Broughton, however, was too brief, too idiosyncratic in interpretation, and too dependent on specific examples (as opposed to typical or normal patterns of behavior) to be convincing.

31. Wrigley ("Fertility Strategy") estimated that 20 percent of pre-industrial couples produced no children who survived them. Some of these were fertile couples whose children died prematurely, but others never produced offspring.

32. E. A. Wrigley, *Population and History* (New York, 1969), pp. 92–94. See also Howell, *Land, Family,* pp. 204–205.

33. G. G. Coulton, *Medieval Village, Manor, and Monastery* (1925; rpt. New York, 1960), p. 244. See also P. P. A. Biller, "Birth Control in the West in the Thirteenth and Early Fourteenth Centuries," *Past and Present* 94 (1982), pp. 3–26.

34. Probably the most thorough discussion of female fertility in early modern England is E. A. Wrigley, "Family Limitation in Pre-Industrial England," *Economic History Review,* 2nd series, 19 (1966), pp. 82–109. See Chapter IV for a discussion of infant and child mortality (esp. note 14).

35. "Ballad of a Tyrannical Husband," in *Reliquiae Antiquae,* vol. II, ed. Thomas Wright and James Orchard Halliwell (London, 1845), pp. 196–199.

36. For discussions of the working lives of women and men in the medieval countryside, see Hanawalt, "Women's Contribution"; Hilton,

"Women in the Village"; Power, "Working Woman"; Middleton, "Sexual Division of Labor"; Michael Roberts, "Sickles and Scythes: Women's Work and Men's Work at Harvest Time," *History Workshop* 7 (1979), pp. 3–28. These patterns of work match well the child care responsibilities of women by keeping most work done by women in the immediate vicinity of the home. For the importance of child care in shaping women's work, see Judith K. Brown, "A Note on the Division of Labor by Sex," *American Anthropologist*, 72 (1970), pp. 1073–1078. Although the sexual division of labor in the medieval countryside was quite variable, Shahar has argued that proscribed tasks reflected the lower status of women's work; women worked at whatever their household economies demanded regardless of whether the task was customarily associated with men, but men never performed certain domestic tasks associated with women (spinning is the classic example). See *Fourth Estate*, p. 242.

37. Hanawalt, "Women's Contribution."

38. William Langland, *Piers Plowman: The A Version*, ed. George Kane (London, 1960), passus VII, lines 264–285, pp. 341–344. The peasant croft has been little considered in the historical literature. See Britton, *Community*, pp. 157–159, and Teresa McLean, *Medieval English Gardens* (New York, 1980), esp. pp. 172–248.

39. Very little is known about the diet of countrypeople in medieval England, but one recent study of commodities specified in maintenance agreements has underlined the primary importance of corn (used in producing both bread and ale). See Christopher Dyer, "English Diet in the Later Middle Ages," in *Social Relations and Ideas*, ed. T. H. Aston et al. (Cambridge, 1983), pp. 191–216.

40. William Langland, *Piers Plowman: An Edition of the C Text*, ed. Derek Pearsall (Berkeley, Calif., 1979), passus IX, lines 70–83, p. 164.

41. Louise A. Tilly and Joan W. Scott, *Women, Work, and Family* (New York, 1978), pp. 43–60; Ester Boserup, *Woman's Role in Economic Development* (New York, 1970), pp. 15–81; Olwen Hufton, "Women and the Family Economy in Eighteenth-Century France," *French Historical Studies* 9 (1975), pp. 1–22, and "Women, Work and Marriage in Eighteenth-Century France," in *Marriage and Society: Studies in the Social History of Marriage*, ed. R. B. Outhwaite (New York, 1981), pp. 186–203.

42. "Ballad of a Tyrannical Husband."

43. "A Woman is a Worthy Thing," in *The Oxford Book of Medieval English Verse*, ed. Celia and Kenneth Sisam (Oxford, 1970), p. 521.

44. Some scholars still maintain that women's wages were not necessarily lower than those of men (Hilton, "Women in the Village," pp. 102–103, and Hanawalt, "Women's Contribution"), but most evidence

belies this viewpoint. See, for example, Thorold Rogers whose analyses of labor rates led him to treat women's work as exemplary of low-paid employment (*Agriculture and Prices, 1259–1400*, pp. 252–302, esp. p. 266). See also Beveridge, "Wages in the Winchester Manors"; Kathleen Casey, "The Cheshire Cat: Reconstructing the Experience of Medieval Women," in *Liberating Women's History*, ed. Berenice A. Carroll (Urbana, Ill., 1976), pp. 230–231 (for a table of wages based on the figures of Thorold Rogers). For other scholars who agree that women's wages were usually lower, see Power, *Medieval Women*, p. 60; Middleton, "Sexual Division of Labor"; Shahar, *Fourth Estate*, p. 242.

45. Dorothea Oschinsky, *Walter of Henley and Other Treatises on Estate Management and Accounting* (Oxford, 1971), p. 427.

46. Middleton, "Sexual Division of Labor," pp. 159–162.

47. Middleton, "Sexual Division of Labor," p. 159.

48. Hilton, "Women Traders" and Kowaleski, "Women's Work."

49. The average daily consumption of ale by the English peasantry is unknown, but the normal monastic allowance was one gallon of good ale per day, often supplemented with a second gallon of weak ale. L. F. Salzman, *English Industries of the Middle Ages* (Oxford, 1923), p. 286. The extant records provide, unfortunately, no information whatsoever about ale-buyers. William Langland, however, implied that poorer people were the most likely to resort regularly to ale-buying when he urged officials to punish (from the Attwater translation, p. 21):

> Brewers and bakers   butchers and cooks
> For these are this world's men   that work the most harm
> For the poor people that   must buy piece-meal.

50. For the assize, see *The Statutes of the Realm*, Vol. 1 (London, 1810), pp. 199–204. For discussions of its enforcement, see Helen M. Cam, *The Hundred and the Hundred Rolls* (1930; rpt. New York, 1960), p. 211; Hilton, "Women in the Village," p. 104; Britton, *Community*, p. 25. In Brigstock, some brewers purchased long-term licenses (*licencia braciandi*) to cover several months of brewing activity. See the Appendix for basic information on brewing in Brigstock.

51. In Brigstock, for example, the 3,797 ale amercements levied against women accounted for 51 percent of their 7,416 appearances before the court (these figures include appearances by isolated individuals).

52. Estimates of how many women in Brigstock actually brewed commercially can be only tentative. It is extremely difficult to trace female individuals in manorial courts because women usually changed their names upon marriage. Hence, one woman could be counted twice; first under her natal surname and second under her marital name. This bias is partially offset by the fact that the counts of individual women and

counts of individual female brewers suffer from the same handicap. Of the 843 individual females counted in the surname groups of Brigstock, 311 (37 percent) were cited for brewing activities. This count excludes brewing by isolated individuals (outside of the reliable 277 surnames in the manor). A second method of measuring the proportion of women in Brigstock who brewed commercially also yields high levels. The chronic underrepresentation of women in the Brigstock court can be offset by assuming that the number of women on the manor was roughly equal to the known number of males (1,149 males). In such a case, 311 women brewed out of a possible 1,149 women in the village (27 percent),

53. For a comprehensive survey of the processes involved in ale and beer production in preindustrial England, see H. A. Monckton, *A History of English Ale and Beer* (London, 1966), pp. 11–82.

54. R. K. Field, "Worcestershire Peasant Buildings," pp. 105–145. Many of the households listed in Field's appendix boasted equipment used in brewing. For example, the goods belonging to the cottager Thomas atte Frythe of early fifteenth-century Stoke Prior included a brass pot, a mashing vat, and barrels for storing both ale and liquor (p. 138).

55. The precise use of "ale-wife" in Middle English has yet to be fully researched and analyzed. *The Oxford English Dictionary* cites its use in some versions of *Piers Plowman* as synonymous with brewster. It also notes that the term need not indicate marital status because wife in Middle English often simply signified woman. *The Middle English Dictionary,* Vol. 1 (Ann Arbor, 1956), pp. 181–184, defines ale-wife as barmaid, but presents no contemporary usages to support this definition. The term does not appear in the manorial records of Brigstock because the clerks wrote in Latin. In this discussion, ale-wife applies only to major brewers (30 or more citations) on the assumption that contemporaries would have used this term only to designate women who frequently brewed and sold ale. These 38 women accounted for 2,265 of the 3,844 ale amercements—59 percent.

56. Of Brigstock's 38 ale-wives, 28 (74 percent) were identified as wives throughout their brewing careers. Five additional ale-wives (13 percent) brewed both when married and during widowhood. The marital status of the 5 remaining ale-wives (13 percent) was unstated. Most brewers in Brigstock only appeared in the courts during the years that they were brewing and selling ale. Eleven brewers (from among the 85 who accumulated 10 or more citations) did appear in the courts before they embarked on their careers as ale-sellers. Nine of these brewers were cited as married women at least 2 years before they began producing ale commercially. The gap between known marriage and the beginning of a brewing career stretched as high as 14 years. Both the average and

the median for these 9 married brewers were the same; 6 years elapsed between the first reference in the court as a wife and the first brewing amercement. This long interval suggests that brewing for profit was often undertaken a considerable number of years after marriage. Of the 27 brewers (from the group of those paying 10 or more amercements) who appeared in the court after the end of their ale careers, the intervals stretched from 2 to 27 years, but clustered around the average of 9 years and the median of 8 years—suggesting that commercial ale production was normally abandoned in later life.

57. For examples, see N.R.O., 14/4/1301 and 10/8/1321 (Alice), 8/4/1316 (Emma), and 24/11/1313 (Richard).

58. Of Brigstock's 36 traceable ale-wives (2 ale-wives were isolated individuals who cannot be linked to any households in the community), 30 (83 percent) had presumed kin (shared reliable surname) who were also brewers. Wives, husbands, and daughters were assessed for ale sales sequentially (with different persons in the household accepting legal responsibility at various times); nonhousehold kin were frequently assessed in the same court sessions (indicating that they were both sellling ale within the same time period—probably in competition with one another).

59. The average length of an ale-wife's career was 20.6 years. Although the aletasters usually made about 9 annual presentments in the surviving records, ale-wives averaged only 3 to 4 amercements each year.

60. The wife of Richard Gilbert was chosen for detailed analysis because her career most exemplified the average pattern. She received 58 citations (average for all ale-wives was 59). She brewed for 17 years (1328–1345), and she averaged 3.4 amercements per year. Between 1328 and 1334, she received amercements in about half of the surviving ale presentments. In 1335, 1336, and 1338, she was amerced in less than 1 of every 5 aletasters' reports. In 1337, however, she was amerced on 9 out of 10 possible occasions. In 1339, 1340, 1341, 1342, and 1344 she received no ale amercements. In 1343, she was amerced once, and she paid 3 amercements in 1345 (a year for which 13 ale presentments survive). Although her career might indicate that ale-wives brewed less regularly toward the end of their careers, the histories of other ale-wives do not support this notion. Margery Golle, for example, brewed between 1306 and 1345. Although she was fairly active between 1311 and 1322, she brewed irregularly from 1323 to 1331 (in many years she received no citations), but then resumed an active career in the 1330s.

61. For analyses of brewers in Iver and Houghton-cum-Wyton, see my "Gender, Family and Community: A Comparative Study of the English Peasantry, 1287–1349," Diss. University of Toronto 1981, pp.

262–272, 320–328. In contrast to the trends observed in Brigstock, Iver, and Houghton-cum-Wyton, Richard Smith found that ale-sellers in Redgrave and Rickinghall were not only economically underprivileged but also often unmarried (see "Life-Cycles," pp. 150–178). Although they did not consider the marital statuses of brewers, both DeWindt (*Land and People*, pp. 237–238) and Britton (*Community*, pp. 87–88) found that producers of ale were, unlike brewers in Redgrave and Rickinghall, neither poor nor itinerant. Clearly, the subject merits further comparative study.

62. In Brigstock, women so dominated the brewing industry that it is impossible to trace change over time. In bread sales, however, female participation rose steadily from 21 percent of the market in the late thirteenth century to 83 percent in the 1340s (see Table 7.2). In Iver, female brewers, who controlled 23 percent of the market in the early 1330s, held 33 percent of all ale sales by the late 1340s. In Houghton-cum-Wyton, men controlled almost one-fifth of the ale market in the early fourteenth century, but were negligible participants in the industry (7 percent) by the 1340s.

63. Many studies have shown that women who make significant economic contributions to their family economies gain considerable domestic power and prestige. See Ernestine Friedl, "The Position of Women" and Stanley Chojnacki, "Dowries and Kinsmen in Early Renaissance Venice," *Journal of Interdisciplinary History* 5 (1975), pp. 571–600. Because such benefits can clearly be significant and highly valued by women, they should not be neglected or belittled. But power associated with the private sphere commonly lacks the authority and breadth of public power (see Reiter, "Men and Women").

64. Of these 10 major ale-wives, 6 only appeared in court on one or two occasions not related to brewing, and they always appeared with their husbands.

65. For examples of such cases, see N.R.O., 21/9/1318 and 12/10/1318 (Margery accused of slandering Richard Boys; she refused to answer accusation without her husband who was impleaded jointly with her); 28/11/1325 (Margery accused of slandering Galfridus ad Solarium by calling him a thief; she refused to respond without her husband who again was sued jointly with her).

66. Because women's court roles were so severely limited, one cannot straightforwardly compare the public benefits acquired (or not acquired) by males and females through commercial brewing. Since women started from a position of strong public disability, any advancement—women pledging, women pleading more cases alone, women developing larger court networks with non-kin—would have indicated a growth in public

authority. Because men were not so legally restricted, their public advancement can be best analyzed through tracing public behavior that was relatively unusual for males—the holding of public office.

67. Only 9 percent of Iver's males held public office, but 22 percent of the men involved in commercial brewing achieved official power. Of Iver's 72 officeholders, 44 (61 percent) sold ale. As a rule, officeholders were especially committed brewers; they averaged 8.6 amercements (against a 5.4 average for all male brewers).

68. "Ballad of the Tyrannical Husband."

69. "How the Goodwife Taught Her Daughter," in Rickert, *Babees Book,* p. 40, and "Abuse of Women," in *Secular Lyrics of the XIVth and XVth Centuries,* ed. Rossell Hope Robbins (Oxford, 1952), p. 36.

70. Hyphenated surnames are used here to emphasize the dual familial ties of women like Agnes Penifader-Kroyl and her sister Cristina Penifader-Power. This usage is ahistorical; married women usually (although not invariably) were identified by their husbands' surnames.

71. Although technically defined as persons to whom one is related by birth, cognates in the Kroyl-Penifader analysis include all members of a subject's marital and natal families. Affines include all persons, excluding spouse, to whom a subject was related through marriage. See the Appendix for a fuller discussion of these categories, as well as a general introduction to the Kroyl-Penifader study.

72. Henry Kroyl junior had 17 multiplex contacts with his brother John; the intensity of this relationship was followed at a far distance by 2 relationships with nonrelatives, who each had 10 multiplex contacts with Henry Kroyl junior. It should be noted that Henry Kroyl junior never had contact in the Brigstock court with his other two brothers William Kroyl and Robert Kroyl. Because William Kroyl ceased to appear in the courts after 1322, his lack of interaction with Henry Kroyl junior must not be overemphasized. Robert Kroyl, however, appeared in the courts for nearly three decades.

73. William Penifader and his brother Robert Penifader II shared 5 multiplex contacts; although both had a few relationships with nonrelatives that exceeded this fraternal association, it was nevertheless one of the most important associations in both of their networks. John Kroyl's relationship with his brother Henry (17 multiplex contacts) was surpassed only by one relationship with a nonrelative, William Werketon (33 multiplex contacts).

74. Henry Cocus had a premarital network of 40 contacts with 28 people, including 8 multiplex contacts with his father. All his other associations were single contacts, except for 2 contacts each with 4 nonrelatives. Henry Cocus' marriage settlement was concluded on New Year's Day 1304, but his father had died by July 1302 (heriot paid in N.R.O.,

6/7/1302). Henry Cocus' postmarital network of 161 contacts with 85 people included 8 multiplex interactions with his brother William (only 1 relationship surpassed this fraternal friendship—9 multiplex contacts with William Golle).

75. Agnes Penifader-Kroyl had 12 multiplex contacts with her husband, 6 multiplex contacts with her brother-in-law John Kroyl, and 5 multiplex contacts with William Werketon. William Werketon was an important associate of both brothers (7 contacts with Henry Kroyl junior, 33 contacts with John Kroyl).

76. These women were: Leticia Bate-Swargere (1 contact with her husband, 1 with her son, and 2 with presumed nonrelatives); Matilda Helkok-Lambin (4 contacts with presumed nonrelatives); Juliana Leche-Fisher (1 contact with her husband, 7 contacts with presumed nonrelatives); Agnes Tolle-Kroyl (2 contacts with her husband, 2 contacts with presumed nonrelatives, and 1 contact with a Matthew Kroyl whose relationship to her is unknown).

77. Beatrice Helkok-Cocus' postmarital network included 1 contact with her father, 4 with her husband, 2 with her in-laws, and 7 with presumed nonrelatives. Cecilia Breche-Koyk's postmarital network included 2 contacts with her brother, 6 with her husband, and 9 with presumed nonrelatives. Emma Kyde-Tappe's postmarital network included 1 contact with her paternal uncle, 5 contacts with her husband, and 14 with presumed nonrelatives.

78. Searle cites the use of *domina domus* in "Seigneurial Control," p. 40 (note 125).

79. Shahar, *Fourth Estate,* p. 77.

80. Shahar, *Fourth Estate,* pp. 98–106.

81. Langland, *Piers Plowman, C Text,* lines 82–83 (Pearsall edition, p. 164). I have used Eileen Power's translation from *Medieval Women,* p. 74.

Chapter VI. Widows

1. Alice Avice first appeared in the Brigstock records in 1292, and she was widowed by 1316 (when the manorial clerk first identified her as a widow). Her marital court network included only one person besides her husband with whom she had multiple contacts (2 contacts with Robert Moke). For examples of her activities in court as a married woman, see N.R.O., 5/4/1311 (ale amercement); 12/10/1302 (guilty of disrespect toward the bailiff and defendant in a plea of trespass brought by William Scharp); 6/3/1292 (acquisition of a quarter-virgate with her husband); 10/11/1301 (separate pleas of trespass pursued with her husband against Alice ad Solarium and Mablia Tulke).

2. Widowed by 1316, Alice Avice last appeared in the courts of Brigstock in 1332. During widowhood, her court network included multiple contacts with 5 persons (her son Peter, a possible son Henry Grace, Galfridus ad Solarium, Adam Prepositus, and Adam Kyde). For examples of her activities in court as a widow, see N.R.O., verso of file 31 (payment of 2 shillings with Adam Kyde in 1319 rental); ?/3/1316 (transfer of three and one-half rods from her free bench to Henry Grace—possibly one of her sons—who then conveyed the property to her son Peter); 20/1/1317 (lease of a small *domus* for 20 years from Emma Scharp); 28/9/1331 (amercement for having an obnoxious dung heap); 21/9/1321 (plea of trespass against Emma Stoyle); 3/3/1317 (pledge for daughters Strangia and Alice in their receipt of land).

3. Both sides of this attempt to estimate the duration of marriages in Brigstock are subject to error. First, because few merchets were recorded in the Brigstock courts, a woman could have been married for many years before her first court appearance as a wife. Second, because all widows did not have to pay heriots or reliefs, many years could also elapse between the onset of widowhood and a court citation indicating the woman's changed status. But since more heriots or reliefs were paid than merchets, the termination of marriages can be more accurately dated than their beginnings. As a result, these calculations probably underestimate the normal length of marriage in Brigstock.

4. Razi never directly calculated the duration of marriage in *Life, Marriage,* but two sets of figures suggest the conclusions offered here. First, Razi calculated that most marriages occurred between the ages of 18 and 22 years, with young men being older than their prospective wives by several years (pp. 60–64). Second, Razi estimated that most men in Halesowen at age 20 had a life expectancy of 25 to 28 years (pp. 43–45). If we estimate from these figures that young men marrying at 22 years could expect to die at the age of 45 to 48 years, the duration of their marriages would be 23 to 26 years. Needless to say, this estimate is extremely rough, especially because it ignores female life expectancies (for which Razi gives no data). For a debate about the accuracy of Razi's calculations, see Poos and Smith, "Legal Windows?" and Razi, "Use of Manorial Court Rolls."

5. Stone (*Family, Sex and Marriage,* p. 55) estimated that "the median duration of marriage in Early Modern England was probably somewhere between seventeen to twenty years." See also Laslett, *Family Life and Illicit Love,* p. 184.

6. Of the 843 women identified in the reliable surnames of Brigstock, 106 are known to have been widowed at least once during their lives (12.5 percent). Male widowhood cannot be traced because a husband's

public status did not change when his wife died—he paid no fines, he lost no lands, he did not alter his position as head of household. If both sexes enjoyed roughly equal expectancies of life, about half of all wives and half of all husbands would have lost their spouses, but we simply have no data that allow us to calculate sexual differences in life expectancy in the medieval countryside (see Razi, *Life, Marriage,* pp. 34–45). In his study of widowhood in rural France, Alain Bideau found that roughly half of all marriages were ended by the death of the husband, see "A Demographic and Social Analysis of Widowhood and Remarriage: The Example of the Castellany of Thoissey-en-Dombes, 1670–1840," *Journal of Family History* 5 (1980), esp. pp. 32–33.

7. Peter Laslett, *Family Life and Illicit Love,* p. 200; André Burguière, "Réticences théoriques et intégration pratique du remariage dans la France d'Ancien Régime—dix-septieme-dix-huitieme siècles," in *Marriage and Remarriage in Populations of the Past,* ed. J. Dupâquier et al. (New York, 1981), pp. 41–48; Bideau, "Widowhood and Remarriage."

8. See Chapter IV, note 12.

9. For some of the many discussions of the tenurial rights of widows, see Homans, *English Villagers,* esp. pp. 181–182; Faith, "Peasant Families"; Shahar, *Fourth Estate,* pp. 236–239. Variations in the customary laws that governed free bench will be discussed more fully below.

10. Titow found that 9 to 15 percent of the tenants on the manors of the Winchester, Glastonbury, and Worcester estates were women (most of whom were widows); see *English Rural Society,* p. 87. At Waltham and High Easter in 1328, nearly one-fourth of the land was held by women (a figure that excludes landholding by wives, whose properties were explicitly identified under their husbands' lands). See Poos, "Population and Resources," pp. 214–215. Hilton found that 1 in every 7 tenants at Ombersley in 1419 was a widow, see "Women in the Village," p. 99. Barbara English found that women held one-sixth of the bovates and one-third of the cottar holdings in late thirteenth-century Holderness, see *The Lords of Holderness, 1086–1260* (Oxford, 1979), p. 191. Of the 60 persons listed in the Brigstock rental for 1319, 11 (18 percent) were women of whom at least 6 were widows. See N.R.O., file 31. Similar rates have been found in early modern villages. In Aldenham between 1611 and 1701, from 10.4 to 18.2 percent of households were headed by widows (see W. Newman Brown, "The Receipt of Poor Relief and Family Situation 1636–1690," in *Land, Kinship and Life-Cycle,* ed. Smith, pp. 405–422). Laslett's survey of preindustrial households led him to conclude that about 13 percent were headed by widows (see "Mean Household Size in England Since the Sixteenth Century," in *Household and Family,* ed. Laslett, p. 147).

11. For examples, see N.R.O., 14/4/1317 (identified as wife); 20/7/1321 (identified as widow); 12/3/1322 (identified with no indication of marital status).

12. N.R.O., ?/2/1322.

13. For example, women of unknown status in the Brigstock samples were pledged by kin very infrequently (18 percent versus 46 percent of all female criminals; 14 percent versus 29 percent of all female receivers of land; 0 percent versus 24 percent of all female litigants). In the crime sample, women of unknown status were also much more likely than other women to be cited for crimes associated with householding.

14. Joel T. Rosenthal has described how the experiences of aristocratic widows were similarly varied and diverse in his article, "Aristocratic Widows in Fifteenth-Century England," in *Women and the Structure of Society,* ed. Barbara J. Harris and Jo Ann K. McNamara (Durham, N.C., 1984), pp. 36–47. Probably widowed in the summer of 1318, Alice Penifader sought excused absences from several court meetings that autumn. In January 1319, she (identified by the forename Dulcia) paid to be excused from attending court until Michaelmas, and in the following October (again identified as Dulcia), she was fined again to avoid court suit for a year. She never again merited notice by the clerk. See N.R.O., 31/8/1318, 4/1/1319, and 4/10/1319.

15. The classic discussion of the effect of land availability on remarriage is J. Z. Titow, "Some Differences Between Manors and Their Effects on the Condition of the Peasant in the Thirteenth Century," *Agricultural History Review* 10 (1962), pp. 1–13. See also Houston and Smith, "A New Approach to Family History?" pp. 123–124; Rosamund Faith, "Berkshire: Fourteenth and Fifteenth Centuries," in *Peasant Land Market,* ed. Harvey, p. 114; Jack Ravensdale, "Population Changes and the Transfer of Customary Land on a Cambridgeshire Manor in the Fourteenth Century," in *Land, Kinship and Life-Cycle,* ed. Smith, pp. 197–225. For a general introduction to remarriage in early modern England (where remarriages constituted 25 to 30 percent of all marriages), see R. Schofield and E. A. Wrigley, "Remarriage Intervals and the Effect of Marriage Order on Fertility," in *Marriage and Remarriage,* ed. Dupâquier, pp. 211–227. Eight of the 106 widowed women in Brigstock remarried (7.5 percent). Five of the 34 widows traced in Iver remarried (15 percent).

16. Razi, *Life, Marriage,* p. 63.

17. Razi's finding that widows in Halesowen after the plague (when slackening demand for land had lowered the incidence of remarriage) gave birth to proportionally more illegitimate children lends support to the notion that most widows preferred to remain sexually active and,

hence, likely preferred to remarry if they could find second partners. See *Life, Marriage*, pp. 138–139.

18. The advantages of remaining unmarried were even evident to St. Jerome who complained that widows failed to find second husbands because they preferred liberty over wifely submission (*et quia maritorum expertae dominatum viduitatis praeferunt libertatem*). Quoted in Shahar, *Fourth Estate*, p. 97.

19. Of the 45 widows of officeholders, 29 (64 percent) were active in local life, trading lands, pursuing disputes, committing offenses, and the like. Of the 61 widows of nonofficeholders, only 23 (38 percent) were active in such matters.

20. No data correlating age with remarriage are available for medieval English villages, but one study of rural remarriage has shown clearly that young widows were especially likely to remarry and that age much less dramatically affected the likelihood of a widower remarrying (see Bideau, "Widowhood and Remarriage"). See also Schofield and Wrigley, "Remarriage Intervals," pp. 213–219. Rosenthal found that age at widowhood influenced the likelihood of remarriage for aristocratic widows, see "Aristocratic Widows," p. 40. Data on four remarried widows in Brigstock are unavailable, but three of the other four survived their first husbands for exceptionally long lengths of time: 6 years, 16 years, 31 years, 42 years.

21. It is, of course, possible that aging affected the status of women and men differently. Le Roy Ladurie claimed, for example, that elderly men in Montaillou were objects of ridicule whereas women gained, rather than lost, prestige as they aged (see *Montaillou*, pp. 196, 216). This possibility cannot be checked for medieval English villages and received no attention in Laslett's lengthy discussion of aging in early modern England in *Family Life and Illicit Love*, pp. 174–213. More than likely, customs in fourteenth-century Montaillou differed dramatically from practices in contemporary England because of social and demographic divergences between southern ("Mediterranean") and northern Europe. See R. M. Smith, "The People of Tuscany and Their Families in the Fifteenth Century: Medieval or Mediterranean?" *Journal of Family History* 6 (1981), pp. 107–128.

22. Richard Smith has described how the elderly constituted a significant portion of the rural poor because of the "poverty cycle" of conjugal households, see "Some Issues," pp. 68–85. See also Clark, "Some Aspects of Social Security."

23. John Popelin paid a merchet for his daughter Isabella in 1327; his widow Alice paid a merchet for their daughter Johanna in 1334; when their son William married in 1338, Alice Popelin guaranteed his

future inheritance of a semi-virgate. See St. George's Chapel (Windsor Castle), IV.B.1 (merchets paid 17/10/1327 and 26/9/1334) and B.A.S., m. 20 (grant of land to William). The Penifaders of Brigstock provide another example of a widow's disintegrating household. When Robert Penifader died in 1318, his daughter Cristina was already married; his daughter Agnes married in the following year.

24. This statement draws on Wrigley's calculations that 20 percent of all couples in a stationary preindustrial population will have no children survive them, 20 percent will produce only daughters, and 60 percent will have at least one son survive them. See "Fertility Strategy."

25. William Popelin almost certainly did not live with his mother after he married in 1338; in 1345, she entered into a maintenance agreement with a married couple to whom she was not related. See B.A.S., m. 36: 5/12/1345.

26. Peter Laslett has argued that both elderly women and men tended to live in their original households, although widows were sometimes incorporated into the households of their married children in order to make use of their assistance in child care (see *Family Life and Illicit Love,* pp. 174–213). Richard Wall found not only that between 71 and 78 percent of all widows in the preindustrial English villages that he examined continued to head their own households but also that more widows than widowers remained independent householders. See "Women Alone in English Society," *Annales de démographie historique* (1981), pp. 312–317.

27. The figure of 101 widows excludes 5 women who remarried so quickly and so permanently that their careers as widows were too brief for consideration. The careers of the other 3 remarried widows have been included in this analysis because they either lived alone for many years before remarriage or else survived their second husbands.

28. N.R.O., 15/7/1311 and 3/1/1314.

29. N.R.O., 31/5/1319 and 10/5/1325.

30. N.R.O., 6/9/1331.

31. N.R.O., 6/9/1331 (With), 3/1/1314 (Matilda Cocus), and 25/1/1308 (Edith Cocus). In the same court at which Matilda Cocus was amerced for not providing a servant for herding and plowing, William Golle paid a similar amercement. For an example of a man claiming poverty, see N.R.O., 17/5/1329 (grant of land by Henry Cocus). *"Quia pauper"* entries probably indicated not destitution, but rather temporary lack of resources (see Alfred E. May, "An Index of Thirteenth-Century Peasant Impoverishment? Manor Court Fines," *Economic History Review,* 2nd series, 26 [1973], p. 398).

32. See N.R.O., ?/5/1309 (Emma Werketon); 14/12/1291 (Quena widow of Galfridus); 10/1/1298 (Alice ad Vinarium); ?/5/1309 (Agnes

Geroud); 14/12/1318 (Alice Somonor); 4/1/1319 and 4/10/1319 (Alice or Dulcia Penifader). For examples from Henry Cade's long career, see his fine to relax court suit for a year in N.R.O., 15/12/1301, and his service as a juror in N.R.O., 13/5/1311.

33. P.R.O., SC-2: 194/65, 29/5/1299 (Letia Fox paid 3 pence *pro Dulce serviente sua*).

34. See the verso of N.R.O., file 31. The six widows listed are: Alice Avice (who also paid an amercement for a householder crime), Isabella Leche, Alice Somonor, Emma Talboth, Emma Sephirde, and Alice Tucke.

35. Most instances of female pledging in Brigstock occurred in the decades immediately preceding the plague; this aspect of female pledging will be discussed more fully in Chapter VII. At Wakefield, widows might have also been allowed to act as pledges (see Chapter II, note 9).

36. N.R.O., 29/4/1306 and 3/6/1311.

37. For highlights of Matilda Cocus' career as a widow, see N.R.O., 6/7/1302, 26/5/1304, 24/7/1304, 15/7/1311, 3/1/1314, 27/2/1315, and 14/8/1315.

38. For highlights of Emma Sephirde's career as a widow, see N.R.O., 7/9/1302, 9/5/1314, 31/5/1319, and 10/5/1315.

39. For highlights of Alice Somonor's career as a widow, see N.R.O., 24/3/1317, 14/4/1317, 16/6/1317, 14/12/1318, 6/8/1322, and 22/8/1332.

40. Hilton, "Women in the Village," pp. 103–104 (Hilton does not discuss the marital status of the female moneylenders he describes, but they were almost certainly unmarried because wives could not contract debt agreements without involving their husbands); B. A. Holderness, "Widows in Pre-industrial Society: An Essay upon Their Economic Functions," in *Land, Kinship and Life-Cycle,* ed. Smith, pp. 423–442. Widows were defendants in 18 of the 19 debt cases involving widows reported to the court. In many of these cases, moreover, they were being sued for debts owed by their husbands.

41. See Chapter V, note 56, for the marital statuses of ale-wives. Of the 106 widows traced in Brigstock, 22 sold ale at least once (21 percent); of all the women identified in Brigstock, about one-third sold ale on at least one occasion (see Chapter V, note 52). The 3 women who brewed intensely as widows were: Alice Goldhop the wife of Hugh Helkok who acquired only 1 ale amercement when married and accumulated another 37 during her widowhood; Margery the widow of William Durant who brewed 13 times as a wife and 25 times as a widow; and Matilda the widow of Hugh Tubbe who accumulated 93 ale citations while married and brewed on 30 more occasions while widowed. Widows cited for commercial baking were: Alice widow of John Dogge (2 baking amercements as a wife, 1 as a widow); Emma Sephirde widow of

Peter Swetman (6 baking amercements as a widow); Elicia widow of Richard Aylward (4 baking amercements as a wife, 2 as a widow); Alice widow of Henry Pidenton (1 baking amercement as a widow); Strangia widow of Robert Pidenton (1 baking amercement as a widow).

42. The variable customs that provided for widows have been much discussed in the historical literature. See especially Homans, *English Villagers,* esp. pp. 181–182 (where he claims that the variety of custom indicates its comparative unimportance); and Faith, "Peasant Families," esp. p. 91 (where she notes that, despite variety, provisions were "durable and firmly established"). Custom, of course, did not necessarily reflect practice. For example, Ravendale's study of the remarriages of widows in Cottenham has shown that the lord of that manor usually waived (for a fee) the customary forfeiture of a widow's free bench if she remarried; see "Population Changes." It is worth noting that, since widows of all landholders could claim some portion of their husbands' properties, the only landless widows were widows of landless men. Faced with supporting themselves and their families without the wage-earning power of an adult male, such women probably numbered among the poorest members of rural society. But they appear rarely in manorial records because of their landless status.

43. Many of these differences likely arose from different tenures of land that were unspecified in the court records, but the results were certainly confusing to contemporaries; about 1 of every 10 widows in Brigstock endured some sort of legal inquiry into her rights as a land-holder (see Table 6.5).

44. N.R.O., file 31.

45. Of the 106 widows studied, 55 conveyed land on at least one occasion (52 percent). Of the 106 conveyances made by these widows, 52 explicitly stated that the properties being conveyed were from the widow's free bench (49 percent), and 67 (63 percent) conveyed land outside of the family (this figure includes transfers that conveyed land from a widow through the heir of her husband to a third party).

46. N.R.O., 17/2/1335 (Cimiterio), and 1/8/1343 (Tubbe). Hilton found that many rural lessors were widows, see *Medieval Society,* p. 163.

47. N.R.O., 6/9/1297 and 17/8/1302. Both inquisitions were held to determine whether a widow could sell half of her lands. Although neither explicitly mentioned free bench, both were implicitly considering free bench tenure.

48. N.R.O., 15/9/1335 (Heyr). N.R.O., 17/8/1302 (Helkok); 28/1/1318 (Coleman); 16/3/1302 (Chapman). Of the 106 conveyances made by widows, the clerk made no mention of free bench restrictions in 54 cases (51 percent). For examples of widows conveying land on other manors, see Jones, "Bedfordshire: The Fifteenth Century," pp.

249–250, and Lomas, "South-East Durham," p. 300, both in *Peasant Land Market,* ed. Harvey.

49. N.R.O., 20/1/1317.

50. N.R.O., 11/7/1340 (Alice widow of Henry son of Peter), and 20/3/1315 (Alice Tulke). An obvious but imponderable question about two-step transfers is: Who profited? Heirs, eager to realize the value of their inheritances, might have often pressured widows to release portions for immediate sale. Such impatience might have been the motive, for example, behind Alice the widow of Adam Talbot's transfer of future access to her free bench through the heir to a third party; she retained effective control over the free bench land for her life, but the heir was able to realize immediately the value of the land (see N.R.O., 10/9/1333). But widows, desirous of more extensive control over their free bench lands, might have often coerced heirs into agreeing to alienations of their lands. Heirs almost certainly, for example, obtained no financial benefit from agreeing to two-step transfers that conveyed land to their noninheriting siblings (8 cases found in Brigstock). In the final analysis, of course, both a widow and the heir of her husband had to agree to the advantages offered by a proposed two-step transfer.

51. To be included in this analysis, a widow needed (a) to have paid a relief or heriot indicating the beginning of widowhood and (b) to have transferred land on at least one occasion; 22 women met both these criteria.

52. However, 16 of these 41 widows conveyed land to children only as the first step of two-step transfers that conveyed land outside of the family. To be sure, a widow's child might have profited as much from such a transfer as did the widow herself, but only 25 widows conveyed properties to children that were retained by the children.

53. To look at the figures from a different perspective, of the 54 widows involved in land conveyances, 16 conveyed land only to children, 29 conveyed land only to nonrelatives (including those who used two-step transfers), and 9 conveyed land to both relatives and nonrelatives.

54. N.R.O., ?/3/1332; 7/5/1333; 17/2/1335; 10/3/1335.

55. These 30 widows include all widows who could be traced in the courts during both their married and their widowed years. Of these 30, the breakdown was as follows: 19 widows exceeded both the number of persons contacted and the number of contacts made during their married years; 8 widows had smaller networks than they had built as wives; 3 widows had networks equivalent to those of their married years. On the average, the traced careers of these women as wives lasted 16.9 years; their average career as widows lasted 9.5 years.

56. A widow was classified as publicly inactive if she never traded land and merited only one citation (essoin, plea, petty crime, and the

like) after her payment of heriot or relief. Of the 54 inactive widows in Brigstock, 38 (70 percent) had husbands who never held local office.

57. Only 12 widows were identified from the pre-plague records of Houghton-cum-Wyton, raising the possibility that many women were widows for so brief a time that their widowhoods escaped notice in the extant records. Of these 12 widows, 3 (25 percent) definitely remarried.

58. The composition of Iver's free bench is never explicitly described in the extant records, but one court entry implies that widows controlled an unseparated one-third of their husbands' holdings. In 1341, William le Coke's transfer of property to John Snape was followed by his widowed mother's conveyance of her right to one-third of the property (B.A.S., m. 24, 2/5/1341). Of the 34 widows in Iver, only 16 can be fully studied because they lost their husbands during the well-documented years from 1332 to 1348. The following discussion is based largely on the experiences of these 16 widows.

59. B.A.S., m. 17, 7/5/1337.

60. B.A.S., m. 9, 5/5/1335 (animal trespass by Alice widow of Roger Schepherde); m. 40, 21/11/1346 (John Palmer cited for illegally felling trees on land of Dionysia widow of Salamon Blake); m. 20, 1/4/1338 (Juliana widow of Peter Godefrey cited for illegally felling trees on the tenement of her husband's heir); m. 41, 3/5/1346 (Margery widow of John Lawrence ordered to repair a ditch).

61. B.A.S., m. 21, 4/7/1338 (Sprot custody); and m. 14, 7/10/1336 (merchet paid by the widowed Agnes Ram for her daughter).

62. B.A.S., m. 37, 14/1/1346 (Lawrence); m. 36, 5/12/1345 (Popelin).

63. The widows who transferred land in Iver were: (1) Alice Popelin who (a) transferred a small parcel to her daughter Margery (B.A.S., m. 18, 14/7/1337, (b) transferred property to her daughter Johanna and her husband Peter Pekele (B.A.S., m. 19, 1/12/1337), and (c) granted future access to her messuage and semi-virgate to her son William when he married (B.A.S., m. 20, 1/4/1338); (2) Alice Coke who released her one-third right in a tenement to her son who then conveyed the entire tenement to John Snape (B.A.S., m. 24, 2/5/1341; (3) Cecilia Blanchard who leased land to John Snape and sold another property to Peter Peckule (B.A.S., m. 44, 4/12/1348); (4) Alice Shepherde (Bercarius) who (a) leased 3 rods to John Aleyn (B.A.S., m. 32, 9/11/1342) and (b) joined by her daughter, conveyed 3 rods outside of the family (B.A.S., m. 35, 27/9/1345). These 4 widows represent one-fourth of the 16 widows whose careers could be reconstructed from the Iver records.

64. Katerina Peys, for example, was a widow by 1335 (B.A.S., m. 8, 7/7/1335) and remained active in the courts until her death by plague

(B.A.S., m. 52, 6/5/1349). During her long widowhood, she brewed frequently (see B.A.S., m. 45, 15/6/1348 for one ale amercement), provided the lord with security that she would not remarry without permission (B.A.S., m. 12, 29/7/1336), pursued a debt dispute with Alice Gentyl (see B.A.S., m. 17, 7/5/1337), raised a just hue against several men (B.A.S., m. 17, 8/5/1337), paid a fine for the illegal fishing of her son (B.A.S., m. 17, 7/5/1337), and paid for the trespass of a colt owned by her (B.A.S., m. 20, 1/4/1338).

Chapter VII. Medieval Countrywomen in Perspective

1. Macfarlane, *English Individualism.*
2. Illich, *Gender.*
3. See W. K. Lacey, *The Family in Classical Greece* (Ithaca, N.Y., 1968) and Sarah B. Pomeroy, *Goddesses, Whores, Wives, and Slaves: Women in Classical Antiquity* (New York, 1975).
4. The notion of a distinctive northern pattern has been most developed by Richard Smith in "People of Tuscany," "Hypothèses sur la nuptialité," and "Some Reflections." If his arguments are proven to be accurate, they will imply long-term stability in the lives of Englishwomen, with changes occurring less across the centuries than between the geographic regions of Europe. But Smith's findings are not uncontested. As this book was going to press, David Herlihy published a new study, based largely on Tuscan data, asserting a general medieval household pattern that varied minimally by region; see *Medieval Households* (Cambridge, Mass., 1985). See also David Herlihy and Christiane Klapisch-Zuber, *Les Toscans et leur familles* (Paris, 1978).
5. Although women shared many characteristics—reproductive capabilities, second-rank public status, discontinuity in public opportunity—that distinguished them from men, they did not necessarily possess the social cohesiveness and identity to comprise a discrete social group. Such sharp distinctions characterized the public opportunities of daughters, wives, and widows that there were, arguably, three types of adult females in Brigstock, rather than a single female prototype. Moreover, women—even those who share common experiences—usually identify more strongly as members of other social groups (families, classes, races) than as members of a group defined by gender. For a discussion of the common traits of femaleness, see Michele Zimbalist Rosaldo, "Woman, Culture and Society: A Theoretical Overview," in *Woman, Culture and Society,* ed. Michelle Zimbalist Rosaldo and Louise Lamphere (Stanford, 1974), pp. 17–42.
6. For an illuminating discussion of the intersection of public and

private forces in creating gender rules, see Joan Kelly-Gadol, "The Doubled Vision of Feminist Theory," *Feminist Studies* 5 (1979), 216–227.

7. Whyte, *The Status of Women,* p. 10.

8. See the Appendix for a full discussion of methods used to trace social stratification in Brigstock.

9. Middleton, "Sexual Division of Labor."

10. As observed by Karen Sacks, "women who perform social labor have a higher status vis-à-vis men of their own class than do women who labor only in the domestic sphere." See "Engels Revisited: Women, the Organization of Production, and Private Property," in *Toward an Anthropology of Women,* ed. Reiter, p. 233.

11. Only a few scattered exceptions to the general exclusion of women from politics have been found. In Halesowen in the late fourteenth and early fifteenth centuries, a few female aletasters were elected (Hilton, "Women in the Village," pp. 105–106). Annie Abram has identified a few instances of women elected churchwardens and feudal women holding offices or participating in elections. See A. Abram, *English Life and Manners in the Late Middle Ages* (London, 1913), pp. 36–37.

12. For information on the status of women before royal and mercantile courts, see Pollock and Maitland, *English Law,* and Bateson, *Borough Customs, Vol. II.*

13. For recent studies on the working lives of medieval English townswomen, see Hilton, "Women Traders," and Kowaleski, "Women's Work." See also the studies of urban women in preindustrial continental towns by Martha Howell and Natalie Z. Davis in Hanawalt's *Women and Work in Preindustrial Europe.*

14. The best studies of the lives of feudal women remain Margaret Wade Labarge, *A Baronial Household of the Thirteenth Century* (1965; rpt. Totowa, N.J., 1980), and H. S. Bennett, *The Pastons and their England,* 2nd edition (1932; rpt. Cambridge, 1977).

15. de Pisan, *The Treasure of the City of Ladies,* p. 145.

16. Chaucer, general prologue and prologue to the Wife of Bath's tale in *The Canterbury Tales.*

17. See *The Book of Margery Kempe,* ed. Sanford Brown Meech and Hope Emily Allen, Early English Text Society, vol. 212 (1940; rpt. London, 1961), quote on p. 9, and Clarissa W. Atkinson, *Mystic and Pilgrim: The Book and World of Margery Kempe* (Ithaca, N.Y., 1983).

18. Norman Davis, ed., *Paston Letters and Papers of the Fifteenth Century* (Oxford, 1971), and Bennett, *Pastons and their England.*

19. Labarge, *Baronial Household.*

20. See the Appendix for a full explanation of the methods used to reconstruct the demographic and economic history of Brigstock.

21. See Chapter V, note 62.

22. Crimes against persons accounted for 59 percent of reported crimes in 1301–1304, fell to 26 percent in 1318–1322, and remained at that level in 1340–1343.

23. The proportion of women who used kin to pledge for their land transactions changed over time, but in no discernible pattern. Of women using pledges, 20 percent used kin in 1301–1303, 35 percent used kin in 1314–1316, 44 percent used kin in 1331–1333, and 16 percent used kin in 1343–1345. In the sample of civil pleas, changes were similarly uneven: 25 percent assisted by kin in 1301–1303, 8 percent in 1314–1316, 46 percent in 1331–1333, and 11 percent in 1343–1345. In both instances, moreover, the significance of pledging data is skewed by the propensity of women involved in land transfers and civil pleas to act jointly with men (usually their husbands).

24. Joan Kelly-Gadol, "Did Women Have a Renaissance?" in *Becoming Visible: Women in European History,* ed. Renate Bridenthal and Claudia Koonz (New York, 1977), pp. 137–164.

25. For similar trends in an early modern community, see Mary Prior, "Women and the Urban Economy: Oxford 1500–1800," in *Women in English Society 1500–1800,* ed. Mary Prior (London, 1985), esp. pp. 108–110.

26. The assumption of improved female status after the plague runs throughout most writings on Englishwomen in the Middle Ages, but no single study has comparatively analyzed women's status before and after 1348. For a summary of some of the arguments in favor of high female status after the plague, see Hilton, "Women in the Village." See also P. J. P. Goldberg, "Female Labour, Service and Marriage." For a survey of the English economy in these years, see John Hatcher, *Plague, Population and the English Economy 1348–1530* (London, 1977).

27. For women in early modern England, no work has yet superseded the study by Alice Clark, *Working Life of Women in the Seventeenth Century* (1919; rpt. London, 1982).

Appendix. A Note on Method

1. Homans, *English Villagers;* Raftis, *Tenure and Mobility.*

2. Keith Wrightson, "Medieval Villagers in Perspective," *Peasant Studies* 7 (1978), pp. 203–217; Zvi Razi, "The Toronto School's Reconstitution of Medieval Peasant Society: A Critical View," *Past and Present* 85 (1979), pp. 141–157; Poos and Smith, "Legal Windows?"; Razi, "Use of Manorial Court Rolls."

3. Raftis, *Warboys;* DeWindt, *Land and People;* Britton, *Community;* Smith, "Life-Cycles"; Razi, *Life, Marriage.*

4. Much of what follows is based on methodological approaches discussed in my article, "Spouses, Siblings and Surnames: Reconstructing Families from Medieval Village Court Rolls," *Journal of British Studies* 23 (1983), pp. 26–46. Some points made there, however, have been modified to suit the particular requirements of this research project. This ongoing process of methodological refinement has also produced different calculations for Brigstock, Iver, and Houghton-cum-Wyton from those reported in my dissertation in 1981.

5. Choosing adequate source collections is a crucial prerequisite to successful family reconstitutions. Based on my experiences with the archives of Brigstock, Iver, and Houghton-cum-Wyton, I developed four criteria for judging collections of sources: (1) quantity (roughly 8–10 courts per year), (2) quality (including information on tithings, inheritances, and marriages as well as adequate coverage of women), (3) geographical coherence, and (4) supplementary sources. See "Spouses, Siblings." The records of few manors, however, will meet all these standards. In this study, the extant manorial records for Brigstock (averaging 9 courts per year from 1287 to 1348 with only 6 gaps, none of more than 3 years) vastly exceed the modest sources available for Iver and Houghton-cum-Wyton. Yet even the archive of Brigstock does not include many valuable types of entries (such as merchet payments) or many sources to supplement the manorial court rolls (no surveys, no contemporary custumals, no entry in the 1279 Hundred Rolls, no detailed assessments from the lay subsidies, and only brief accounting notes on the versos of some court rolls). Although these sources would have certainly been useful, the focus of this study on gender relations especially required a nearly complete series of court rolls, the greatest asset of Brigstock's archive. The collections for both Iver and Houghton-cum-Wyton are certainly inadequate for in-depth analyses, but sufficed for the comparative purposes used in this study.

6. Probably the best guide to the process of extracting data for historical reconstructions is Alan Macfarlane, *Reconstructing Historical Communities* (London, 1977). Althouh my eschewing of computers at early stages of reconstitution might seem unusual, it is an approach advised by Macfarlane and used in even the most quantified studies of manorial rolls (see Razi, *Life, Marriage*). But as computers become more refined and precise, they will be useful at earlier and earlier stages of historical reconstruction.

7. For the citation to John Wolf Kroyl, see N.R.O., ?/5/1338. For examples of the various identifications of this person as an aletaster for Brigstock, see N.R.O., 11/6/1339 (Wolf Kroyl), 2/7/1339 (John Kroyl), and 13/8/1339 (John Wolf).

8. J. A. Raftis, *A Small Town in Late Medieval England: Godman-chester 1278-1400* (Toronto, 1982), p. 153.

9. B.A.S., m. 47, 6/6/1349 and m. 78, 6/9/1360.

10. See Tables A.7, A.14, and A.17.

11. For a discussion of the sorts of relationships usually specified in court rolls, see Smith, "Kin and Neighbors," pp. 252–254. For examples of the limited genealogies drawn from family reconstitutions, see Razi, *Life, Marriage,* pp. 18, 20. Almost no cousins or affines were traced in these tables.

12. Imprecise or unstable surnames were judged to be inadequate guides to family groups. Three main criteria were used: (1) repeated mixing of English and Latin forms (i.e., John ad Fontem/atte Welle); (2) use of unspecific or general modifiers such as personal names (John son of Alice), local areas (John de Felde), common occupations (John le Taylor), and offices (John le Reeve); (3) use of prepositions (John atte Well implies a fluidity absent from John Well). Reliable surnames, in contrast, were judged to be both distinctive and stable. Most reliable surnames lacked the three indicators of instability cited above, but a fair measure of discretion was required to distinguish unstable from reliable surnames. Some surnames derived from unique personal names or distant towns, for example, and thus were clearly precise and reliable.

13. In the text, a person denoted as being related to another either shared a reliable surname or was known to be related from the clerk's identification. On occasion, finer distinctions were made and have been noted. Nonrelatives were always, in fact, *presumed* nonrelatives because of the fact that many relationships could not be reconstructed from the records.

14. This method was used by both DeWindt, *Land and People,* pp. 169–170, and Razi, *Life, Marriage,* pp. 24–26, but neither adjusted their figures for the different number of courts extant for each period. The count for Brigstock included all males cited in the 277 reliable surnames of Brigstock, plus some firmly identified persons. Only minors, obvious transients, and unidentified males were excluded.

15. Many other historians have remarked on the correlation between increased land sales and times of economic difficulty. For example, Bruce Campbell's analysis of grain prices and land sales in Coltishall led him to conclude that "consecutive years of harvest failure reduced the peasantry to such a state that they were obliged to sell land in order to buy food" (see "Inheritance and the Land Market," in *Land, Kinship and Life-Cycle,* ed. Smith, pp. 107–127, quote from p. 113).

16. Beckerman, "Customary Law," p. 112.

17. These calculations include only those ale citations to which legible

amercements were attached. Alfred May's attempt to measure poverty through levels of court amercements ("An Index of Thirteenth-Century Peasant Impoverishment?") was severely criticized by J. B. Post, "Manorial Amercements and Peasant Poverty," *Economic History Review,* 2nd series, 28 (1975), pp. 304–311. Some of Post's criticisms do not apply to this analysis of Brigstock amercements (since it is based on only one type of manorial levy). And Post's worries about the representativeness of brewers and their amercements are belied by the wide dispersal of brewing activity within Brigstock. The trends shown in Table A.3, moreover, do not stand on their own as a single measure of growing impoverishment, but instead are supported by other measurements—field crimes, land transactions, and debt cases. As Post argued, "it is grossly optimistic to suppose that a simple statistic will index the details of [progressive peasant impoverishment]." In Brigstock, many independent measurements suggest economic hardship in the decades that preceded the plague.

18. Kershaw, "Great Famine." Unfortunately, the Brigstock samples, designed to illuminate broad changes over a half-century, do not permit detailed analysis of the effects of the crisis years (between 1315 and 1322) on local economy and society.

19. Maddicott, *Demands of the Crown.*

20. Wrightson, "Medieval Villagers," and Razi, "A Critical View."

21. Anne DeWindt, "Peasant Power Structures."

22. Ideally, all samples would have covered the same years. But this was not possible because the views of frankpledge used for the sample of crimes survived in different series and were of varying quality from the court sessions used for the samples of land transactions and civil litigation. It should be noted that three court sessions (?/?/1322, 11/12/1332, and 31/12/1332) were not included in the sample of land transactions because they were too damaged to be photocopied and were unavailable to me at the time of sampling. Moreover, since my notes indicated that only three land transfers were recorded in these courts, it seemed pointless to subject these fragile membranes to further wear and tear.

23. The categorization of properties by size was fairly straightforward because most transfers of land clearly designated their extent. All properties designated "less than 2 rods" were either so described by the clerks or were described as consisting of some unmeasured small property (e.g., fither, butt, selion, or small *domus* with or withhold curtilage). Properties in the category "over 2 rods" were so described by the clerk. All properties of unstated or vague extent were excluded from analyses of land size.

24. Most anthropological studies of social networks have focused on

very small groups. See Jeremy Boissevain, *Friends of My Friends: Networks, Manipulators and Coalitions* (Oxford, 1974), pp. 97–146; Bruce Kapferer, "Norms and the Manipulation of Relationships in a Work Context," in *Social Networks in Urban Situations,* ed. J. Clyde Mitchell (Manchester, 1969), pp. 181–244. Two recent applications of network theory by English historians have, nevertheless, dealt with large numbers of individual networks. In one case, the authors reported impressive details about kin linkages, but revealed little about the social quality and meaning of these connections. See Keith Wrightson and David Levine, *Poverty and Piety,* pp. 73–109. In the other case, the analysis combined all kin into one category and obscured possible variations between contacts with different types of relatives; see Smith, "Kin and Neighbors." Both studies addressed relations between kin and non-kin, not relations with different types of kin.

25. Succinct descriptions of network analysis can be found in J. Clyde Mitchell, "Social Networks," *Annual Review of Anthropology* 3 (1974), pp. 279–299, and J. A. Barnes, *Social Networks* (Reading, Mass., 1972).

26. Robert Penifader received 8 citations for official activities. His land dealings included numerous small transfers and one grant of a full virgate of meadow (N.R.O., 8/8/1314).

27. Emma Penifader and Alice II Penifader were both cited for work defaults in 1304 (N.R.O., 4/9/1304). Emma Penifader was never noted in later courts. Alice II Penifader's next known appearance in the courts occurred four decades after her first, when she leased land to her nephew (N.R.O., 5/8/1345). These lost histories probably reflect untraced marriages rather than early death or emigration. Because women usually dropped their natal surnames upon marriage, they cannot be traced if their marriage records are lost. As a result, the potential social importance of the affinal connections created by such marriages also cannot be examined.

28. For Cristina Penifader's marriage to Richard Power of Cranford (located some six miles south of Brigstock), see N.R.O., 28/7/1317.

29. Henry Kroyl senior was cited 26 times for official duties. At his death, he possessed a full virgate of land (N.R.O., 8/9/1329).

30. Boissevain, *Friends,* pp. 28–32; Kapferer, "Norms," pp. 226–227.

31. Farley, *Domesday-Book,* I, p. 149a. A translation of the Domesday entry for Iver can be found in William E. Page, ed., *Victoria History of the Country of Buckingham,* I (London, 1926), pp. 257–258.

32. Page, *VCH Buckingham,* III, p. 286.

33. See, for example, B.A.S., m. 35, 27/9/1345.

34. Radulph Couhurde rented 25 cows for a term of one year. See B.A.S., m. 36, 5/12/1345.

35. For a holding that included fishing rights, see John de Thorneye's

properties in B.A.S., m. 47, 6/6/1349. John Snape and Robert Wolward rented fisheries in the same court. For amercements paid for sales of fish, see Thomas Gonere, William Pundere, and John le Lord in B.A.S., m. 14, 7/10/1336.

36. The common waters of the community are mentioned in B.A.S., m. 14, 7/10/1336 and m. 18, 14/7/1337. In the Iver courts of 1344–1346, the Prior of Harmondsworth (located just south of Iver) was repeatedly summoned to answer for his trespasses on the Iver fisheries. See B.A.S., membranes 33 through 42.

37. A full history of the ownership of Iver manor is given in W. H. Ward and K. S. Block, *A History of the Manor and Parish of Iver* (London, 1933), pp. 22–39.

38. In areas of demographic pressure, land demand usually sufficed to keep all tenements in good repair. Citations for waste or abandonment of holdings are common, for example, in many English court rolls after the plague, when lower population levels enabled many peasants to relinquish or ignore marginal holdings in favor of better properties. Wastage citations in Iver occurred as follows: 1332, 1 citation; 1333, 1 citation; 1335, 15 citations; 1337, 1 citation; 1338, 5 citations; 1344, 1 citation; 1345, 7 citations; 1346, 6 citations; 1349, 1 citation.

39. Farley, *Domesday-Book,* I, p. 204b. A translation of the entries for Houghton and Wyton can be found in William Page et al., eds., *Victoria History of the County of Huntingdon,* I (London, 1926), p. 343.

40. William Henry Hart and Posonby A. Lyons, eds., *Cartularium Monasterii de Ramseeia,* I (London, 1884), pp. 363–373.

41. Page, *VCH Huntingdon,* II, pp. 178–181, 253–254.

42. Only 16 references to land transfers (most of which were accomplished without permission and were therefore voided by the court) survive in the records of Houghton-cum-Wyton before the plague. The essential stability of landholding on this manor can also be seen by comparing the mid-thirteenth-century survey described above to another survey taken in the early twelfth century (see Hart and Lyons, *Cartularium,* III, pp. 278–280). See also the description of Houghton-cum-Wyton in the royal survey of 1279: W. Illingworth and J. Caley, eds., *Rotuli Hundredorum tempore Henrici III et Edwardi I* (London, 1818), II, p. 601. For the tendency of peasants to fragment their holdings unless prevented by lords, see Miller, *Ely,* p. 135.

43. See, for example, the courts for Houghton-cum-Wyton printed in W. O. Ault, ed., *Court Rolls of the Abbey of Ramsey and the Honor of Clare* (New Haven, Conn., 1928), pp. 239–259.

Bibliography

Manuscript Sources

Brigstock

Public Record Office (London)
    Series SC-2: 194/65
        court roll: Nov. 1298–Oct. 1299
Northamptonshire Record Office (Northampton)
    Montagu Collection Box X364A
        court roll 1:   Feb. 1287–June 1287
        court roll 2:   July 1287–Aug. 1287
        court roll 3:   Nov. 1291–Sept. 1292
        court roll 4:   June 1295–Sept. 1295
        court roll 5:   July 1295
        court roll 6:   Aug. 1295–Sept. 1295
        court roll 7:   March 1297–Nov. 1297
        court roll 8:   Dec. 1297–Oct. 1298
        court roll 9:   April 1300–Sept. 1300
        court roll 10:   Dec. 1300–Sept. 1301
        court roll 11:   Oct. 1301–Oct. 1302
        court roll 12:   Feb. 1303–Sept. 1303
        court roll 13:   Dec. 1303–Sept. 1304
        court roll 14:   Nov. 1305–Oct. 1306
        court roll 15:   July 1307–Aug. 1307

court roll 16: Sept. or Oct. 1307
court roll 17: Nov. 1307
court roll 18: Dec. 1307–Jan. 1308
court roll 19: Jan. 1308–Feb. 1308
court roll 20: March 1308
court roll 21: March 1309–June 1310
court roll 22: March 1311–June 1311
court roll 23: June 1311–July 1311
court roll 24: Jan. 1312
Montagu Collection Box X364B
court roll 25: Nov. 1313–Oct. 1314
court roll 26: Nov. 1314–Sept. 1315
court roll 27: Nov. 1315–Jan. 1316
court roll 28: March 1316–April 1316
court roll 29: July 1316–Sept. 1316
court roll 30: Oct. 1316–Sept. 1317
court roll 31: July 1318–Oct. 1319
court roll 32: Oct. 1320–Sept. 1321
court roll 33: Feb. 1322–Sept. 1322
court roll 34: March 1325–Sept. 1325
court roll 35: Nov. 1325–Sept. 1326
court roll 36: Jan. 1328–Sept. 1328
court roll 37: Nov. or Dec. 1328–Sept. 1329
court roll 38: Feb. 1330–April 1330
Montagu Collection Box X365
court roll 39: Dec. 1330–Sept. 1331
court roll 40: March or April 1332–Oct. 1332
court roll 41: Nov. 1332–Sept. 1333
View for Sept. 1340
court roll 42: Oct. 1334–Sept. 1335
court roll 43: May 1336–Sept. 1336
court roll 44: Oct. 1336–Sept. 1337
court roll 45: March 1338–Sept. 1338
court roll 46: Oct. 1338–Sept. 1339
court roll 47: Oct. 1339–Sept. 1340
court roll 48: Oct. 1340–Sept. 1341
court roll 49: Oct. 1342–Nov. 1342
court roll 50: Jan. 1343–Sept. 1343
court roll 51: Nov. 1343–Sept. 1344
court roll 52: Jan. 1345–Sept. 1345
court roll 53: Jan. 1348–March 1348
court roll 54: April 1348–Sept. 1348

Montagu Collection Box X371
   custumal of 1391
   Miscellaneous Ledger 141
   extracts from manorial records

Iver

Buckinghamshire Archaeological Society (Aylesbury)
   128/53 (courts for Jan. 1332–Sept. 1376)
St. George's Chapel, Windsor Castle (Windsor)
   XV.55.1 (courts for Oct. 1287–Oct. 1288)
   XV.55.3 (court for May 1288)
   XV.55.4 (court for Oct. 1288)
   XV.55.5 (court for April 1333)
   XV.55.6 (courts for March–Nov. 1333)
   IV.B.1 (extracts from manorial records)

Houghton-cum-Wyton

British Library (London)
   Additional Charters 34912 (accounts for 1290)
   Additional Charters 39693 (accounts for 1310)
   Additional Charters 34338 (court for Nov. 1292)
   Additional Charters 39597 (court for Jan. 1294)
   Additional Charters 39756 (court for Nov. 1306)
   Additional Charters 39586 (court for Dec. 1309)
   Additional Charters 34324 (court for Jan. 1313)
   Additional Charters 34897 (court for Jan. 1316)
   Additional Charters 34898 (court for Jan. 1325)
   Additional Charters 39761 (court for Dec. 1331)
Public Record Office (London)
   Series SC-6 878/14 (accounts for 1297)
   Series SC-6 878/15 (accounts for 1297)
   Series SC-6 878/16 (accounts for 1302)
   Series SC-6 878/17 (accounts for 1307)
   Series SC-6 878/18 (accounts temp. Edward I or Edward II)
   Series SC-6 878/19 (accounts for 1312)
   Series SC-6 884/4 (accounts for 1314)
   Series SC-6 878/20 (accounts for 1316)
   Series SC-6 878/21 (accounts for 1319)
   Series SC-6 878/22 (accounts for 1320)
   Series SC-6 878/23 (accounts for 1325)
   Series SC-6 879/1 (accounts for 1337)

Series SC-2 179/5 (court for Nov. 1288)
Series SC-2 179/7 (court for Nov. 1290)
Series SC-2 179/9 (courts for Dec. 1296–Nov. 1297)
Series SC-2 179/10 (court for Dec. 1299)
Series SC-2 179/11 (court for Oct. 1301)
Series SC-2 179/12 (court for Jan. 1306)
Series SC-2 179/13 (courts for July 1306–July 1311)
Series SC-2 179/15 (court for Nov. 1308)
Series SC-2 179/16 (court for Nov. 1311)
Series SC-2 179/19 (court for Oct. 1320)
Series SC-2 179/20 (court for Nov. 1321)
Series SC-2 179/21 (court for Oct. 1322)
Series SC-2 179/22 (court for Dec. 1326)
Series SC-2 179/25 (court for Dec. 1328)
Series SC-2 179/26 (court for Dec. 1332)
Series SC-2 179/30 (court for Jan. 1340)
Series SC-2 179/32 (court for Nov. 1347)
Series SC-2 179/33 (court for Oct. 1349)
Series E179 122/4 (tax for 1327–1328)
Series E179 122/7 (tax for 1332–1333)
Series E179 122/14 (tax for 1340–1341)

Printed Sources

Ault, W. O., ed., *Court Rolls of the Abbey of Ramsey and the Honor of Clare* (New Haven, Conn., 1928).
Baildon, William Paley, ed., *Court Rolls of the Manor of Wakefield, Vol. I (1274–1297)*, Yorkshire Archaeological Society 29 (Leeds, 1901).
Baildon, William Paley, ed., *Court Rolls of the Manor of Wakefield, Vol. II (1297–1309)*, Yorkshire Archaeological Society 36 (Leeds, 1906).
Bateson, Mary, ed., *Borough Customs, Vol. II*, Selden Society 21 (London, 1906).
Calendar of Fine Rolls Preserved in the Public Record Office, 1307–1319 (London, 1912).
Calendar of Inquisitions Miscellaneous Preserved in the Public Record Office, vol. I (London, 1916).
Calendar of the Patent Rolls Preserved in the Public Record Office, 1292–1301 (London, 1895).
Chaucer, Geoffrey, *The Complete Works of Geoffrey Chaucer*, ed. F. N. Robinson (Boston, 1933).

Farley, Abraham, ed., *Domesday-Book seu Liber Censualis Willelmi Primi,* 2 vols. (London, 1783).

Glasscock, Robin E., ed., *The Lay Subsidy of 1334* (London, 1975).

Hart, William Henry, and Posonby A. Lyons, eds., *Cartularium Monasterii de Ramseeia,* Rolls Series 79, 3 vols. (London, 1884–1893).

Illingworth, W., and J. Caley, eds., *Rotuli Hundredorum tempore Henrici III et Edwardi I,* 2 vols. (London, 1812–1818).

Langland, William, *The Book Concerning Piers the Plowman,* trans. and ed. Donald and Rachel Attwater (1907; rpt. London, 1959).

Langland, William, *Piers Plowman: The A Version,* ed. George Kane (London, 1960).

Langland, William, *Piers Plowman: An Edition of the C Text,* ed. Derek Pearsall (Berkeley, Calif., 1979).

Maitland, F. W., ed., *Select Pleas in Manorial and Other Seignorial Courts,* Selden Society 2 (London, 1889).

Maitland, Frederic William, and William Paley Baildon, eds., *The Court Baron,* Selden Society 4 (London, 1891).

Meech, Sanford Brown, and Hope Emily Allen, eds., *The Book of Margery Kempe,* Early English Text Society, vol. 212 (1940; rpt. London, 1961).

Oschinsky, Dorothea, ed., *Walter of Henley and Other Treatises on Estate Management and Accounting* (Oxford, 1971).

de Pisan, Christine, *The Treasure of the City of Ladies,* trans. Sarah Lawson (Harmondsworth, 1985).

Rickert, Edith, ed. and trans., *The Babees Book: Medieval Manners for the Young* (London, 1923).

Robbins, Rossell Hope, ed., *Secular Lyrics of the XIVth and XVth Centuries* (Oxford, 1952).

Sisam, Celia and Kenneth, eds., *The Oxford Book of Medieval English Verse* (Oxford, 1970).

The Statutes of the Realm, vol. 1 (London, 1810).

Turner, G. J., ed., *Select Pleas of the Forest,* Selden Society 13 (London, 1901).

Wright, Thomas, and James Orchard Halliwell, *Reliquiae Antiquae,* vol. II (London, 1845).

Secondary Works

Abram, A., *English Life and Manners in the Late Middle Ages* (London, 1913).

Abram, A., "Women Traders in Medieval London," *Economic Journal* 26 (1916), pp. 276–285.

Adkins, W. Ryland D., and R. M. Serjeantson, eds., *Victoria History of the County of Northampton,* 4 vols. (London, 1902–1937).

Amundsen, Darrel W., and Carol Jean Diers, "The Age of Menarche in Medieval Europe," *Human Biology* 45 (1973), pp. 363–369.

Ariès, Philippe, *Centuries of Childhood: A Social History of Family Life,* trans. Robert Baldick (New York, 1962).

Atkinson, Clarissa W., *Mystic and Pilgrim: The Book and World of Margery Kempe* (Ithaca, N.Y., 1983).

Attreed, Lorraine C., "From *Pearl* Maiden to Tower Princes: Towards a New History of Medieval Childhood," *Journal of Medieval History* 9 (1983), pp. 43–58.

Barnes, J. A., *Social Networks* (Reading, Mass., 1972).

Beard, Mary Ritter, *Woman as a Force in History* (1946; rpt. New York, 1962).

Beckerman, John, "Customary Law in English Manorial Courts in the Thirteenth and Fourteenth Centuries," Diss. University of London, 1972.

Bennett, H. S., *The Pastons and their England,* 2nd edition (1932; rpt. Cambridge, 1977).

Bennett, Judith M., "Gender, Family and Community: A Comparative Study of the English Peasantry, 1287–1349," Diss. University of Toronto, 1981.

Bennett, Judith M., "Spouses, Siblings and Surnames: Reconstructing Families from Medieval Village Court Rolls," *Journal of British Studies* 23 (1983), pp. 26–46.

Bennett, Judith M., "The Tie That Binds: Peasant Marriages and Families in Late Medieval England," *Journal of Interdisciplinary History* 15 (1984), pp. 111–129.

Beresford, Maurice, and John G. Hurst, *Deserted Medieval Villages* (London, 1971).

Berkner, Lutz K., "Rural Family Organization in Europe: A Problem in Comparative History," *Peasant Studies Newsletter* 1 (1972), pp. 145–156.

Berkner, Lutz K., "The Stem Family and the Developmental Cycle of the Peasant Household: An Eighteenth-Century Austrian Example," *American Historical Review* 77 (1972), pp. 398–418.

Beveridge, William, "Wages in the Winchester Manors," *Economic History Review* 7 (1936–1937), pp. 22–43.

Bideau, Alain, "A Demographic and Social Analysis of Widowhood and Remarriage: The Example of the Castellany of Thoissey-en-Dombes, 1670–1840," *Journal of Family History* 5 (1980), pp. 28–43.

Biller, P. P. A., "Birth Control in the West in the Thirteenth and Early Fourteenth Centuries," *Past and Present* 94 (1982), pp. 3–26.

Birrell, Jean R., "The Forest Economy of the Honour of Tutbury in the Fourteenth and Fifteenth Centuries," *University of Birmingham Historical Journal* 8 (1962), pp. 114–134.

Birrell, Jean, "Peasant Craftsmen in the Medieval Forest," *Agricultural History Review* 17 (1969), pp. 91–107.

Birrell, Jean, "Who Poached the King's Deer? A Study of Thirteenth-Century Crime," *Midland History* 7 (1982), pp. 9–25.

Boissevain, Jeremy, *Friends of My Friends: Networks, Manipulators and Coalitions* (Oxford, 1974).

Boserup, Ester, *Woman's Role in Economic Development* (New York, 1970).

Brand, John, *Observations on the Popular Antiquities of Great Britain* (1848–1849; rpt. New York, 1970).

Brand, Paul A., and Paul R. Hyams, untitled contribution to "Debate: Seigneurial Control of Women's Marriage," *Past and Present* 99 (1983), pp. 123–133.

Bridges, John, *The History and Antiquities of Northamptonshire*, 2 vols., ed. Peter Whalley (London, 1791).

Britnell, R. H., "The Proliferation of Markets in England, 1200–1349," *Economic History Review,* 2nd series, 34 (1981), pp. 209–221.

Britton, Edward, "The Peasant Family in Fourteenth-Century England," *Peasant Studies* 5, no. 2 (1976), pp. 2–7.

Britton, Edward, *The Community of the Vill: A Study in the History of the Family and Village Life in Fourteenth-Century England* (Toronto, 1977).

Brown, Judith K., "A Note on the Division of Labor by Sex," *American Anthropologist* 72 (1970), pp. 1073–1078.

Brown, R. Allen, H. M. Colvin, and A. J. Taylor, *The History of the King's Works: Volume II, The Middle Ages* (London, 1963).

Cam, Helen M., *The Hundred and the Hundred Rolls* (1930; rpt. New York, 1960).

Cam, Helen M., *Liberties and Communities in Medieval England: Collected Studies in Local Administration and Topography* (London, 1963).

Carroll, Berenice A., ed., *Liberating Women's History* (Urbana, Ill., 1976).

Chaytor, Miranda, "Household and Kinship: Ryton in the Late 16th and Early 17th Centuries," *History Workshop* 10 (1980), pp. 25–60.

Chojnacki, Stanley, "Dowries and Kinsmen in Early Renaissance Venice," *Journal of Interdisciplinary History* 5 (1975), pp. 571–600.

Clanchy, Michael, "Law and Love in the Middle Ages," in *Disputes and Settlements: Law and Human Relations in the West,* ed. John Bossy (Cambridge, 1983), pp. 47–68.

Clark, Alice, *Working Life of Women in the Seventeenth Century* (1919; rpt. London, 1982).

Clark, Elaine, "Some Aspects of Social Security in Medieval England," *Journal of Family History* 7 (1982), pp. 307–320.

Coulton, G. G., *Medieval Village, Manor, and Monastery* (1925; rpt. New York, 1960).

Dale, Marian K., "The London Silkwomen of the Fifteenth Century," *Economic History Review* (1933), pp. 324–335.

Davenport, F. G., *The Economic History of a Norfolk Manor 1086–1565* (1906; rpt. New York, 1967).

Davis, Natalie Zemon, " 'Women's History' in Transition: The European Case," *Feminist Studies* 3 (1976), pp. 83–103.

Davis, Norman, ed., *Paston Letters and Papers of the Fifteenth Century* (Oxford, 1971).

DeWindt, Anne, "Peasant Power Structures in Fourteenth-Century King's Ripton," *Mediaeval Studies* 38 (1976), pp. 236–267.

DeWindt, Anne Rieber, and Edwin Brezette DeWindt, *Royal Justice in the Medieval English Countryside*, 2 vols. (Toronto, 1981).

DeWindt, Edwin Brezette, *Land and People in Holywell-cum-Needingworth: Structures of Tenure and Patterns of Social Organization in an East Midlands Village, 1252–1457* (Toronto, 1972).

Donahue, Charles, Jr., "The Policy of Alexander the Third's Consent Theory of Marriage," in *Proceedings of the Fourth International Congress of Medieval Canon Law*, ed. Stephen Kuttner (Vatican City, 1976), pp. 251–281.

Dupâquier, J., et al., eds., *Marriage and Remarriage in Populations of the Past* (New York, 1981).

Dyer, Christopher, *Lords and Peasants in a Changing Society: The Estates of the Bishopric of Worcester, 680–1540* (Cambridge, 1980).

Dyer, Christopher, "English Diet in the Later Middle Ages," in *Social Relations and Ideas*, ed. T. H. Aston et al. (Cambridge, 1983), pp. 191–216.

English, Barbara, *The Lords of Holderness, 1086–1260* (Oxford, 1979).

Erickson, Carolly, *The Medieval Vision* (New York, 1976).

Faith, Rosamund Jane, "Peasant Families and Inheritance Customs in Medieval England," *Agricultural History Review* 14 (1966), pp. 77–95.

Faith, Rosamund, untitled contribution to "Debate: Seigneurial Control of Women's Marriage," *Past and Present* 99 (1983), pp. 133–148.

Field, R. K., "Worcestershire Peasant Buildings, Household Goods and Farming Equipment in the Later Middle Ages," *Medieval Archaeology* 9 (1965), pp. 105–145.

Friedl, Ernestine, *Vasilika: A Village in Modern Greece* (New York, 1962).

Friedl, Ernestine, "The Position of Women: Appearance and Reality," *Anthropological Quarterly* 40 (1967), pp. 97–108.

Gilligan, Carol, *In a Different Voice: Psychological Theory and Women's Development* (Cambridge, Mass., 1982).

Gillis, John R., *Youth and History: Tradition and Change in European Age Relations 1770–Present* (New York, 1974).

Given, James Buchanan, *Society and Homicide in Thirteenth-Century England* (Stanford, 1977).

Goldberg, P. J. P., "Female Labour, Service and Marriage in the Late Medieval Urban North," forthcoming in *Northern History.*

Goody, Jack, "Strategies of Heirship," *Comparative Studies in Society and History* 15 (1973), pp. 3–20.

Goody, Jack, *Production and Reproduction: A Comparative Study of the Domestic Domain* (Cambridge, 1976).

Goody, Jack, *The Development of the Family and Marriage in Europe* (Cambridge, 1983).

Goody, Jack, Joan Thirsk, and E. P. Thompson, eds., *Family and Inheritance: Rural Society in Western Europe 1200–1800* (Cambridge, 1976).

Hajnal, J., "European Marriage Patterns in Perspective," in *Population in History: Essays in Historical Demography,* ed. D. V. Glass and D. E. C. Eversley (Chicago, 1965), pp. 101–143.

Hallam, H. E., "Some Thirteenth-Century Censuses," *Economic History Review,* 2nd series, 10 (1958), pp. 340–361.

Hallam, H. E., "Further Observations on the Spalding Serf Lists," *Economic History Review,* 2nd series, 16 (1963), pp. 338–350.

Hallam, H. E., *Rural England 1066–1348* (Glasgow, 1981).

Hanawalt, Barbara A. (a.k.a. Barbara Hanawalt Westman), "The Peasant Family and Crime in Fourteenth-Century England," *Journal of British Studies* 13, no. 2 (1974), pp. 1–18.

Hanawalt, Barbara A., "Violent Death in Fourteenth- and Early Fifteenth-Century England," *Comparative Studies in Society and History* 18 (1976), pp. 297–320.

Hanawalt, Barbara A., "Childrearing among the Lower Classes of Late Medieval England," *Journal of Interdisciplinary History* 8 (1977), pp. 1–22.

Hanawalt, Barbara A., "Community Conflict and Social Control: Crime and Justice in the Ramsey Abbey Villages," *Mediaeval Studies* 39 (1977), pp. 402–423.

Hanawalt, Barbara A., *Crime and Conflict in English Communities, 1300–1348* (Cambridge, Mass., 1979).

Hanawalt, Barbara A., ed., *Women and Work in Preindustrial Europe* (Bloomington, Ind., 1986).

Harris, Olivia, "Households and Their Boundaries," *History Workshop* 13 (1982), pp. 143–152.

Harris, Olivia, "Households as Natural Units," in *Of Marriage and the Market,* 2nd edition, ed. Kate Young et al. (London, 1984), pp. 136–155.

Hartmann, Heidi, "Capitalism, Patriarchy, and Job Segregation by Sex," in *Women and the Workplace,* ed. Martha Blaxall and Barbara Reagan (Chicago, 1976), pp. 137–169.

Harvey, Barbara F., "The Population Trend in England Between 1300 and 1348," *Transactions of the Royal Historical Society,* 5th series, 16 (1966), pp. 23–42.

Harvey, Barbara, *Westminster Abbey and Its Estates in the Middle Ages* (Oxford, 1977).

Harvey, P. D. A., *A Medieval Oxfordshire Village: Cuxham 1240–1400* (Oxford, 1965).

Harvey, P. D. A., ed., *The Peasant Land Market in Medieval England* (Oxford, 1984).

Hatcher, John, *Rural Economy and Society in the Duchy of Cornwall 1300–1500* (Cambridge, 1970).

Hatcher, John, *Plague, Population and the English Economy 1348–1530* (London, 1977).

Helmholz, R. H., *Marriage Litigation in Medieval England* (London, 1974).

Helmholz, R. H., "Infanticide in the Province of Canterbury during the Fifteenth Century," *History of Childhood Quarterly* 2 (1975), pp. 379–390.

Herlihy, David, "Vieiller à Florence au Quattrocento," *Annales économies, sociétés, civilisations* 24 (1969), pp. 1338–1352.

Herlihy, David, *Medieval Households* (Cambridge, Mass., 1985).

Herlihy, David, and Christiane Klapisch-Zuber, *Les Toscans et leurs familles* (Paris, 1978).

Hill, Christopher, "Note: Household and Kinship," *Past and Present* 88 (1980), p. 142.

Hilton, Rodney H., *The Economic Development of Some Leicestershire Estates in the 14th and 15th Centuries* (London, 1947).

Hilton, R. H., *A Medieval Society: The West Midlands at the End of the Thirteenth Century* (London, 1966).

Hilton, R. H., *The English Peasantry in the Later Middle Ages* (Oxford, 1975).

Hilton, R. H., "Lords, Burgesses and Hucksters," *Past and Present* 97 (1982), pp. 3–15.

Hilton, Rodney, "Women Traders in Medieval England," *Women's Studies* 11 (1984), pp. 139–155.

Homans, George Caspar, *English Villagers of the Thirteenth Century* (1941; rpt. New York, 1970).

Houston, Rab, and Richard Smith, "A New Approach to Family History?" *History Workshop* 14 (1982), pp. 120–131.

Howell, Cicely, *Land, Family and Inheritance in Transition* (Cambridge, 1983).

Hufton, Olwen, "Women and the Family Economy in Eighteenth-Century France," *French Historical Studies* 9 (1975), pp. 1–22.

Hufton, Olwen, "Women, Work and Marriage in Eighteenth-Century France," in *Marriage and Society: Studies in the Social History of Marriage*, ed. R. B. Outhwaite (New York, 1981), pp. 186–203.

Hufton, Olwen, "Women in History: Early Modern Europe," *Past and Present* 101 (1983), pp. 125–141.

Hyams, Paul R., "The Origins of a Peasant Land Market in England," *Economic History Review*, 2nd series, 23 (1970), pp. 18–31.

Illich, Ivan, *Gender* (New York, 1982).

Kapferer, Bruce, "Norms and the Manipulation of Relationships in a Work Context," in *Social Networks in Urban Situations*, ed. J. Clyde Mitchell (Manchester, 1969), pp. 181–244.

Kellum, Barbara A., "Infanticide in England in the Later Middle Ages," *History of Childhood Quarterly* 1 (1973–1974), pp. 367–388.

Kelly-Gadol, Joan, "The Social Relation of the Sexes: Methodological Implications of Women's History," *Signs* 1 (1976), pp. 809–823.

Kelly-Gadol, Joan, "Did Women Have a Renaissance?" in *Becoming Visible: Women in European History*, ed. Renate Bridenthal and Claudia Koonz (New York, 1977), pp. 137–164.

Kelly-Gadol, Joan, "The Doubled Vision of Feminist Theory," *Feminist Studies* 5 (1979), pp. 216–227.

Kershaw, Ian, "The Great Famine and Agrarian Crisis in England, 1315–1322," *Past and Present* 59 (1973), pp. 3–50.

King, Edmund, *Peterborough Abbey 1086–1310: A Study in the Land Market* (Cambridge, 1973).

Kosminsky, E. A., *Studies in the Agrarian History of England in the Thirteenth Century*, ed. R. H. Hilton (Oxford, 1956).

Krause, J., "The Medieval Household: Large or Small?" *Economic History Review*, 2nd series, 9 (1957), pp. 420–432.

Kuehn, Thomas, *Emancipation in Late Medieval Florence* (New Brunswick, 1982).

Kussmaul, Ann, *Servants in Husbandry in Early Modern England* (Cambridge, 1981).

Labarge, Margaret Wade, *A Baronial Household of the Thirteenth Century* (1965; rpt. Totowa, N.J., 1980).

Lacey, W. K., *The Family in Classical Greece* (Ithaca, N.Y., 1968).

Laslett, Peter, with Richard Wall, eds., *Household and Family in Past Time* (Cambridge, 1972).

Laslett, Peter, *Family Life and Illicit Love in Earlier Generations* (Cambridge, 1977).

Le Roy Ladurie, Emmanuel, *Montaillou: The Promised Land of Error,* trans. Barbara Bray (New York, 1978).

Levett, Ada Elizabeth, *Studies in Manorial History,* ed. H. M. Cam, M. Coate, and L. S. Sutherland (1938; rpt. London, 1962).

Macfarlane, Alan, *Reconstructing Historical Communities* (London, 1977).

Macfarlane, Alan, *The Origins of English Individualism: The Family, Property and Social Transition* (Oxford, 1978).

Maddicott, J. R., *The English Peasantry and the Demands of the Crown 1294–1341,* Past and Present Supplement 1 (Oxford, 1975).

May, Alfred N., "An Index of Thirteenth-Century Peasant Impoverishment? Manor Court Fines," *Economic History Review,* 2nd series, 26 (1973), pp. 389–402.

McClure, Peter, "Patterns of Migration in the Late Middle Ages: The Evidence of English Place-Name Surnames," *Economic History Review,* 2nd series, 32 (1979), pp. 167–182.

McIntosh, Marjorie Keniston, "The Privileged Villeins of the English Ancient Demesne," *Viator* 7 (1976), pp. 295–328.

McIntosh, Marjorie K., "Servants and the Household Unit in an Elizabethan English Community," *Journal of Family History* 9 (1984), pp. 3–23.

McLean, Teresa, *Medieval English Gardens* (New York, 1980).

Middleton, Christopher, "The Sexual Division of Labor in Feudal England," *New Left Review* 113–114 (1979), pp. 147–168.

Middleton, Chris, "Peasants, Patriarchy and the Feudal Mode of Production in England: A Marxist Appraisal: Part 1. Property and Patriarchal Relations Within the Peasantry," *Sociological Review* 29 (1981), pp. 105–135.

Middleton, Chris, "Peasants, Patriarchy and the Feudal Mode of Production in England: Part 2. Feudal Lords and the Subordination of Peasant Women," *Sociological Review* 29 (1981), pp. 137–154.

Miller, Barbara D., *The Endangered Sex: Neglect of Female Children in Rural North India* (Ithaca, N.Y., 1981).

Miller, Edward, *The Abbey and Bishopric of Ely* (Cambridge, 1951).

Miller, Edward, "England in the Twelfth and Thirteenth Centuries: An Economic Contrast?" *Economic History Review,* 2nd series, 24 (1971), pp. 1–14.

Miller, Edward, and John Hatcher, *Medieval England: Rural Society and Economic Change 1086–1348* (London, 1978).

Mitchell, J. Clyde, "Social Networks," *Annual Review of Anthropology* 3 (1974), pp. 279–299.

Monckton, H. A., *A History of English Ale and Beer* (London, 1966).

Morgan, Lewis Henry, *Ancient Society,* ed. Leslie A. White (1877; rpt. Cambridge, Mass., 1964).

Morris, William Alfred, *The Frankpledge System* (New York, 1910).

Noonan, John T., Jr., "Power to Choose," *Viator* 4 (1973), pp. 419–434.

Owst, G. R., *Literature and Pulpit in Medieval England,* 2nd edition (New York, 1961).

Page, Frances M., *The Estates of Crowland Abbey* (Cambridge, 1934).

Page, William E., ed., *Victoria History of the County of Buckingham,* 4 vols. (London, 1905–1927).

Page, William, Granville Proby, and S. Inskip Ladds, eds., *Victoria History of the County of Huntingdon,* 3 vols. (London, 1926–1936).

Payer, Pierre J., *Sex and the Penitentials: The Development of a Sexual Code, 550–1150* (Toronto, 1984).

Pettit, Philip A. J., *The Royal Forests of Northamptonshire: A Study in Their Economy, 1558–1714,* Northamptonshire Record Society 23 (Gateshead, 1968).

Pimsler, Martin, "Solidarity in the Medieval Village? The Evidence of Personal Pledging at Elton, Huntingdonshire," *Journal of British Studies* 17, no. 1 (1977), pp. 1–11.

Pinchbeck, Ivy, and Margaret Hewitt, *Children in English Society, Volume I: From Tudor Times to the Eighteenth Century* (London, 1969).

Pollock, Frederick, and Frederic William Maitland, *The History of English Law Before the Time of Edward I,* 2 vols., 2nd edition (1898; rpt. Cambridge, 1968).

Pollock, Linda A., *Forgotten Children: Parent-Child Relations from 1500 to 1900* (Cambridge, 1983).

Pomeroy, Sarah B., *Goddesses, Whores, Wives, and Slaves: Women in Classical Antiquity* (New York, 1975).

Poos, L. R., "Population and Resources in Two Fourteenth-Century Essex Communities: Great Waltham and High Easter, 1327–1389," Diss. University of Cambridge, 1983.

Poos, L. R., "Population Turnover in Medieval Essex: The Evidence of Some Early Fourteenth-Century Tithing Lists," in *The World We Have Gained: Essays in Honour of Peter Laslett,* ed. Lloyd Bonfield, Richard Smith, and Keith Wrightson (Oxford, 1986).

Poos, L. R., "The Rural Population of Essex in the Later Middle Ages," *Economic History Review,* 2nd series, 38 (1985), pp. 515–530.

Poos, L. R., and R. M. Smith, " 'Legal Windows Onto Historical Populations'? Recent Research on Demography and the Manor Court in Medieval England," *Law and History Review* 2 (1984), pp. 128–152.

Post, J. B., "Ages at Menarche and Menopause: Some Medieval Authorities," *Population Studies* 25 (1971), pp. 83–87.

Post, J. B., "Manorial Amercements and Peasant Poverty," *Economic
History Review,* 2nd series, 28 (1975), pp. 304–311.

Postan, M. M., "Some Economic Evidence of Declining Population in the
Later Middle Ages," *Economic History Review,* 2nd series, 2 (1950),
pp. 221–246.

Postan, M. M., *The Famulus: The Estate Labourer in the XIIth and
XIIIth Centuries,* Economic History Review Supplements 2 (Cambridge, 1954).

Postan, M. M., "The Charters of the Villeins," in *Carte Nativorum,* ed.
C. N. L. Brooke and M. M. Postan, Northamptonshire Record Society
20 (Oxford, 1960), pp. xxviii–lx.

Postan, M. M., *The Medieval Economy and Society* (1971; rpt. Harmondsworth, 1975).

Postan, M. M., *Essays on Medieval Agriculture and General Problems
of the Medieval Economy* (Cambridge, 1973).

Postan, M. M. and J. Titow, "Heriots and Prices on Winchester Manors," *Economic History Review,* 2nd series, 11 (1959), pp. 392–411.

Power, Eileen, *Medieval Women,* ed. M. M. Postan (Cambridge, 1975).

Prior, Mary, "Women and the Urban Economy: Oxford 1500–1800," in
Women in English Society 1500–1800, ed. Mary Prior (London,
1985), pp. 93–117.

Raftis, J. Ambrose, *The Estates of Ramsey Abbey: A Study in Economic
Growth and Organization* (Toronto, 1957).

Raftis, J. Ambrose, *Tenure and Mobility: Studies in the Social History
of the Mediaeval English Village* (Toronto, 1964).

Raftis, J. A., "Social Structures in Five East Midland Villages: A Study
of Possibilities in the Use of Court Roll Data," *Economic History
Review,* 2nd series, 18 (1965), pp. 83–100.

Raftis, J. A., *Assart Data and Land Values: Two Studies in the East
Midlands, 1200–1350* (Toronto, 1974).

Raftis, J. Ambrose, *Warboys: Two Hundred Years in the Life of an English Mediaeval Village* (Toronto, 1974).

Raftis, J. A., ed., *Pathways to Medieval Peasants* (Toronto, 1981).

Raftis, J. A., *A Small Town in Late Medieval England: Godmanchester
1278–1400* (Toronto, 1982).

Rapp, Rayna, Ellen Ross, and Renate Bridenthal, "Examining Family
History," *Feminist Studies* 5 (1979), pp. 174–200.

Razi, Zvi, "The Toronto School's Reconstitution of Medieval Peasant
Society: A Critical View," *Past and Present* 85 (1979), pp. 141–157.

Razi, Zvi, *Life, Marriage and Death in a Medieval Parish: Economy, Society and Demography in Halesowen, 1270–1400* (Cambridge, 1980).

Razi, Zvi, "Family, Land and the Village Community in Later Medieval England," *Past and Present* 93 (1981), pp. 3–36.

Razi, Zvi, "The Use of Manorial Court Rolls in Demographic Analysis: A Reconsideration," *Law and History Review* 3 (1985), pp. 191–200.

Reiter, Rayna R., ed., *Toward an Anthropology of Women* (New York, 1975).

Reynolds, Glynis, "Infant Mortality and Sex Ratios at Baptism as Shown by the Reconstruction of Willingham, a Parish at the edge of the Fens in Cambridgeshire," *Local Population Studies* 22 (1979), pp. 31–37.

Riegelhaupt, Joyce F., "Saloio Women: An Analysis of Informal and Formal Political and Economic Roles of Portuguese Peasant Women," *Anthropological Quarterly* 40 (1967), pp. 109–126.

Roberts, Michael, "Sickles and Scythes: Women's Work and Men's Work at Harvest Time," *History Workshop* 7 (1979), pp. 3–28.

Rogers, Susan Carol, "Female Forms of Power and the Myth of Male Dominance: A Model of Female/Male Interaction in Peasant Society," *American Ethnologist* 2 (1975), pp. 727–756.

Rosaldo, Michelle Zimbalist and Louise Lamphere, eds., *Woman, Culture and Society* (Stanford, 1974).

Rosenthal, Joel T., "Aristocratic Widows in Fifteenth-Century England," in *Women and the Structure of Society,* ed. Barbara J. Harris and Jo Ann K. McNamara (Durham, N.C., 1984), pp. 36–47.

Royal Commission on Historical Monuments, *An Inventory of the Historical Monuments in the County of Northampton, Vol. I: Archaeological Sites in Northeast Northamptonshire* (London, 1975).

Russell, Josiah Cox, *British Medieval Population* (Albuquerque, 1948).

Russell, J. C., "Demographic Limitations of the Spalding Serf Lists," *Economic History Review,* 2nd series, 15 (1962), pp. 138–144.

Russell, Josiah C., "The Preplague Population of England," *Journal of British Studies* 5, no. 2 (1966), pp. 1–21.

Sacks, Karen, *Sisters and Wives: The Past and Future of Sexual Equality* (1979; rpt. Urbana, Ill., 1982).

Salzman, L. F., *English Industries of the Middle Ages* (Oxford, 1923).

Sanday, Peggy R., "Toward a Theory of the Status of Women," *American Anthropologist* 75 (1973), pp. 1682–1700.

Scammell, Jean, "Freedom and Marriage in Medieval England," *Economic History Review,* 2nd series, 27 (1974), pp. 523–537.

Scammell, Jean, "Wife-Rents and Merchet," *Economic History Review,* 2nd series, 29 (1976), pp. 487–490.

Scheper-Hughes, Nancy, "Vernacular Sexism: An Anthropological Response to Ivan Illich," *Feminist Issues* 3 (1983), pp. 28–37.

Schofield, Roger, and E. A. Wrigley, "Infant and Child Mortality in England in the Late Tudor and Early Stuart Period," in *Health, Medicine and Mortality in the Sixteenth Century,* ed. Charles Webster (Cambridge, 1979), pp. 61–95.

Schofield, Roger, and E. A. Wrigley, "English Population History from Family Reconstitution: Summary Results 1600–1799," *Population Studies* 37 (1983), pp. 157–184.

Searle, Eleanor, *Lordship and Community: Battle Abbey and Its Banlieu 1066–1538* (Toronto, 1974).

Searle, Eleanor, "Freedom and Marriage in Medieval England: An Alternative Hypothesis," *Economic History Review,* 2nd series, 29 (1976), pp. 482–486.

Searle, Eleanor, "Seigneurial Control of Women's Marriage: The Antecedents and Function of Merchet in England," *Past and Present* 82 (1979), pp. 3–43.

Searle, Eleanor, untitled contribution to "Debate: Seigneurial Control of Women's Marriage," *Past and Present* 99 (1983), pp. 148–160.

Segalen, Martine, *Love and Power in the Peasant Family: Rural France in the Nineteenth Century,* trans. Sarah Matthews (Chicago, 1983).

Shahar, Shulamith, *The Fourth Estate: A History of Women in the Middle Ages,* trans. Chaya Galai (London, 1983).

Sharpe, J. A., "Domestic Homicide in Early Modern England," *Historical Journal* 24 (1981), pp. 29–48.

Sheehan, Michael M., *The Will in Medieval England* (Toronto, 1963).

Sheehan, Michael M., "The Formation and Stability of Marriage in Fourteenth-Century England: Evidence of an Ely Register," *Mediaeval Studies* 33 (1971), pp. 228–263.

Sheehan, M. M., "Choice of Marriage Partner in the Middle Ages: Development and Mode of Application of a Theory of Marriage," *Studies in Medieval and Renaissance History,* new series, 1 (1978), pp. 3–33.

Shorter, Edward, "Illegitimacy, Sexual Revolution, and Social Change in Modern Europe," *Journal of Interdisciplinary History* 2 (1971), pp. 237–272.

Shorter, Edward, "Female Emancipation, Birth Control, and Fertility in European History," *American Historical Review* 78 (1973), pp. 605–640.

Smith, Daniel Scott, "Child-Naming Practices as Cultural and Familial Indicators," *Local Population Studies* 32 (1984), pp. 17–27.

Smith, Richard M., "English Peasant Life-Cycles and Socio-Economic Networks: A Quantitative Geographical Case Study," Diss. University of Cambridge, 1974.

Smith, R. M., "Kin and Neighbors in a Thirteenth-Century Suffolk Community," *Journal of Family History* 4 (1979), pp. 219–256.

Smith, R. M., "Some Reflections on the Evidence for the Origins of the 'European Marriage Pattern' in England," in *The Sociology of the*

Family: New Directions for Britain, ed. Chris Harris, Sociological Review Monograph 28 (Keele, Eng., 1979), pp. 74–112.

Smith, R. M., "The People of Tuscany and Their Families in the Fifteenth Century: Medieval or Mediterranean?" *Journal of Family History* 6 (1981), pp. 107–128.

Smith, R. M., "Rooms, Relatives and Residential Arrangements: Some Evidence in Manor Court Rolls 1250–1500," *Annual Report of the Medieval Villiage Research Group* 30 (1982), pp. 34–35.

Smith, R. M., "Hypothèses sur la nuptialité en Angleterre aux XII–XIV siècles," *Annales, économies, sociétés, civilisations* 38 (1983), pp. 107–136.

Smith, R. M., "Some Thoughts on 'Hereditary' and 'Proprietary' Rights in Land under Customary Law in Thirteenth and Early Fourteenth Century England," *Law and History Review* 1 (1983), pp. 95–128.

Smith, Richard M., ed., *Land, Kinship and Life-Cycle* (Cambridge, 1984).

Stenton, Doris Mary, *The English Woman in History* (London, 1957).

Stone, Lawrence, *The Family, Sex and Marriage in England 1500–1800* (New York, 1977).

Stuard, Susan Mosher, ed., *Women in Medieval Society* (Philadelphia, 1976).

Thorold Rogers, James E., *A History of Agriculture and Prices in England, Vol. I: 1259–1400* (Oxford, 1866).

Tilly, Charles, "Population and Pedagogy in France," *History of Education Quarterly* 13 (1973), pp. 113–128.

Tilly, Louise A., and Joan W. Scott, *Women, Work, and Family* (New York, 1978).

Titow, J. Z., "Some Differences Between Manors and Their Effects on the Condition of the Peasant in the Thirteenth Century," *Agricultural History Review* 10 (1962), pp. 1–13.

Titow, J. Z., *English Rural Society 1200–1350* (London, 1969).

Trexler, Richard C., "Infanticide in Florence: New Sources and First Results," *History of Childhood Quarterly* 1 (1973), pp. 98–116.

Trexler, Richard C., *Public Life in Renaissance Florence* (New York, 1980).

Vinogradoff, Paul, *Villainage in England: Essays in English Mediaeval History* (1892; rpt. Oxford, 1968).

Wall, Richard, "The Age at Leaving Home," *Journal of Family History* 3 (1978), pp. 181–202.

Wall, Richard, "Household and Kinship," *History Workshop* 12 (1981), p. 199.

Wall, Richard, "Inferring Differential Neglect of Females from Mortality Data," *Annales de démographie historique* (1981), pp. 119–140.

Wall, Richard, "Woman Alone in English Society," *Annales de démographie historique* (1981), pp. 303–317.

Wall, Richard, with Jean Robin and Peter Laslett, eds., *Family Forms in Historic Europe* (Cambridge, 1983).

Ward, W. H., and K. S. Block, *A History of the Manor and Parish of Iver* (London, 1933).

Whyte, Martin King, *The Status of Women in Preindustrial Societies* (Princeton, 1978).

Wrightson, Keith, "Medieval Villagers in Perspective," *Peasant Studies* 7 (1978), pp. 203–217.

Wrightson, Keith, "Household and Kinship in Sixteenth-Century England," *History Workshop* 12 (1981), pp. 151–158.

Wrightson, Keith, *English Society 1580–1680* (London, 1982).

Wrightson, Keith, and David Levine, *Poverty and Piety in an English Village: Terling, 1525–1700* (New York, 1979).

Wrigley, E. A., "Family Limitation in Pre-Industrial England," *Economic History Review,* 2nd series, 19 (1966), pp. 82–109.

Wrigley, E. A., "Mortality in Pre-Industrial England: The Example of Colyton, Devon, Over Three Centuries," *Daedalus* 97 (1968), pp. 546–580.

Wrigley, E. A., *Population and History* (New York, 1969).

Wrigley, E. A., "Ferlility Strategy for the Individual and the Group," in *Historical Studies of Changing Fertility,* ed. Charles Tilly (Princeton, 1978), pp. 135–154.

Young, Charles, *The Royal Forests of Medieval England* (Philadelphia, 1979).

Index

313

Women (*Cont.*)
  case studies of, 10
  under common law, 25, 28, 107–8,
    110, 114
  compared to men, 6–9, 21–47, 64,
    169, 177–81, 206, 215–17
  crimes of violence against, 26
  as criminals, 38–41, 191–93, Ta-
    ble 2.4
  effect of household status on, 7–9,
    128
  feudal, 3–4, 9, 185–89
  golden age of, 4–6, 177–78
  ideals of behavior, 5–6, 25, 37, 45,
    140, 177
  as landholders, 6–8, 32–36, 191,
    Tables 2.3, 7.3
  legal activity of, 6–8, 27–32
  as litigants, 27–32, 194, Tables 2.2,
    5.2, 7.5
  modern, 3–5
  as mothers, 42, 44–45, 68, 140
  as pledges, 24–25, 154–55, 193–94,
    Table 6.3
  political activity of, 5–8, 22–27,
    31

  in religion, 3, 45, 188
  and social rank, 5–6, 180–89, Ta-
    ble 7.1
  status of, 10, 42–47, 179–80, 197–
    98
  and tithings, 24, 160
  urban, 3–4, 9, 119, 160, 185–89,
    197
  use of familial pledges by, 38, 136,
    193, Table 5.9
  as victims of crimes, 26, 30, 38–40,
    193
  as villagers, 6–8, 36–42, 169
  as workers, 3–4, 6, 32–33, 36, 83,
    115–29, 186–87, 197–98
Work. *See also* Ale-wives; Servants;
    Wage-laborers
  of daughters, 57, 70, 73, 82–84
  of husbands, 115–129
  of men, 32–33
  of sons, 57, 70, 73, 82–84
  of wives, 115–129
  of women, 3–4, 6, 32–33, 36, 83,
    115–29, 186–87, 197–98
Wrightson, Keith, 212–13
Wrigley, E. A., 59, 68